FLORIDA

GETTING STARTED GARDEN GUIDE

Grow the Best Flowers, Shrubs, Trees,
Vines & Groundcovers

D1308329

Published in 2013 by Cool Springs Press, an imprint of the Quayside Publishing Group, 400 First Avenue North, Suite 400, Minneapolis, MN 55401

Original edition published as Florida Gardener's Guide, © 2002 Cool Springs Press

The information in this book is true and complete to the best of our knowledge. All recommendations are made without any guarantee on the part of the author or Publisher, who also disclaims any liability incurred in connection with the use of this data or specific details.

Cool Springs Press titles are also available at discounts in bulk quantity for industrial or sales-promotional use. For details write to Special Sales Manager at Cool Springs Press, 400 First Avenue North, Suite 400, Minneapolis, MN 55401 USA. To find out more about our books, visit us online at www.coolspringspress.com.

Library of Congress Cataloging-in-Publication Data

MacCubbin, Tom, 1944-
  Florida getting started garden guide : grow the best flowers, shrubs, trees, vines & groundcovers / Tom MacCubbin and Georgia B. Tasker.
      p. cm.
  Includes bibliographical references and index.
  ISBN 978-1-59186-546-9 (softcover)
  1. Gardening--Florida. 2. Tropical plants--Florida. 3. Landscape gardening--Florida.
I. Tasker, Georgia. II. Title.

SB453.2.F6M225 2013
635.09759--dc23

2013009477

Acquisitions Editor: Billie Brownell
Design Manager: Brad Springer
Layout: S.E. Anglin

Printed in China

10 9 8 7 6 5 4 3 2 1

FLORIDA

GETTING STARTED GARDEN GUIDE

Grow the Best Flowers, Shrubs, Trees, Vines & Groundcovers

Tom MacCubbin and Georgia B. Tasker

COOL
SPRINGS
PRESS
Home and Garden Experts™

MINNEAPOLIS, MINNESOTA

ACKNOWLEDGMENTS

This author would like to acknowledge the information provided on plant growth and care by Tom Wichman and Celeste White, horticulturalists at the University of Florida's Orange County Extension Service. Their vast experience in plant culture helped add detailed information to the listings. I would also like to express appreciation to the many University of Florida Extension specialists who have contributed information over the years that increased my knowledge of the plants contained within this book.

—*Tom MacCubbin*

Gardeners, professional and amateur, are a generous group by nature, readily offering cuttings, seeds, or plants as well as knowledge to those who share their interests. From this wellspring of generosity I have received a great deal of kindly help. Special mention goes to the horticulturists at Fairchild Tropical Botanic Garden, and to members of many orchid and plant societies, where an abundance of local knowledge resides. Any mistakes or omissions are my own.

—*Georgia Tasker*

CONTENTS

GARDENING
IN FLORIDA

Welcome to gardening in Florida, a state of remarkable contrasts. Our state is not all beaches, nor is it all orange groves. It is not all rhododendrons, nor is it all palm trees.

It is an exciting and sometimes unexpected mix of all these things. We have freshwater marshes, seven thousand lakes, sandy ridges, mucky swamps, and more miles of coastal area than just about any other state. To garden here is to experience firsthand the stuff we're made of, from the high pines of the Panhandle to the 25-million-year-old central sandy ridge to the relatively new geology of the southern peninsula.

The Natural Terrain in Florida

The rock beneath our impertinent finger of land is limestone. The peninsula is some 400 miles long and about 100 miles wide (not counting the Panhandle). It is warmed on the southeast by the Gulf Stream and occasionally chilled in the northwest by arctic fronts.

Gardeners in the northwestern part of the state, north of Tallahassee, know of remnants of Appalachian plants that were pushed south in the last Ice Age meltwater. Imagine coming across mountain laurel and yew trees in ravines and on bluffs around the Apalachicola River—and all this so near white sand and saw palmetto.

Around Gainesville, gardeners are familiar with live oaks hung with Spanish moss, pine trees in the flatwoods, bear grass, deer tongue (wild vanilla), wax myrtle, scrub oak, and sweetbay magnolias that bloom in the summer. The climate is subtropical in this area, where Marjorie Kinnan Rawlings wrote *Cross Creek* and immortalized the area's plants, animals, seasons, and two-footed critters.

When traveling south through the pine landscapes of the Ocala National Forest, you'll come upon one of our rarest landscapes, the scrub, where the sand pine and rosemary, the myrtle oaks, and wiregrass have staked out their spot on high dunes millions of years old. The scrub is arid and populated by many of our most

Bromeliad

interesting plants and animals, including the endangered scrub jay and the gopher tortoise.

From the chain of lakes that feeds the Kissimmee River, which empties into Lake Okeechobee, the land begins to flatten out, to gradually sink toward the sea. Vast pond apple forests once grew south of the lake before it was diked. At that time water ran from the lake through the sawgrass into the cypress strands and around the tree islands until it reached the Gulf of Mexico on the west coast or drained into the Atlantic Ocean on the east through rivers and finger glades.

By the time you reach the southern end of the peninsula, you'll be gardening where temperate and tropical mix in a rich blend, where gumbo limbo, fiddlewood, strongbark, and blolly romance the oak and flirt with the mastic, where a particular kind of slash pine and its companions grow in highly endangered, scattered shards of pine rockland, and where wild coffee snuggles up to the pigeon plum and paradise tree.

On the upper Florida Keys, where West Indian plants make a fragile forest, you'll have to dig into fossilized coral or build a raised bed. The rock here was a reef once, and only a thin layer of leaf litter disguises these stony skeletons. By the time you reach the middle and lower Keys, limestone has resurfaced. Slash pines and silver palms eke out a meager existence, and mangroves surround it all.

This is how we look in our more natural gardens, those we have left and are trying to hang on to.

Planted Gardens in Florida

Our planted gardens are very different from the natural areas, although there has been a trend toward native gardens in the past decade.

Gardening has tended to be more relaxed and leisurely in North Florida than in the southern part of the state. In northern Florida, gardens are influenced by the Southern states: dogwoods, redbuds, azaleas, camellias, and rhododendrons are prized garden plants, making spring a glorious season. Alfred B. Maclay State Gardens in Tallahassee features azaleas and camellias, and there are displays of these shrubs at Eden Gardens State Park.

Central Florida has felt the ripple effects of Walt Disney World for years. The lavish use of color, which is Disney's specialty, is not as intense in home landscapes, but the color impulse is quickened here. In Winter Park, older sections of Orlando, and neighboring small towns, azaleas, laurel oaks, and cabbage palms are garden mainstays. The Harry P. Leu Gardens in downtown Orlando has a huge collection of camellias, roses, palms, cycads, bamboo, and a wonderfully tranquil lakefront walk.

Lake Wales, a tiny town south of Orlando, has one of the state's most elegant gardens. This is Bok Tower Gardens, designed by the Frederick Law Olmsted firm, which is famous for having designed New York City's Central Park. Bok's carillon, majestically rising atop Iron Mountain (a high point at 295 feet), overlooks reflecting pools and is surrounded by gentle, classic garden walks around huge old azaleas and beneath live oaks.

Tourist attractions and winter homes of the wealthy have influenced the home gardens on both southern coasts, from McKee Jungle Gardens (now McKee Botanical Gardens) in Vero Beach; to Jungle Larry's Caribbean Gardens near Naples (which was pioneer botanist Henry Nehrling's old garden in the 1920s); to Henry Flagler's White Hall in Palm Beach; to Henry Ford's winter home in Fort Myers next door to Thomas Edison's; to John Ringling's estate in Sarasota.

On the west coast, the former home of Marie Selby in Sarasota is now a botanical garden specializing in epiphytes, or air plants, including orchids and bromeliads. The grounds are on a small peninsula that juts into Sarasota Bay, surrounded by mangroves and native plants. Here you will find huge ficus—as well as in other areas of the coast, such as the Thomas Edison home in nearby Fort Myers—along with a hibiscus collection, water garden, and bamboo stands.

Thomas Edison, like other early South Florida garden and plant lovers, collected plants from around the world. His home looks onto the Caloosahatchee River; behind it is his large collection of tropical fruit trees. Edison loved palms, and he lined his street in Fort Myers with royal palms, a legacy that still stretches all the way to Fort Myers Beach.

The Deering brothers, among the founders of the giant farm machinery company International Harvester, spent winters in Miami. James built the Italianate palace and formal gardens called Vizcaya; Charles settled farther south and kept his surroundings more naturalistic, though he had a mango grove, a lawn sweeping down to Biscayne Bay, and royal palms brought in from the Everglades.

In Palm Beach, the Society of the Four Arts Garden, a treasure bequeathed to the town of Palm Beach by the garden club back in 1938, is enchanting. It was designed to show people how to grow various plants on the island, and today its Japanese garden, water garden, and small formal fountains are to be cherished.

Fairchild Tropical Botanic Garden in Coral Gables was begun in the 1930s by palm enthusiast Robert Montgomery and named for David Fairchild, one of this country's most esteemed plant explorers. It has one of the world's best palm collections. The 83-acre garden features long vistas over man-made lakes built by the Civilian Conservation Corps, collections of tropical flowering trees, vines, and shrubs, a new 12,500-square-foot butterfly conservatory and a science village, which houses the garden's scientists and graduate students and their laboratories.

Gardeners in Miami Beach, Coral Gables, and Coconut Grove have different garden styles, and they utilize an increasing number of tropical plants to express them. The popularity of crotons, ixoras, and fruit trees is a legacy of early gardeners.

Today you will find intimate little gardens of exuberant tropical foliage and color in South Beach and more manicured gardens elsewhere. Coral Gables has the wealth to keep gardeners busy clipping and shearing, whereas Coconut Grove is far lusher, if not overgrown, with many different plants used more playfully.

The Key West Tropical Forest and Botanical Garden specializes in the native flora of the Florida Keys and Caribbean, including a small collection of Cuban palms, two butterfly gardens, and wetlands.

Gardening with Native Plants

Few can resist flowering plants from the tropics or the big, glorious tropical leaves of the aroid and banana families. Yet native plants are increasing in popularity as more gardeners understand the need for habitat restoration and natural gardens for birds, butterflies, and wildlife. The Florida Native Plant Society has 37 chapters around the state. Many people are planting native trees and shrubs as a hedge against cold, drought, and hurricanes. And there is an increasing awareness of the dangers of too many pesticides, which has made the insect and disease resistance of many natives more appealing. Often the cover of large native trees can be used to create the right microclimate for tropical plants, and gardeners are increasingly sophisticated about using these trees.

Creating Your Own Garden: Climate and Soil

Climate

Soil, climate, and microclimate are the parameters within which you will work. Begin by finding your location on the United States Department of Agriculture's hardiness zone map (see page 15). The most recent map divides the state into areas with the same annual minimum temperatures, from Zones 8 through 11. Zones 8, 9, and 10 are subdivided into Zone 8A, Zone 8B, Zone 9A, Zone 9B, Zone 10A, and Zone 10B. Zone 10B, however, has greatly expanded up the eastern coast as the climate warms, and the other zones also are moving northward.

Most of the state is considered subtropical, whereas North Florida is similar to Texas, Louisiana, and Georgia. Extreme southern Florida is tropical, while Central Florida is hotter in the summer and cooler in the winter than

Philodendron

is South Florida, which is favored by southeastern breezes in the summer and far from the impact of most cold fronts in winter.

Florida's winter is December through February, spring is March and April, summer is May through September, autumn is late October and November. The widest variation in seasons occurs in the north, the least in the south.

Superimposed on the temperate seasons are the two tropical ones: wet and dry. The rainy season spans May through October, with the beginning and the end of the season having the most rainfall. Thunderstorms and lightning strikes occur more often in Florida than in any other state. The hurricane season begins June 1 and ends the last day of November.

A booming population has put a severe strain on the state's fresh water supply, which is rain-fed and obtained from underground aquifers. It serves not only Florida's millions of people, but also its agriculture and natural resources. No gardener can afford the luxury of using limitless supplies. Although common sense would tell us to group plants by their water needs, we must go a step further and design gardens that reduce water (and fertilizer) use. Once you become adept at reading plants, you may learn to fertilize only when the plants tell you they require it. Leaves that are generally paler, that are yellow between the veins, and plants that produce fewer blooms are three signs of fertilizer need.

Soil

Soils in the northern and western parts of the Florida Panhandle tend to be poorly draining clay, whereas the southern Panhandle and highlands are sloping, sandy-loamy soils, particularly around the Tallahassee hills. The central ridge is sandy with some underlying limestone to the west of the ridge. Most of Central Florida (with the exception of the ridge) is flat, with poorly drained, sandy soils; the area is commonly called pine flatwoods.

In South Florida, the central Everglades marshes and swamps are flanked by marl and sand over limestone or outcroppings of limestone. On the West Coast, shells of countless sea creatures have been crushed and washed ashore, making a coarse, calcareous substrate.

Most plants prosper in slightly acid to neutral soils, though there is a long list of plants, both native and exotic, that will tolerate high-pH (alkaline) soils. The alkalinity may cause leaf yellowing from magnesium, manganese, or iron deficiency, and foliar sprays of micronutrients are recommended in these areas three or four times a year. Use iron drenches annually to help plants in such soils.

Live Oak

In both sands and rocky soils, certain mineral elements will leach away in heavy rains. (Sandy and rocky soils both require irrigation, but limestone will hold water longer in little niches and crevices.)

A good many of the newer developments in Coastal and South Florida are built on fill, or land that has been sheared of its organic top layer and dredged for raising the houses above standing water. The fill material tends to be highly alkaline with extremely poor drainage because of compaction. You may have to build up mounds of good soil to plant in these conditions. Eventually, the roots of trees and shrubs will penetrate the compacted rocky soil and loosen it.

Increasing Pests and Diseases

New and exotic insects and diseases regularly invade Florida, where climate is conducive for their survival. In the 1960s and 1970s, lethal yellowing of palms swept through South Florida and killed more than 100,000 Jamaica tall coconuts and a long list of other susceptible palms. It still exists and kills palms, although at a less rapid rate.

King and queen sago cycads were practically eliminated by Asian cycad scale.

Citrus canker caused thousands of backyard citrus trees to be cut down in the late 1990s. That episode was followed by citrus greening, a serious bacterial disease spread by minute insects called psyllids. Green fruit become misshapen and leaves develop yellow patches. There is no cure, and the U.S. Department of Agriculture says the disease may jeopardize the future of citrus in the United States.

Ficus white fly keeps many weeping fig hedges denuded; the rugose white fly now affecting gumbo limbos causes so much sooty mold to collect on the tree's leaves and plants (or anything else) beneath it that it's hard to recommend planting the trees at the moment. Croton scale also attacks gumbo limbo, crotons, and some 50 other hosts in Florida. Natural predators do exist, although horticultural oil and soap sprays may be used against the insects.

The disease called laurel wilt is spread by red bay ambrosia beetle and first occurred in Florida in 2005. It threatens native red bay (*Persea borbonia*), avocado (*Persea americana*) and other members of the laurel family. The fungus plugs up the xylem and phloem of an infected tree, causing wilt and death.

Often new insect infestations will break out, spread rapidly, and then gradually come under control of natural predators.

Gardening Across the State

Because of the broad range of plants that can be grown in Florida, from temperate in the north to tropical in the south, the *Florida Getting Started Garden Guide* was written by two authors: Tom MacCubbin, urban horticulturist in Orlando, has written about the more northern and central Florida plants, and Georgia Tasker, a writer with Fairchild Tropical Botanic Garden, has covered the more southern ones. Regional information is provided for plants that may be grown differently in different areas. Some tropical plants may be grown in Central and North Florida as annuals or container plants, whereas some northern flowers may be used as annuals in winter in South Florida.

Planting times may differ as well. In South Florida, vegetables and flowers are planted in the winter, whereas trees and shrubs are usually planted at the beginning of summer.

Wherever you garden, remember that all our gardens are connected, that our natural areas are affected by what goes on into our planted yards, and our planted yards benefit from a knowledge of what grows in our natural areas. So garden carefully, and may you have all the sun and all the rain you require.

How to Use This Book

Each profile in this garden guide provides you with information about a plant's particular characteristics, habits, and basic requirements for active growth as well as our personal experiences and knowledge of the plant. We have included the information you need to help you realize each plant's fullest potential. Only when a plant performs at its best can one appreciate it fully. You will find such pertinent information as mature height and spread, seasonal colors (if any), sun and soil preferences, water requirements, fertilizing needs, pruning and care, and pest information. Each section is clearly marked for easy reference.

Sun Requirements
Symbols represent the range of sunlight suitable for each plant. The icon representing *Full Sun* means the plant needs to be sited in a full sun (8–10 hours daily) location. The *Part Sun* symbol means the plant likes full sun, but will appreciate a few hours of protection from the harsh, late afternoon sun. *Part Shade* indicates the plant can be situated where it receives partial sun all day, morning sun, or dappled shade. *Full Shade* means the plant needs a shady location protected from direct sunlight. Some plants can be grown in more than one range of sunlight, so you will sometimes see more than one sun symbol.

Full Sun   Part Sun   Part Shade   Shade

Additional Benefits
Many plants offer benefits that further enhance their appeal. The following symbols indicate some of the more important additional benefits:

 Native

 Fall or other seasonal color

 Drought-tolerant

 Attracts beneficials, such as insects, bees, and butterflies

 Attracts hummingbirds

 Edible for animals

Companion Planting and Design
Landscape design ideas are provided as well as suggestions for companion plants to help you achieve striking and personal results from your garden. This is where many people find tremendous satisfaction when gardening.

Try These
Try some of our favorite cultivars or related species.

USDA Hardiness Zone Map

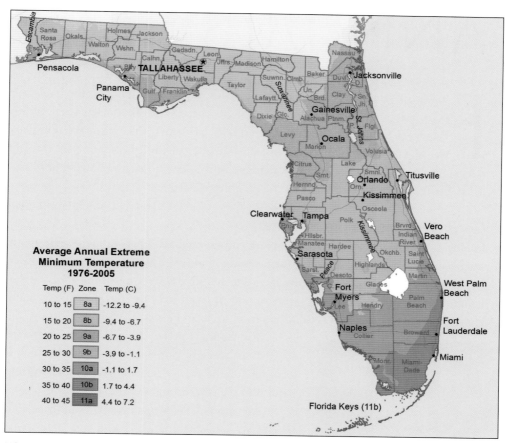

USDA Plant Hardiness Zone Map, 2012. Agricultural Research Service, U.S. Department of Agriculture. Accessed from http://planthardiness.ars.usda.gov.

Hardiness Zones

Cold-hardiness zone designations were developed by the United States Department of Agriculture (USDA) to indicate the minimum average temperature in an area. A zone assigned to an individual plant indicates the lowest temperature at which the plant can be expected to survive over a winter. Florida has zones ranging from 8a to 11a. Though a plant may grow (and still grow well) in zones other than its recommended cold-hardiness zone, it is a good indication of which plants to consider for your landscape. Unless otherwise noted in the plant's profile, all plants in this book are suitable for all of Florida.

ANNUALS FOR FLORIDA

Florida gardeners have learned that a quick way to add color to the landscape is to use annual flowers. Most can be purchased with blooms at local garden centers to bring home and create an instant garden. As the name annual implies, the plants last only a season or two but offer plenty of color for six to eight weeks. A few, including geraniums, impatiens, and coleus, continue growing until seasonal changes in temperature causes the plantings to decline.

Considerations Before Planting

In Florida you have to learn when to plant certain annuals. There are two main types: warm season and cool season. Warm-season annuals usually grow well between March and November. Then as the days shorten and temperatures dip into the 40s Fahrenheit or lower at night, it's time to add the cool-season types. They are usually planted November through February in most areas of Florida.

Torenia

Most annuals prefer the bright locations with at least six to eight hours of sun. When picking a location for the flower bed, remember the shifting pattern of the sun throughout the year.

Give annual flowers some of your best soil. It pays to enrich sandy sites with lots of organic matter. Work in liberal quantities of compost, peat moss, garden soil, and manure. Test the soil acidity, as annuals prefer a pH around 6.5. Make adjustments as needed, following test recommendations. (For rocky alkaline soils or poorly drained soils, build raised beds.)

Starting Your Annuals

Some gardeners like to start annuals from seed. It's difficult to pass the seed racks at garden centers and not purchase several packs. Remember the proper growing season must be followed, and starting flowers from seed takes a little time. Very few seeds can be planted directly in the garden to grow. Most must be sown in pots or cell packs and need six to eight weeks to be ready for the garden. If you decide to start your own transplants,

Dianthus

choose an easy-to-grow annual such as marigold, salvia, impatiens, or zinnias for first attempts.

Use a germination or good potting mix for the sowings, and cover the seed lightly. Keep the seed containers moist. Most seeds germinate within a week. Give the seeds the suggested light level noted on the seed packet. Most need full sun immediately. Feed the seedlings with a liquid fertilizer solution to have plants for the garden in a few weeks.

Gardeners wishing to skip seedling culture can find a large selection of transplants at local garden centers. They are usually available at the proper time for planting in Florida. For years flowers were marketed in cell packs, but recently the 4-inch pot or larger containers have become the standard sizes for the garden. These plants are usually well rooted and in bloom, ready to create the instant garden. Buy those with the fewest open flowers to make sure the plants haven't bloomed themselves out while still small.

Growing Tips

Check the label for each type of annual selected for the garden to note the spacing needed. Plant annuals at the same depth that they were growing in the containers or a little higher. If planted too deep, some rot rather quickly. After planting, give the soil a good soaking. Many gardeners also like to add a light mulch layer up to an inch thick. If you do, keep the mulch back from the stems a few inches. The new plants need watering every day for the first week or two. Make sure you moisten the rootballs. Gradually taper off the watering to an as-needed basis. When the surface inch of soil starts to feel dry to the touch, it's usually time to water established plantings.

Annual flowers also need frequent feedings. Many gardeners like to use a liquid or granular fertilizer every three to four weeks for in-ground plantings—more frequently with container plantings. Consider using slow-release fertilizers that make feedings easier following label instructions.

Ageratum

Ageratum houstonianum

Botanical Pronunciation
A-jer-AY-tum hyous-tone-e-AY-num

Other Name Floss flower

Bloom Period and Seasonal Color
Spring to summer blooms in white, blue

Mature Height x Spread
8 inches to 2 feet x 18 inches

Ageratum is an ideal compact plant to use along walkways or as a carpet of blossoms leading up to shrub plantings. Plantings are usually full of easy-to-see blooms as the small flowers are born in tight clusters that are held well above the plant, creating a blanket of color. Ageratum varieties provide the sometimes all too elusive blue colorations as well as pure whites. Ageratum can be planted in beds, container gardens, planter boxes, and hanging baskets. One or two plants can fill a hanging basket. This is a great annual to use as a contrast color with other bright annuals and in patriotic red, white, and blue plantings for national holidays. (TM)

When, Where, and How to Plant

Ageratum is a tender annual that is grown during the warm seasons. Transplant to the garden whenever temperatures are consistently above 32 degrees Fahrenheit, or be ready to protect the plants from cold weather. Plantings can extend into the summer, but seasonal weather often causes the plants to decline. Add plenty of organic matter to sandy soil, and till the ground to a depth of 6 to 8 inches. Thoroughly moisten dry soils, and then add the transplants. Give ageratum a 12- to 18-inch spacing because most sprawl out over the garden soil. To prevent root rot problems, do not plant too deeply. Immediately after planting, thoroughly moisten the soil.

Growing Tips

Add a light mulch layer. Keep the mulch several inches back from the stems of the plants. Ageratum need frequent watering for the first few weeks. In sandy soils daily watering may be needed. Ageratum growing in containers may need more frequent watering. Check these plants daily, and water when the surface soil feels dry to the touch. Feed container plantings every other week with a water-soluble product; in-ground plantings, monthly with a general garden fertilizer. Slow-release fertilizers can be substituted using label instructions.

Regional Advice and Care

Gardeners in South Florida can plant ageratum from October through April. Central Florida residents may also plant during these months but most likely will lose plants due to cold during the winter. North Florida residents should delay planting until March. Ageratum may have caterpillars, mites, and garden flea hoppers as pests. Handpick pests from the plantings, or treat them with a natural pesticide.

Companion Planting and Design

Ageratum is a great border plant to stage with taller fall through spring plantings of bush daisy, dusty miller, marigolds, salvia, snapdragons, and petunias as a backdrop.

Try These

Some popular varieties include the 'Aloha Blue', 'Blue Danube', 'Blue Horizon', 'Diamond Blue', and 'Hawaii' selections. Blue is a hard color to find in flowers. But you won't be disappointed with variety 'Blue Horizon', which has a good blue color.

Angelonia

Angelonia angustifolia

Botanical Pronunciation
an-ga-LONE-e-ah an-GUS-ta-fol-e-ah

Other Name Summer snapdragon

Bloom Period and Seasonal Color
Spring through fall in purple, lavender, blue, pink, and white

Mature Height x Spread
12 to 24 inches x 18 inches

A few years ago there was little mention of angelonia for home flower gardens. Plants were considered erratic and inconsistent growers. Well now this plant is a great find at your local garden center, becoming one of the most colorful and reliably long-lived annuals in home and commercial landscapes. Many live so long they are often grown like perennials or even listed as perennials in garden guides. Angelonia are cheery plants for the landscape sending up spikes of assorted colors opening throughout the spring through late fall growing seasons until the very cold weather arrives. Use them in beds as accents or feature them in container gardens. Flowers are suitable for arrangements too. (TM)

When, Where, and How to Plant
Give angelonia a full sun location for best flowering. Plantings normally begin in early spring and continue through fall. The quality of soil does not seem to matter too much, but it is best to grow them in a well-drained site. Most gardeners find working liberal quantities of organic matter, including peat moss, compost, or garden soil, into Florida sands helps keep maintenance to a minimum and promotes the best growth. Seeds are available, but most gardeners prefer to obtain started plants in bloom. Small to large plants are available in containers of various sizes from garden centers for late winter through fall planting.

Growing Tips
Plantings are drought-tolerant but grow best with at least weekly watering. Many like to add a thin layer of mulch over the surface of the soil to reduce the need for frequent watering and help control weeds. Feed every three to four weeks with a traditional fertilizer, or use a slow-release product that can feed flower beds and containers for three or more months.

Regional Advice and Care
Caterpillars and aphids are occasional pests. Some can be handpicked from the plants or controlled with natural sprays. Start planting in late winter or early spring in North Florida. In other areas of the state angelonia can be grown nearly year-round. New varieties are self-cleaning, but it never hurts to cut off old stems of blooms.

Companion Planting and Design
Because angelonia are a little taller than many annuals, they are best used as a backdrop or central feature of a planting. Use with annuals like marigolds, salvia, begonias, and verbena, or stage with long-lived perennials, including bush daisy, perennial salvia, and seasonal bulbs. In containers use them in the center, and add other sprawling flowers around the sides.

Try These
Enjoy bright, long-lasting purple, lavender, pink, and white blooms of the new 'Serena' series. The plants are prolific flower producers and require little grooming. Another good selection with blue or white blossoms is in the 'Angleface' series. All selections offer a lot of vigor for spring through fall gardens.

Celosia

Celosia spp.

Botanical Pronunciation
see-LOW-she-ah

Other Name Cockscomb

Bloom Period and Seasonal Color
Fall to late spring blooms in yellow, orange, red, and pink

Mature Height x Spread
10 inches to 36 inches x 36 inches

When you mention celosia, you likely have a flower form in mind, but there are at least three groups on the market. One is the plumosa type with the upright plumes of feathery blossoms. Another is the compact cockscomb type with rounded to flattened dense inflorescence. Both selections come in a good array of colors. The third common selection is what's called the wheat celosia with upright rounded spikelike displays of mainly pinkish flowers. Each celosia selection can provide color for the warmer months when used as focal points, in massive beds, as a backdrop, or in container gardens. All but the wheat celosia have trouble during the summer months when the seasonal rains soak the bloom clusters and encourage rot. Many selections also dry well for use in arrangements. (TM)

When, Where, and How to Plant
Celosia is a warm-season annual that's affected by frosts and freezes. It's also affected by rainy, damp weather, which causes flower clusters to rot. In warmer locations plantings can begin during fall and continue into spring. Celosia can be planted in full sun in ground beds, container gardens, or planter boxes. Add plenty of organic matter to sandy soil, and till the ground to a depth of 6 to 8 inches. Thoroughly moisten dry soils, and then add the transplants. Give celosia a 10- to 12-inch spacing. To prevent root rot problems, do not plant too deeply. Where possible, remove the declining blooms to allow new shoots to develop. Celosia gives about six to eight weeks of good color before needing replacement.

Growing Tips
Many gardeners like to add a light mulch layer. Keep the mulch several inches back from the plant stems. Celosia need frequent watering for the first few weeks. In sandy soils daily watering may be needed until the roots grow out into the surrounding soil. Gradually reduce watering to times when the surface inch of soil feels dry to the touch. Feed every three to four weeks with a traditional fertilizer, or use a slow-release product for flower beds and containers for three or more months.

Regional Advice and Care
North Florida gardeners should delay plantings until March or April. Central and South Florida gardeners can plant September through May but must be ready to give winter protection during cold weather. Celosia may have caterpillars as pests. Handpick the pests from the plants, or apply a control recommended by the University of Florida.

Companion Planting and Design
Plant a bed of mixed colors or cluster with zinnias, marigolds, salvia, or green shrubs. Make them an accent feature in dish gardens with an herbal border.

Try These
Good varieties include 'Bombay', 'Castle Mix', 'Flamingo Feather', 'Fresh Look', 'Pink Candle', and 'Red Velvet'. Bright spikes of color are sure to catch your attention and that of visitors. 'Castle Mix' appears to be brighter than others and comes in a good variety of colors.

Coleus

Solenestemon scutellarioides

Botanical Pronunciation

so-leh-ne-STEM-un scoo-te-lar-e-OID-ez

Bloom Period and Seasonal Color

Year-round foliage in pink, green, bronze, or red mixes

Mature Height x Spread

1 to 2 feet x 2 feet

Ranging from lance type to broad, rounded leaves, the foliage of coleus is the focal point of the plant. Coleus offers a feast of colorful foliage with mixes that have every color of the rainbow or varieties with pink, green, bronze, or red foliage. The variously shaped leaves are interestingly edged with a slightly toothed shape to a ruffled border. Coleus provides good, reliable eye-catching color whether filling a flower bed or serving as a backdrop for other plantings. The most useful varieties for the landscape are those that grow from 1 to 2 feet tall. You will find coleus with the most sun tolerance among the newer varieties. Regional growers often have their own selections of new coleus. (TM)

When, Where, and How to Plant

Coleus are available at garden centers year-round. Most plantings are made March through October. Coleus can be planted in ground beds, container gardens, and planter boxes. Add plenty of organic matter to sandy soil, and till in to a depth of 6 to 8 inches. Thoroughly moisten dry soils, and then add the transplants, spacing 12 to 18 inches apart and thoroughly moistening the soil again. With the long Florida growing season, coleus may grow too tall for the planting site. When this happens, cut the plants back to the desired height.

Growing Tips

Many gardeners add a light mulch layer. Keep the mulch several inches back from the stems of the plants. Coleus need frequent watering for the first few weeks. In sandy soils daily watering may be needed until the roots grow out into the surrounding soil. Gradually reduce watering to times when the surface inch of soil feels dry to the touch. Check these plants daily and water when the surface soil feels dry. Feed every three to four weeks with a traditional fertilizer, or use a slow-release product that can feed flower beds and containers for three or more months.

Regional Advice and Care

North Florida gardeners can expect to replant the coleus after each winter. Unless the plants are given extra winter protection, they are usually lost during the heavy freezes. Central and South Florida gardeners may keep the plants growing for several years. Coleus may have caterpillars and slugs as pests. Handpick the pests from the plants, apply a natural insecticide, or use slug bait.

Companion Planting and Design

Mix many foliage colors together or pick flowering plants with blooms to match the leaves. Coleus are also great plantings to mix with low-growing gingers, ivy, and liriope.

Try These

Some good varieties are found among the 'Carefree', 'Kong', 'Rainbow', and 'Wizard' series. Select a variety for specific light levels. Perhaps it's the crinkled edges of the leaves, but what I like the best is the wide selection of color combinations that form the 'Wizard' mix, which is easy to grow from seed.

Dianthus

Dianthus x *hybrida*

Botanical Pronunciation
die-ANN-thuss HI-bra-dah

Other Name Pinks

Bloom Period and Seasonal Color
Fall through spring blooms in pink, white, or red

Mature Height x Spread
8 to 18 inches x 18 inches

Modern dianthus are known to most gardeners as pinks, partially because so many selections come in a range of pink hues and partially because the fringed edge of each flower petal appears as if it has been trimmed with pinking shears. Dianthus is a perennial plant that is treated as an annual in Florida. The dianthus grown in Florida are cool-season flowers that can withstand a light frost. Often with just a little protection, the plants can also survive a light freeze. The plants can be used as a large mass of color in flower beds or just as a small splash along the walkway. Use them in container gardens as a central feature surrounded by spreading flowers or greenery along the sides. (TM)

When, Where, and How to Plant

Start new plantings during fall, and continue through spring. Plant in a sunny location in ground beds, container gardens, and planter boxes. Some gardeners get a few plants through the summer by keeping them in planters that can be moved to a cooler location for the hotter months. Add plenty of organic matter to sandy soil, and till to 6 to 8 inches. Thoroughly moisten dry soils, and then transplant, spacing 10 to 12 inches apart. To prevent root rot problems, do not plant too deeply. Immediately after planting, thoroughly moisten the soil again.

Growing Tips

Keep any light mulch several inches back from their stems. Dianthus need frequent watering for the first few weeks. In sandy soils daily watering

may be needed until the roots grow into the surrounding soil. Gradually reduce watering to times when the surface inch of soil feels dry to the touch. Dianthus growing in containers may need more frequent watering. Feed every three to four weeks with a traditional fertilizer, or use a slow-release product that can feed flower beds and containers for three or more months.

Regional Advice and Care

Dianthus are given similar culture throughout the state. Northern plantings may freeze during winter. Southern plants are often shorter lived due to the hotter spring and summer. Dianthus may have caterpillars as pests. Handpick the pests from the plants, or apply a control recommended by the University of Florida. Some varieties produce dead flowers all at once while the new blossoms begin to emerge. Deadheading at this time keeps the bed attractive. Dianthus can live for more than one growing season, especially during cooler months.

Companion Planting and Design

Plant in container gardens with herb borders, pansies, or ageratum. Add clusters to the garden with dusty miller, salvia, snapdragons, and petunias.

Try These

Good performers include selections from the 'Baby Doll', 'Carpet', 'Charm', 'Duke', 'Lemon Fizz', 'Magic Charm', 'Merry-Go-Round', and 'Telstar' varieties. I like low-growing types with many colors. One that has performed well for me is 'Magic Charm', which is easy to grow from seed.

Dusty Miller

Senecio cineraria

Botanical Pronunciation
sah-NEE-see-oh sin-err-AIR-ee-ah

Bloom Period and Seasonal Color
Grown for its foliage

Mature Height x Spread
12 to 18 inches x 24 inches

The foliage of dusty miller forms a perfect contrast for brightly colored annuals in the flower bed. The fuzzy, gray-green leaves give the garden a silvery look. When planted with bright red salvia or purple petunias, dusty miller provides a tranquil resting spot for the eyes. The shape of the leaves varies, from coarsely toothed to lacelike in appearance, and adds textural interest to the garden. For best performance, plant during the cooler months. Dusty miller proves freezeproof throughout Florida but deteriorates rapidly during summer's rainy days. Dusty miller can be planted in ground beds, container gardens, and planter boxes. Fancy-leaved types easily catch the eye when used as border plants for flower beds or to fill container gardens. (TM)

When, Where, and How to Plant
Plant dusty miller after the rainy season ends and cool weather begins. Fall plantings will last until the hot summer season arrives. Give dusty miller a sunny location for best growth. Add plenty of organic matter to sandy soil, and till the ground to a depth of 6 to 8 inches. Thoroughly moisten dry soils, and then add the transplants, spacing 10 to 12 inches apart. To prevent root rot problems, do not plant too deeply. Immediately after planting, thoroughly moisten the soil again.

Growing Tips
Keep light mulch several inches back from the stems of the plants. Dusty miller needs frequent watering for the first few weeks. In sandy soils daily watering may be needed until the roots grow into the surrounding soil. Gradually reduce watering to times when the surface inch of soil feels dry, and then give the plantings a good soaking. Dusty miller growing in containers may need more frequent watering. Check these plants daily, and water when the surface soil feels dry. Feed every three to four weeks with a traditional fertilizer, or use a slow-release product that can feed flower beds and containers for three or more months.

Regional Advice and Care
For most of Florida the months for planting are October through April. South Florida residents may delay dusty miller planting until late fall, when the cooler temperatures favor best growth. In North and Central Florida dusty miller often survives into early summer. As the hot, damp weather arrives for the summer, most plantings rapidly decline and should be replaced. Dusty miller may have caterpillars as pests. Handpicking the pests from the plants is best.

Companion Planting and Design
Add plants with contrasting colors to this garden. Some great combinations would include dusty miller with red salvia, pink celosia, purple petunias, and red begonias.

Try These
Good varieties for the landscape include 'Cirrus', 'Silver Dust', 'Silver Lace', and 'Silver Queen'. The silvery the foliage the better, and if it has fancy leaves, that is special too. You will love the foliage of 'Silver Lace' with its fernlike appearance.

Geranium

Pelargonium x *hortorum*

Botanical Pronunciation
pel-er-GON-ee-um hor-TORE-ham

Other Name Common geranium

Bloom Period and Seasonal Color
Fall through spring blooms in pink, red, and lavender plus white and blends

Mature Height x Spread
18 to 24 inches x 36

A beloved bedding plant, the geranium produces colorful flowers on plants that are bright green with rounded leaves. The foliage can have dark patterns called zonal markings, which provide added interest. Geranium flowers are produced in clusters at the end of long stems and are held well above the foliage. Some members of the genus are perennials, but geraniums in Florida are treated as cool-season annuals. Although a few gardeners sneak the plant through the summer with special protection, most geraniums will need to be replaced with warm-season annuals at the start of the summer rainy season. Geraniums can be planted in ground beds, container gardens, and planter boxes. (TM)

When, Where, and How to Plant

If you are willing to give geraniums winter protection, planting can begin in October. Delay forming large beds until March. Give geraniums a sunny location for best flowering. The plants tolerate some shade, but don't expect a single blossom until they are moved out into the sun. Add plenty of organic matter to sandy soils, and till the ground to a depth of 6 to 8 inches. Thoroughly moisten dry soils, and then add the transplants, spacing 12 to 18 inches apart. To prevent root rot problems, do not plant too deeply. Immediately after planting, thoroughly moisten the soil again.

Growing Tips

Many gardeners like to add a light mulch layer. Keep the mulch several inches back from the stems of the plants. Geraniums need frequent watering for the first few weeks. In sandy soils daily watering may be needed until the roots grow into the surrounding soil. Gradually reduce watering to times when the surface inch of soil feels dry. Geraniums growing in containers may need more frequent watering. Feed every three to four weeks with a traditional fertilizer, or use a slow-release product that can feed flower beds and containers for three or more months.

Regional Advice and Care

Geraniums grow well throughout the state. Northern gardeners should plant only in containers until March, when beds can be created. These geraniums may last a little longer into the summer season. In South and Central Florida it's worth taking the risk of planting during the fall months and tossing a cover over the beds on colder nights. Geraniums may have caterpillars as pests. Handpicking the pests from the plants is best.

Companion Planting and Design

Use in gardens or planters with cool-season annuals and perennials. Pick colors of ageratum, dianthus, salvia, snapdragons, and begonias that contrast with the geranium foliage and blossoms.

Try These

Good selections for Florida include 'Black Velvet', 'Elite', 'Maverick', 'Orbit', 'Pinto', 'Sensation', and 'Summer Showers'. You want plenty of blooms from geraniums to provide a constant display of color. The 'Orbit' hybrids have a good selection of colors and are time tested.

Impatiens

Impatiens walleriana

Botanical Pronunciation
em-PAY-shens wall-eer-e-ANA

Other Name Busy Lizzie

Bloom Period and Seasonal Color
Year-round blooms in all colors

Mature Height x Spread
10 to 24 inches x 24 inches

Gardeners should not dismiss impatiens as too common for their purposes before considering the usefulness of this shade-loving plant. Impatiens provide color in areas where other flowering plants refuse to bloom. One impatiens plant creates a mound of blossoms normally 1 foot or more in diameter, thus making it an economical way to fill a large area with color. In warmer locations, impatiens also can grow almost indefinitely. Where the planting is affected by cold, it often grows back either from stems surviving near the ground line or from seeds. Impatiens can be planted in ground beds, container gardens, planter boxes, and hanging baskets. Usually plantings need shady spots, but during the winter they can often be grown in the full sun locations. (TM)

When, Where, and How to Plant
The major planting time for impatiens in North and Central Florida is March through October; winter is the time for impatiens in South Florida. Add plenty of organic matter to sandy soil, and till the ground to a depth of 6 to 8 inches. Thoroughly moisten dry soils, and then add the transplants, spacing 12 to 14 inches apart. To prevent root rot problems, do not plant too deeply. Immediately after planting, thoroughly moisten the soil. After months of growth, impatiens usually become tall and lanky. Renew desirable growth by pruning the plants back to within 1 foot of the ground.

Growing Tips
Many gardeners like to add a light mulch. Keep it several inches back from the stems of the plants.

Impatiens need frequent watering for the first few weeks. In sandy soils daily watering may be needed until the roots grow out. Gradually reduce watering to times when the surface inch of soil feels dry. Impatiens growing in containers may need more frequent watering. Feed every three to four weeks with a traditional fertilizer, or use a slow-release product that can feed flower beds and containers for three or more months.

Regional Advice and Care
North and Central Florida gardeners must be ready to give impatiens protection during the winter months. Replace impatiens in summer in South Florida. Impatiens may have caterpillars, slugs, and mites. Handpick the pests from the plants, or treat them with a natural pesticide. Nematodes can also be a pest for which there is no easy control. Presently the best recommendations are to replace the soil in infested beds or grow the plants in containers.

Companion Planting and Design
Plant with annuals and perennials in shady spots. Some good flowers include begonias, bromeliads, crossandra, and gingers. Plant with ivy and vinca in beds and containers.

Try These
Garden favorites include selections from the 'Super Elfin', 'Accent', 'Dazzler', 'Shady Lady', 'Splash', and 'Tempo' varieties. If you want lots of vigor and color choose the 'Accent' hybrids. These are well-tested and have given good performance.

Marigold

Tagetes spp.

Botanical Pronunciation
TAH-get-eez

Other Name French marigold

Bloom Period and Seasonal Color
Spring through fall blooms in yellow, orange, red, maroon, and white

Mature Height x Spread
8 inches to 3 feet x 2 feet

What is often referred to as the African marigold is actually the American marigold, *Tagetes erecta*. Both the African marigold and the French marigold, *Tagetes patula*, originated in the Americas. Early explorers took the plants to Europe and Africa, where they were thereafter considered natives. For Florida gardeners, the best time to grow either type is during the warm seasons. Common varieties open yellow, orange, and burnt-color blossoms, but the adventuresome gardener might seek out a white marigold for a more exotic look. Most marigolds have a compact size, which makes them suitable for use in flower beds, along walkways, or in containers. Taller selections are well used as a backdrop or central feature for other plantings. (TM)

When, Where, and How to Plant
In the warmer locations, marigolds may be planted year-round, but for most areas of the state, this is a warm-season annual to plant March through September. Just wait until the cooler weather is over or be prepared to protect the plants with a cover during periods of frost or freezing weather. Marigolds can be planted in full sun in ground beds, container gardens, and planter boxes. Add organic matter to sandy soils, and till the ground to a depth of 6 to 8 inches. Moisten dry soils well, and then add the transplants, spacing 10 to 18 inches apart. Thoroughly moisten the soil again.

Growing Tips
Many gardeners like to add a light mulch layer. Keep the mulch several inches back from the stems of the plants. Marigolds need frequent watering for the first few weeks. In sandy soils daily watering may be needed until the roots grow out into the surrounding soil. Gradually reduce watering frequency to when the surface inch of soil feels dry. Marigolds growing in containers may need more frequent watering. Feed every three to four weeks with a traditional fertilizer, or use a slow-release product that can feed flower beds and containers for three or more months.

Regional Advice and Care
Northern and Central Florida gardeners must give up marigolds when the weather turns cold. Marigolds may have caterpillars, garden flea hoppers, mites, and leaf miners as pests. Handpick the pests from the plants, or apply a natural control.

Companion Planting and Design
Use in ground or in containers with warm-season annuals and perennials. Good combinations include marigolds with ageratum, salvia, torenia, and zinnias. Also mix with herbs and vegetables.

Try These
French marigolds for the garden include the 'Aurora', 'Bolero', 'Janie', 'Queen Sophia', 'Sparky', and 'Tiger Eyes' selections. Good African varieties to try include 'Antigua', 'Inca', 'Moonsong Deep Orange', and 'Moonstruck'. I like marigolds with plenty of color on a compact plant. The bronze-and-gold-colored 'Queen Sophia' selection has been a great performer for small gardens.

Pansy

Viola x wittrockiana

Botanical Pronunciation
veye-OH-la witt-rock-ee-AY-na

Bloom Period and Seasonal Color
Fall and winter blooms in all colors

Mature Height x Spread
10 inches to 12 inches x 12 inches

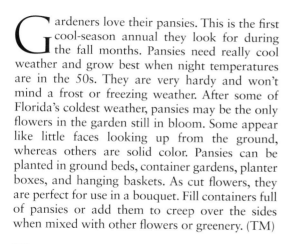

Gardeners love their pansies. This is the first cool-season annual they look for during the fall months. Pansies need really cool weather and grow best when night temperatures are in the 50s. They are very hardy and won't mind a frost or freezing weather. After some of Florida's coldest weather, pansies may be the only flowers in the garden still in bloom. Some appear like little faces looking up from the ground, whereas others are solid color. Pansies can be planted in ground beds, container gardens, planter boxes, and hanging baskets. As cut flowers, they are perfect for use in a bouquet. Fill containers full of pansies or add them to creep over the sides when mixed with other flowers or greenery. (TM)

When, Where, and How to Plant
Wait until there is a consistent chill in the air before planting pansies. It's best to wait until at least late October or November to guarantee good growth. Add plenty of organic matter to sandy soil, and till the ground to a depth of 6 to 8 inches. Thoroughly moisten dry soils, and then add the transplants, spacing 6 to 8 inches apart. The closest spacing gives the best looking garden. To prevent root rot problems, don't plant too deeply. Immediately after planting, thoroughly moisten the soil again. Gardeners should remove old blossoms to keep new flowers forming on the plants.

Growing Tips
Many gardeners like to add a light mulch layer. Keep the mulch several inches back from the stems of the plants. Pansies need frequent watering for the first few weeks. In sandy soils daily watering may be needed until the roots grow out. Gradually reduce watering to times when the surface inch of soil feels dry. Check these plants daily, and water when the surface soil feels dry to the touch. Feed every three to four weeks with a traditional fertilizer, or use a slow-release product that can feed flower beds and containers for three or more months.

Regional Advice and Care
North Florida gardeners can get a slight jump on most pansy growers by adding them to the garden a month or two ahead of schedule. The plants also last longer into the spring season. Pansies may have aphids and slugs as pests. Handpick the pests from the plants, or treat them with a natural pesticide.

Companion Planting and Design
Edge borders or fill entire gardens with a mix of pansy colors. Or use just one selection to contrast with other cool-season dianthus, dusty miller, petunia, and snapdragons.

Try These
Some good varieties for the garden include 'Bolero', 'Cool Wave', 'Flirty Skirts', 'Frizzle Sizzle', 'Joker', and 'Majestic Giants'. Plenty of little faces will appear to be peeking out from among dark green foliage when you plant the 'Cool Wave' hybrids. They give plenty of color over many months.

Petunia

Petunia x hybrida

Botanical Pronunciation
pe-TOON-e-ah hi-BRI-dah

Bloom Period and Seasonal Color
Fall through spring in all colors and blends

Mature Height x Spread
12 to 18 inches x 36 inches

With flowers that range from just over 1 inch to those that are 4 inches in diameter, the petunia offers a wide variety of bedding choices for the cool season. Gardeners growing petunias can count on good coverage from any of the varieties they choose. Their ability to take light frosts plus an extended bloom period from the late fall season right through spring guarantees color at a time when many gardens need it most. Petunias can be planted in ground beds, container gardens, planter boxes, and hanging baskets. Just one petunia can fill a hanging basket when placed in the middle. Obtain selections known for their cascading habits to creep over baskets and planters. (TM)

When, Where, and How to Plant
When the weather starts to cool during October or November, it's the best time to plant petunias. Add plenty of organic matter to sandy soil, and till the ground to a depth of 6 to 8 inches. Thoroughly moisten dry soils, and then add the transplants. Give petunias a 10- to 12-inch spacing. Immediately after planting, thoroughly moisten the soil again. Most plantings tend to grow lanky and full of old blossoms and seedpods. Periodically encourage new growth and extend the life of the plantings with rejuvenation prunings.

Growing Tips
Many gardeners like to add a light mulch layer. Petunias need frequent watering for the first few weeks. In sandy soils daily watering may be needed until the roots grow out into the surrounding soil.

Gradually reduce watering to times when the surface inch of soil feels dry to the touch. Petunias growing in containers may need more frequent watering. Feed every three to four weeks with a traditional fertilizer, or use a slow-release product that can feed flower beds and containers for three or more months.

Regional Advice and Care
North Florida gardeners can often get a head start by planting petunias up to a month ahead of schedule. Plantings in the cooler portions of the state may grow into late spring and early summer. Plantings in North Florida are likely to need protection from the sometimes severe freezing weather. Petunias may have caterpillars and aphids as pests. Handpick pests from the plantings, or treat them with a natural pesticide.

Companion Planting and Design
Mix with greenery or other cool-season plantings in beds, planters, and hanging baskets. Good companions include calendula, dianthus, nicotiana, salvias, and snapdragons. Also cluster them among shrub and bulb plantings.

Try These
Petunia varieties for the garden include selections in the 'Avalanche', 'Bravo', 'Cascade', 'Celebrity', 'Supertunia', and 'Wave' series. Get the most from your petunias with the 'Wave' hybrids. They can last into the warmer months and also have a good selection of colors.

Portulaca

Portulaca grandiflora

Botanical Pronunciation
port-you-LACK-ah grand-eh-FLOR-ah

Other Name Moss rose

Bloom Period and Seasonal Color
Spring through summer blooms in brilliant reds, pinks, oranges, yellows, creams, and white

Mature Height x Spread
3 to 6 inches x 12 inches

Portulaca provides color in the most sun-drenched areas of the summer garden—even when many other plants wither beneath Florida's hot, strong sun. The plump flower buds and spreading growth habit make it a natural for the rock garden or other dry land plantings where a desert look is desired. Breeding efforts have resulted in varieties that provide a full day of color any time the sun shines. Portulaca grows best during the warm months of spring through summer. The plants open flowers for six to eight weeks before gradually declining. Portulaca can be planted in ground beds, container gardens, planter boxes, and hanging baskets. (TM)

When, Where, and How to Plant
This is definitely a warm-season flower. The plantings seem to feed on Florida's hottest days. Start plantings by April, and continue through the summer months into early fall. Cool weather and short days appear to signal the decline for portulaca plantings. Portulaca should be planted in a well-prepared garden site. Add plenty of organic matter to sandy soil, and till the ground to a depth of 6 to 8 inches. Thoroughly moisten dry soils, and then add the transplants, spacing 8 to 10 inches apart and thoroughly moistening the soil again.

Growing Tips
Many gardeners like to add a light mulch layer. Portulaca needs frequent watering for the first few weeks. In sandy soils daily watering may be needed until the roots grow out into the surrounding soil. Gradually reduce watering to times when the surface inch of soil feels dry to the touch. Portulaca growing in containers may need more frequent watering. Check these plants daily, and water when the surface soil feels dry to the touch. Feed every three to four weeks with a traditional fertilizer, or use a slow-release product that can feed flower beds and containers for three or more months.

Regional Advice and Care
South Florida gardeners start planting portulaca a few weeks to a month earlier than do Central or North Florida gardeners. Portulaca may also last longer into the fall in South Florida. Portulaca may have mites as pests. When present, apply a soap spray or a natural control.

Companion Planting and Design
Portulaca is best used as a border or in hanging baskets with taller plants. Plant with marigolds, salvia, vinca, and zinnias; also used to highlight beds of greenery.

Try These
Some good selections to try in Florida gardens are in the 'Happy Hour', 'Margarita', 'Sundial', and 'Toucan' series. Get a wide selection of color from the 'Sundial' hybrids that brighten beds or hanging baskets. The flowers remain open for a long time during the day, which is important.

Salvia

Salvia splendens

Botanical Pronunciation
SAL-vee-ah SPLEN-dens

Other Name Scarlet sage

Bloom Period and Seasonal Color
Year-round blooms in red, salmon, pink, white, and purple

Mature Height x Spread
8 to 18 inches x 24 inches

A warm-season mainstay of the garden, salvia provides some of the brightest color in the landscape. With lots of rocketlike spikes, salvia can be counted on for almost year-round color. For years this plant was known as scarlet sage for its bright red coloration. Red still continues to be the most popular and reliable color, but breeders have now developed some excellent pinks, whites, and violets for added variety. The flowering plant can grow from 8 to 18 inches tall. Salvia gives the best display when planted in clusters for an impressive burst of color. Salvia can be planted in ground beds, container gardens, and planter boxes. Set taller plants to the back of the garden or as the central feature of container gardens. (TM)

When, Where, and How to Plant
The best time to plant a salvia bed is during spring. Plantings often continue through summer and early fall. Give salvia a full sun location. Be careful when purchasing pot-grown plants that they are not overly rootbound and incapable of growing out into the surrounding soil. Add plenty of organic matter to sandy soil, and till the ground to a depth of 6 to 8 inches. Thoroughly moisten dry soil, and then add the transplants, spacing 10 to 16 inches apart. Thoroughly moisten the soil immediately after planting. Keep the plants attractive and encourage new shoots by periodically removing the old flower heads and extra-long stems.

Growing Tips
Many gardeners like to add a light mulch layer. Keep the mulch several inches back from the stems of the plants. Salvias need frequent watering for the first few weeks. In sandy soils daily watering may be needed until the roots grow out into the surrounding soil. Gradually reduce watering to times when the surface inch of soil feels dry, and then give the plantings a good soaking. Salvias growing in containers may need more frequent watering. Check these plants daily, and water when the surface soil feels dry to the touch. Feed every three to four weeks with a traditional fertilizer, or use a slow-release product that can feed flower beds and containers for three or more months.

Regional Advice and Care
North Florida gardeners can expect salvias to be damaged by winter frosts and freezes. Central Florida gardeners can help salvia survive the winter with just a covering during the cold weather. In South Florida, salvia can be grown as a perennial. Salvia may have caterpillars, mites, and slugs as pests. Handpicking the pests from the plants is best.

Companion Planting and Design
A bed of salvia of many types and colors makes a garden. They are ideal additions to dusty miller, marigold, petunia, snapdragon, and wax begonia plantings.

Try These
Try 'Bonfire', 'Hotline', 'Salsa', and 'Sizzler'. Put plenty of color in the garden with selections from the 'Salsa' series. The plants are low to medium in height and vigorous.

Snapdragon

Antirrhinum majus

Botanical Pronunciation
ann-ther-RYE-num MAY-jus

Bloom Period and Seasonal Color
Fall through spring blooms in all colors

Mature Height x Spread
8 inches to 3 feet x 12 inches

The snapdragon is another old-fashioned flower that has been rejuvenated for use in the modern garden. Now there are lower-growing and more colorful snapdragons. Many of these new varieties still have the dragonlike heads that kids young and old like to play with, pushing the sides of the blooms to open the "faces." Breeders have also developed a butterfly series of flower forms. These appear to give a lot more color from the open blooms. New varieties are much more compact, growing from only 8 to 20 inches tall. One thing hasn't changed about snapdragons—they are still perfect in a bouquet. Snapdragons can be planted in ground beds, container gardens, and planter boxes. Use taller varieties as a central feature in beds and containers. (TM)

When, Where, and How to Plant

Snapdragons are available for fall through early spring plantings. The plants are tolerant of frost and light freezes. Give snapdragons a sunny location for best growth. Add plenty of organic matter to sandy soil, and till the ground to a depth of 6 to 8 inches. Thoroughly moisten dry soils, and then add the transplants, spacing 10 to 14 inches apart. To prevent root rot problems, do not plant too deeply. Immediately after planting, thoroughly moisten the soil. Taller varieties often need staking to support the flower spikes. Use a garden wire or individual stakes to prevent wind damage to the plants. Removal of the flowers and seedheads encourages new shoots and prevents the rapid decline of plantings.

Growing Tips

Many gardeners like to add a light mulch layer. Keep the mulch several inches back from the stems of the plants. Snapdragons need frequent watering for the first few weeks. In sandy soils daily watering may be needed until the roots grow out into the surrounding soil. Gradually reduce watering to times when the surface inch of soil feels dry. Snapdragons growing in containers may need more frequent watering. Feed every three to four weeks with a traditional fertilizer, or use a slow-release product that can feed flower beds and containers for three or more months.

Regional Advice and Care

North and Central Florida gardeners should give plantings winter protection to avoid damage. South Florida gardeners should delay plantings until the cooler weather arrives. In the warmer areas the plantings may not last through spring. Snapdragons may have caterpillars as pests. Handpicking the pests from the plants is best.

Companion Planting and Design

Create a bed of a single color, or use a mixture. Plant snapdragons in the middle with pansies, ageratum, and petunias around the sides.

Try These

Some varieties include the 'Aromas', 'Chantilly', 'Bells', 'Chimes', 'Rocket', 'Snapshot', and 'Twinny' selections. I like tall snapdragons you can cut for bouquets. There is a wide color selection and tall-growing plants among the 'Rocket' hybrids.

Torenia

Torenia fournieri

Botanical Pronunciation
tour-EEN-ah four-knee-ER-e

Other Name Wishbone flower

Bloom Period and Seasonal Color
Spring through fall blooms in lavender, white, blue, and pink combinations

Mature Height x Spread
6 to 12 inches x 24 inches

A warm-season plant that covers the ground in a blanket of foliage and flowers, torenia is a plant of many names. Often called the summer pansy because the flowers grow best during warm weather when pansies are long gone, torenia serves the same landscape needs as its namesake. This plant is a must for the garden due to its tolerance of heat, rain, and light shade. All of the flowers are accented with a spot of yellow in the throat of the blossom. Expect the sprawling plants to last for the entire warm season, producing one flush of blooms after another. Torenia can be planted in ground beds, container gardens, planter boxes, and hanging baskets. One plant can fill a basket. (TM)

When, Where, and How to Plant
Start adding torenia to the garden as soon as the cold weather is over. Most gardeners can make the plantings from March through August. Give torenia a full sun to lightly shaded location for best growth. Locate the plantings where they can be seen and enjoyed. In the landscape fill a bed with only torenia or use them as a groundcover. Torenia should be planted in a well-prepared garden site. Add plenty of organic matter to sandy soil, and till the ground to a depth of 6 to 8 inches. Thoroughly moisten dry soils, and then add the transplants, spacing 8 to 12 inches apart and again thoroughly moistening the soil.

Growing Tips
Many gardeners like to add a light mulch layer. Torenia need frequent watering for the first few weeks. In sandy soils daily watering may be needed until the roots grow out into the surrounding soil. Gradually reduce watering to times when the surface inch of soil feels dry to the touch. Torenia growing in containers may need more frequent watering. Feed every three to four weeks with a traditional fertilizer, or use a slow-release product that can feed flower beds and containers for three or more months.

Regional Advice and Care
Torenia need similar care throughout the state. Northern gardens should delay plantings until consistently warm weather arrives. Torenia may have caterpillars and slugs as pests. Handpicking the pests from the plants is best. Gardeners can also apply a *Bacillus thuringiensis* caterpillar control, use slug bait, or apply another control recommended by the University of Florida.

Companion Planting and Design
Plant in a hanging basket, or create a bed of color with the various selections. They also look great as edging with celosia, marigolds, nicotiana, and vinca in the middle.

Try These
Some good varieties to try include 'Catalina', 'Clown', 'Happy Faces', 'Kauai', 'Lemon Drop', and 'Suzie Wong'. I like the vigor of torenia, and the 'Clown' hybrids seem to have plenty of it. There is also a great color assortment among the flowers, produced on compact plants.

Verbena

Verbena x *hybrida*

Botanical Pronunciation
ver-BEAN-ah HI-bri-dah

Other Name Garden verbena

Bloom Period and Seasonal Color
Spring through early winter blooms in blue, purple, red, white, and cream

Mature Height x Spread
10 to 12 inches x 24 inches

Verbena provides some of the best garden blues and purples for the landscape while also sporting attractive foliage. With most verbena varieties growing only 10 to 12 inches tall, the wide-spreading plants are ideal for use as a colorful groundcover to fill flower beds. Verbena leaves are deep green and usually have an attractive scalloped edge, which adds to the beauty of the plantings. Verbena is particularly lovely when filling containers with its vinelike stems of foliage during warm-weather months. The plant is mainly a warm-season annual that tends to trail off in the early winter months. Verbena can be planted in ground beds, container gardens, planter boxes, and hanging baskets. One plant can fill a hanging basket. (TM)

When, Where, and How to Plant
Begin plantings during March and continue through October. Most selections give six to eight weeks of good flowering before needing to be replaced. Give verbena a sunny location for best growth. Add organic matter to sandy soil, and till the ground to a depth of 6 to 8 inches. Thoroughly moisten dry soils, and then add the transplants. Give verbena a 10- to 14-inch spacing. Immediately after planting, again thoroughly moisten the soil.

Growing Tips
Many gardeners like to add a light mulch layer. Just keep the mulch several inches back from the stems of the plants. Verbena plantings need frequent watering for the first few weeks. In sandy soils daily watering may be needed until the roots grow out into the surrounding soil. Gradually reduce watering to times when the surface inch of soil feels dry to the touch. Verbena plantings growing in containers may need more frequent watering. Feed every three to four weeks with a traditional fertilizer, or use a slow-release product that can feed flower beds and containers for three or more months.

Regional Advice and Care
Verbena plantings are cold sensitive and may be damaged by frost and freezes in North and Central Florida gardens. Early plantings should be protected from winter injury with covers when cold weather is expected. Southern gardeners may start planting a month or more ahead of schedule due to warmer growing conditions. Verbena may have caterpillars, mites, and garden flea hoppers as pests. Handpick the pests from the plants, or apply a control recommended by the University of Florida, following label suggestions.

Companion Planting and Design
Fill a hanging basket with color or use them as edging over the sides. Plant in beds with begonias, celosia, dusty miller, geraniums, marigolds, and snapdragons.

Try These
Some good varieties include the 'Obsession', 'Peaches and Cream', and 'Tuscany' selections. It's nice to find plants to use in borders and in hanging baskets. It's equally nice to find a selection of color as you find with the 'Obsession' mix.

Wax Begonia

Begonia x *semperflorens-cultorum*

Botanical Pronunciation
bee-GOHN-e-ah sem-per-FLOOR-ens
cul-TOR-um

Bloom Period and Seasonal Color
Year-round blooms in all shades of pinks and
reds plus some very pure whites

Mature Height x Spread
12 to 18 inches x 18 inches

Begonia is a dependable, minimal care plant that thrives in a variety of garden situations. Attractive almost the entire year, begonias thrive in the shady spots of the garden along with those receiving full sun. The tidy, mounding plants are available with flowers in a variety of colors. The plants flower continuously to create spots of color. Most also have the familiar little spot of yellow stamens in the center of the blossoms. Begonia foliage is very attractive, varying from bright green to bronze in color. All plants are compact and well rounded in shape. Wax begonias can be planted in ground beds, container gardens, planter boxes, and hanging baskets. Some varieties tolerate the sunny sites better than others, so be selective. (TM)

When, Where, and How to Plant
Begonias establish best if planted before days become consistently hot. Where possible, plant beds March through May to have the plants well rooted in the ground by summer. Add plenty of organic matter to sandy soil, and till the ground to a depth of 6 to 8 inches. Thoroughly moisten dry soils, and then add the transplants, spacing 10 to 12 inches apart and again thoroughly moistening the soil. Begonias may grow for several seasons to a year or more before declining. Often the plants become lanky and can be pruned back to renew the compact, attractive growth habit.

Growing Tips
Many gardeners like to add a light mulch layer. Keep the mulch several inches back from the stems of the plants. Wax begonias need frequent watering for the first few weeks. In sandy soils daily watering may be needed until the roots grow out into the surrounding soil. Gradually reduce watering to times when the surface inch of soil feels dry. Wax begonias growing in containers may need more frequent watering. Feed every three to four weeks with a traditional fertilizer, or use a slow-release product that can feed flower beds and containers for three or more months.

Regional Advice and Care
North and Central Florida gardeners usually lose their begonias to frost and freezing weather. Avoid making plantings too late in the year, or provide cold protection. In South Florida begonias can be planted year-round. Wax begonias may have caterpillars and slugs as pests. Gardeners can apply a *Bacillus thuringiensis* caterpillar control or use a slug bait, a soap spray, or a product recommended by the University of Florida.

Companion Planting and Design
Grow with sunny or shady plantings in beds or containers. Create a bed of single to mixed colors, or combine with ageratum, dianthus, dusty miller, torenia, verbena, and zinnias.

Try These
Some good varieties are found in the 'Big', 'Bada Bing', 'Cocktail', 'Fairyland', and 'Pizzazz' selections. Plant the varieties recommended by your garden center. The 'Cocktail' mix has a good assortment of leaf and flower colors for sun or shade.

Zinnia

Zinnia elegans

Botanical Pronunciation
ZIN-knee-ah ell-e-GANS

Bloom Period and Seasonal Color
Spring through fall blooms in pinks, reds, oranges, and plums plus white

Mature Height x Spread
8 inches to 3 feet x 3 feet

The zinnia is a bright, carefree flowering plant with big, long-lasting blossoms. Most zinnias grow a little larger than other garden flowers. Lots of gardeners remember the older varieties, such as 'Giants of California', that grew more than 3 feet tall. Now there are zinnias for every spot. Some grow just 8 inches tall, and others grow in the 12- to 24-inch-tall range. The flowers are big and beautiful, ranging from 2 to 5 inches in diameter. There is an excellent assortment of colors—zinnias are great to enjoy in the garden or cut to bring indoors. Zinnias can be planted in ground beds, container gardens, and planter boxes. Use smaller varieties for borders and larger ones as backdrops or central features in gardens. (TM)

When, Where, and How to Plant

Plant in the ground during early spring before the weather gets too hot and humid. Best plantings are made during March and April to avoid pest problems. Add organic matter to sandy soil, and till the ground to a depth of 6 to 8 inches. Thoroughly moisten dry soils, and then add the transplants, spacing 10 to 20 inches apart, depending on the ultimate size of the variety. After planting, thoroughly moisten the soil. Extend their flowering by removing declining blossoms.

Growing Tips

Many gardeners like to mulch lightly. Zinnias need frequent watering for the first few weeks. In sandy soils daily watering may be needed until the roots grow out. Gradually reduce watering to times when the surface inch of soil feels dry. Zinnias growing in containers may need more frequent watering. Check these plants daily, and water when the surface soil feels dry. Feed every three to four weeks with a traditional fertilizer, or use a slow-release product that can feed flower beds and containers for three or more months.

Regional Advice and Care

North Florida gardeners can enjoy a little longer planting season due to the often cooler spring and early summer weather. Central and South Florida gardeners must plant zinnias early to enjoy the six to eight weeks of good flowering. Zinnias may have caterpillars, leaf spot, and powdery mildew as pests. Caterpillars can be handpicked or treated with a natural *Bacillus thuringiensis* control. Zinnia diseases are best controlled by plantings made during the spring or application of a copper fungicide or another university-recommended fungicide.

Companion Planting and Design

Plant smaller varieties as an edging and use taller types as a central feature of beds and container gardens. They're attractive when mixed with marigolds, nicotiana, salvia, torenia, and verbena.

Try These

Good varieties are 'Benary's Giant', 'Dreamland', 'Magellan', 'Profusion', 'Senora', 'Swizzle', and 'Zahara'. The 'Profusion' and 'Zahara' series are great for the garden and containers due to their vigor and disease resistance. They seem to do well in summer when many varieties have problems.

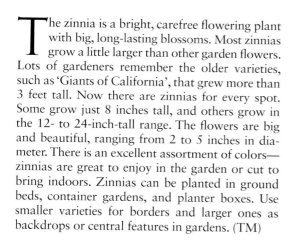

BULBS, CORMS, RHIZOMES, AND TUBERS FOR FLORIDA

Bulbs are plants that have found a niche in time and work quickly to take advantage of it. The temperate bulbs of the northern woods appear in late winter before the snow has melted, rising, flowering, and setting seed before tree leaves return to intercept the light. Crocus, then iris, and squill, by turns, accompany the earth to the spring equinox.

Tropical bulbs must work between wet and dry seasons, finding sustenance in the rainy months, storing within the bulbs the means to get through the dry season, often resting during drought, sending up flowers as or before the rains return.

Caladium

Bulb Options

Amaryllis have become such popular Christmas plants that we forget they are forced to bloom at that time and normally bloom in spring. These are the Dutch amaryllis, which are classified botanically as *Hippeastrum*; the true amaryllis is *Amaryllis belladonna*, which has smaller, fragrant pink flowers that appear in the fall.

Caladiums are summer bulbs in Florida, providing some of the most beautiful leaves anywhere. They are from Central America and northern South America. Early in the last century, Henry Nehrling, a botanist and plantsman living in Gotha, near Orlando, and then in Naples, created about 1,500 caladium hybrids, some of which are still grown today. 'Frieda Hemple' may be one of his best-known hybrids.

Rain lilies, both *Zephyranthes* and *Hebranthes*, are delightful little bulbs to have around because their rain-sparked flowers seem to appear so suddenly. The foliage is like liriope or lilyturf, and you might try using rain lilies instead of liriope in a nice shaded area. Debra DeMarco, a landscape designer in South Miami, often uses society garlic, another bulb, in place of liriope.

Calla Lily

One of the most spectacular of all bulbs is the voodoo lily, an *Amorphophallus*, which is in the aroid family. This tallest of all flowers from Sumatra, *Amorphophallus titanium*, can stand 5 to 6 feet tall. The first reports of the plant seemed so exaggerated that no one believed them.

Several bulbs of this incredible plant were collected in the 1990s and distributed to botanical gardens around the country. One enormous bulb weighs about 70 pounds and flowered twice at Fairchild Tropical Botanical Garden in Miami. When it opens and is ready for pollination, the flower sends out waves of stench to attract pollinating carrion beetles. After pollination, the flower swells slightly and then collapses. The whole flowering episode lasts about three days. A single leaf appears next and may achieve a height of 20 feet. Smaller species, such as *Amorphophallus paeoniifolius*, are grown in South Florida from time to time, and they never fail to attract attention when blooming.

Preparing for Bulbs

Most bulbs are in garden centers (and catalogs) in the fall. If you live in South Florida, you can buy temperate bulbs and store them in the refrigerator's vegetable bin until midwinter. Plant them for spring flowers, and expect them to last only a season. The *Reader's Digest Illustrated Guide to Gardening* offers this advice for refrigerating bulbs: never put them in the same refrigerator bin as fruit, for the ethylene gas from the fruit will kill the bulbs.

Tropical bulbs may be left in the ground year-round in South Florida. The winter's dry season will give them the rest they need, and you should water sparingly until they begin to put up new leaves. Then fertilize and keep the area moist.

Bulbs like a rich soil that drains well, and peat moss, compost, or aged manure can be added to the soil to help it drain and keep it somewhat moist.

As border plants or bedding plants, as accents, as just the right plant for a special place, bulbs bring a charm of their own to the garden. They can make lovely tabletop flowers when forced. As cut flowers, they can be spectacular in clear crystal with nothing but themselves for company.

Achimenes

Achimenes spp.

Botanical Pronunciation
ah-KIM-uh-neez

Other Name Magic flower

Bloom Period and Seasonal Color
Summer through early fall blooms in white, blues, purples, pinks, yellows, and reds

Mature Height x Spread
12 to 18 inches x 24 inches

Gardeners often bypass a great bulb-type plant with a tropical look for the hot, humid gardens. This can be expected as they likely cannot believe the eraser-sized rhizomes can grow into such great flowering plants in just a few months. Achimenes, which is both a common and scientific name, forms a genus of several species and many hybrids. Other common names include magic flower and cupid's bower. Would you believe this is an African violet relative? Plantings fill with up to 2-inch-diameter flowers on sprawling growths, which makes the plants ideal for container culture in hanging baskets and window boxes to display in the filtered sun. In warmer areas of the state they have also been planted as shady site groundcovers. (TM)

When, Where, and How to Plant

Achimenes become active during the warmer days of spring. Ones purchased at garden centers or through mail order companies should be planted when the day temperatures are consistently in the upper 70s to 80s Fahrenheit. Most plantings are in containers filled with a good potting soil mixture. The rhizomes are spaced 3 to 4 inches apart and covered up to an inch deep. If grown in a flower bed or as a groundcover, plant in a prepared, organic matter enriched soil. Keep soil moist but not overly wet, and add mulch. Usually during the summer months rains can provide adequate moisture. If you want to increase the collection during the summer, new plants can be started from cuttings.

Growing Tips

Achimenes can be left in the same containers for a year or two. They multiply quickly, and when pots become congested with rhizomes, it is time to share them with friends. Feed with a liquid fertilizer solution monthly or a slow-release fertilizer made for container plant culture as directed.

Regional Advice and Care

Plants gradually decline in the fall as the days grow shorter. When the foliage turns brown trim it back to the soil and give the planted containers protection from winter in the colder portions of the state. Provide a light watering during the dormant period when the soil becomes dry. In late winter, before spring growth begins, is the best time to separate the rhizomes and replant. Because the rhizomes can multiply rapidly, start new containers with just a few and share others with friends.

Companion Planting and Design

Grow with other shade-loving foliage and flowering plants. Hang baskets from trees or display them on tables. Achimenes can be displayed with impatiens, Amazon lilies, spathiphyllum, bromeliads, and other summer plantings. Blue and pink varieties seem to do the best producing large blooms for about five to six months, but there are also reds and yellow.

Try These

Very few varieties are named, and often you have to find them through mail order companies.

African Iris

Dietes bicolor

Botanical Pronunciation
DYE-et-tees BI-color

Other Name Fortnight lily

Bloom Period and Seasonal Color
Spring and summer blooms in white, cream, and yellow

Mature Height x Spread
2 feet x 1½ feet

Zones 9–10B

Sometimes called fortnight lily, the African iris is considered a hardy (for a tropical plant) and drought-tolerant bulb. Its three outer petals are marked with yellow and are longer than the three inner ones. *Flowers of the World* and other references classify it as *Moraea*. The *Moraea* is from—take your choice—either the name of an eighteenth-century English botanist, Robert More, or the father-in-law of Linnaeus, J. Moraeus. (We do wish these references would get their references straight. No matter.) They bloom off and on throughout the season at roughly two-week intervals, which is why one common name includes the word *fortnight*. *Moraea iridioides* (formerly *Dietes*), the African iris, has large white flowers with orange-brown and blue markings; 'Lemon Drops' and 'Orange Drops' have yellow or orange markings. (GBT)

When, Where, and How to Plant
Plant any time during the year, spacing 18 to 24 inches. Plant in full sun. Enrich the planting hole of the rhizome with organic matter, such as compost, peat moss, and pine-bark mulch. Sand will help increase drainage. Put a little bone meal in the bottom of the planting hole, which should be 2 to 3 inches deep. Cover the hole, fertilize with 1 to 2 teaspoons of a slow-release fertilizer, and then mulch; water. If drainage is a problem, grow *Dietes bicolor* in raised beds using a mix of peat moss or compost and sand, plus slow-release fertilizer and potting mix.

Growing Tips
If using a granular fertilizer, 2 to 3 pounds per 100 square feet of bulb bed is sufficient. Bulbs already contain enough stored food to go through their first flowering. Rhizomes also store water as well as food, which is one reason these are said to be drought-tolerant. But they will profit in their flowering capacity if you water them regularly: two to three times a week if it does not rain. Reduce watering after flowering.

Regional Advice and Care
Where cold is a problem, grow tropical bulbs in pots to bring inside in winter. Grasshoppers and snails love *Dietes*. The product for use to fight grasshoppers is *Nosema locustae*, a protozoa that has various commercially packaged names. It causes grasshoppers to produce fewer eggs. For snails or garden slugs, protect African iris with copper screen barriers or, in dry seasons, with diatomaceous earth.

Companion Planting and Design
The African iris is a versatile perennial that is useful as a border plant along woodsy paths or at the edges of planting beds, even in rock gardens.

Try These
The yellow flowers of the fortnight lily are quite lovely.

African Lily

Agapanthus africanus

Botanical Pronunciation
ag-ah-PAN-thus af-re-CAN-us

Other Name Lily-of-the-Nile

Bloom Period and Seasonal Color
Spring through early summer blooms in white
or blue

Mature Height x Spread
3 feet x 18 inches

Gardeners who want color in a great accent plant love the durable African lilies. The plants give an eye-catching flower display, shooting up an inflorescence that's topped with a ball-like cluster of blue or white flowers. Each blossom is 1 to 2 inches long. When not in bloom, the plants provide dark green straplike foliage from year-round greenery. After the plants have flowered, cut the old stalks back to near the ground to allow the plant's energy to go into bulb production, or allow the plant to continue seed development. Add African lilies to the perennial flower bed, or spot them among shrub plantings throughout the landscape. Some gardeners also like to grow the plants in containers for the patio or entrance area. (TM)

When, Where, and How to Plant
Rhizomes of African lilies are best planted from October through March in the Florida landscape. Container grown plants are available from garden centers for planting throughout the year. They grow best in areas with six to eight hours of sun and bright light for the remaining portions of the day. Select areas that do not flood during the rainy season. All bulbs should be planted in well-drained soil. When planting in containers, use a loose potting mix and large containers. African lilies grow well in sandy soils as long as they are given plenty of water and all the nutrients needed for growth. Work liberal quantities of compost or peat moss and manure into the planting site. African lilies should be set in the soil with the tops of the rhizomes just below the surface of the ground. Space

the rhizomes 12 inches apart, and then provide adequate water to moisten the soil thoroughly.

Growing Tips
A light mulch can be added to maintain soil moisture and supply some nutrients. Water weekly during the drier months. Do not overwater during the summer, as root rot may be a problem. The African lily needs a light feeding once in March, May, and September. Use a general landscape or slow-release fertilizer, following label instructions for bulbs or perennial plantings. African lilies may be affected by caterpillars and grasshoppers. Handpick pests from the plants, or treat them with a pest-control product recommended by the University of Florida, following label instructions.

Regional Advice and Care
African lilies grow best in North and Central Florida gardens. In the colder portions of the state, protect them from the more severe freezes. Plantings in South Florida are usually short-lived. Remove declining flower heads as needed, or save them for dried arrangements.

Companion Planting and Design
African lily is a workhorse of the bulbs, planted in clusters as a groundcover among perennials and shrubs. Grow as a backdrop for flowerbeds of annuals, tropicals, and other bulbs.

Try These
Several selections with blue color are available. I prefer the dark blue ones.

Amaryllis

Hippeastrum hybrids

Botanical Pronunciation
hip-ee-ASS-strum

Other Name Barbados lily

Bloom Period and Seasonal Color
Winter and spring blooms in red, pink, orange, salmon, and white

Mature Height x Spread
2 feet x 12 inches

A favorite Christmas present for Florida gardeners, the amaryllis today has become a true knockout. 'Apple Blossom' and 'Red Lion' are old-time hybrids that are recommended for South Florida gardens by amaryllis expert Dr. Alan Meerow with the USDA Subtropical Research Station in Miami. *Hippeastrum* 'Dancing Queen' is a luscious orange-and-white double. Another double is salmon-light orange flowering *Hippeastrum* 'Smoked Salmon'. Butterfly amaryllis, *H. papilio*, can be found in mail order catalogs and at plant sales. It is a light greenish white overlain with crimson-maroon markings. Another red cousin is the Jacobean lily, *Amaryllis formosissima*, which looks like a cross between an orchid and an amaryllis. (GBT)

When, Where, and How to Plant
Plant in September, October, November, or again in late winter to early spring. Plant in an enriched soil, blending two parts peat moss with one part sand and one part pine-bark mulch or chips, either in the soil or in pots. You may prefer to dig the whole bed and replace soil with this mix. Add bone meal to the bottom of the individual planting holes, placing the bulbs just at the soil level or slightly above, spaced a foot or a little more apart. Add a couple of teaspoons of 6-6-6 or slow-release fertilizer for each bulb after backfilling, and then mulch to help keep the soil evenly moist. Remove spent flower stalks before the plants form seeds (which occurs quickly). This practice will direct energy back into bulb formation.

Growing Tips
Fertilize at least three times a year. When flowers begin to form, spray with a 20-20-20. A foliar micronutrient spray also is helpful, particularly if you see leaves beginning to turn yellow before flowering. After flowering, keep watering the plants until the leaves turn yellow, and then allow them to rest. Some may not die back. But when plants seem to go into a slowdown or resting stage, withhold water for a while, or dig and refresh the planting bed.

Regional Advice and Care
Plant bulbs in pots to bring indoors when freezing is predicted. Grasshoppers and snails can demolish amaryllis leaves quickly. The protozoa product containing *Nosema locustae*, mentioned for African iris, can be useful for amaryllis. Also check at night for snails in pots and under mulch, and handpick them to remove.

Companion Planting and Design
After the holiday season is over, you can plant amaryllis in the garden as border plants or in beds of their own. Amaryllis plants are useful at the feet of leggy shrubs or in pots on the pool deck.

Try These
My favorite is 'Apple Blossom', which is white with pink edges and piping, although 'Red Lion' has a stunning velvet finish and is the color of Merlot wine. 'Dancing Queen' is just flat-out awesome.

Amazon Lily

Eucharis grandiflora

Botanical Pronunciation
YOU-kah-riss grand-eh-FLOR-ah

Other Name Eucharis lily

Bloom Period and Seasonal Color
Mainly winter months with narcissuslike blossoms in white

Mature Height x Spread
18 inches x 24 inches

Zones 9–11

The snow-white blossoms of the Amazon lily held high above the plant resemble those of a large narcissus. Flowering is sporadic but usually occurs during the winter and early spring months. The plant could bloom at almost any time of the year, however. The large, rounded, deep green foliage may reach 6 inches in diameter. This plant works well in the shady gardens of Central and South Florida. Grow it with other perennials, or use it as a groundcover in front of other greenery. Many gardeners prefer to grow the Amazon lily in containers, where they can control the water and fertilizer to encourage more reliable flowering. Potted Amazon lilies can be grown on the porch or patio or at an entrance. (TM)

When, Where, and How to Plant

Amazon lilies can be planted at any time of the year. Division of clumps is best done during the fall through early spring months. They grow best in areas with filtered sun but have produced good foliage and flowers in shady areas under trees. Foliage exposed to full sun usually burns. Work liberal quantities of compost or peat moss and manure into the planting site. Plant the Amazon lily with the tip of the bulb at the surface of the soil. Space bulbs 3 to 4 inches apart. In a container, add 3 to 4 bulbs to an 8-inch pot. After planting, provide adequate water to moisten the soil thoroughly. Flowering can usually be encouraged by alternating moist and dry periods for about a month. After the treatment, feed the plants to start growth and flowers. After the plants have flowered, cut the old stalks back to near the ground.

Growing Tips

A light mulch can be added to maintain soil moisture and supply some nutrients with in-ground plantings. Keep planting sites moist, watering weekly during the drier times of the year. Amazon lilies need a light feeding once in March, May, and September. Gardeners can use general landscape product or slow-release fertilizer, following label instructions for bulbs or perennial plantings. Plants in containers can be fed monthly during the warmer months with a water-soluble fertilizer at label rates. Water when the surface soil begins to dry.

Regional Advice and Care

Amazon lilies are quite cold-sensitive. North Florida and some colder areas of Central Florida should restrict plantings to container gardens. Amazon lilies may be affected by caterpillars and slugs. Handpick pests from the plants, or treat with a natural pest-control product. Remove declining flower stalks as needed to keep plants attractive.

Companion Planting and Design

This is a groundcover and flowering plant for the shade. It can be used in beds or pots as a substitute for hostas. Plant with caladiums, gingers, impatiens, and begonias.

Try These

Only the species is available in Florida.

Blood Lily

Scadoxus multiflorus

Botanical Pronunciation
ska-DOX-us mul-ti-FLOOR-us

Bloom Period and Seasonal Color
Spring to early summer blooms in red

Mature Height x Spread
18 inches to 2 feet x 18 inches

Perhaps the name really tells the story about the blood lily flowers. These bright red attention-getters pop up along with the spring foliage to form a 6-inch or larger ball of color. One of Florida's most exotic bulbs, the blood lily can be grown with perennials or added to plantings in front of shrubs. Or it can be grown in containers on a porch or patio or near an entrance. Many gardeners like to add the plants to rest areas, where visitors can stop and study the inflorescence made up of many individual blooms. The bright green foliage sprouts each spring; the long, ovate leaves remain attractive until fall when the plants go dormant. Only one species of blood lily is commonly marketed in Florida. (TM)

When, Where, and How to Plant

Most blood lilies are planted from January through March in the Florida garden. Container plants are often available year-round and can be added to the landscape at any time. Make divisions from fall through early winter when the plants are dormant. They grow best in an area with filtered sun for most of the day but can also be grown under the more intense shade of trees. Blood lilies tolerate sandy soil but are easier to maintain if the soil is improved with organic matter before planting. Work liberal quantities of compost or peat moss and manure into the planting site. Blood lily bulbs should be planted with the tips just below the surface of the soil. Space the bulbs 6 to 8 inches apart. In a 6- or 8-inch pot, several bulbs may be grown. After the plants have flowered, most gardeners cut the old stalks back to near the ground to allow the plant's energy to go into bulb production.

Growing Tips

After planting, provide adequate water to moisten the soil thoroughly. A light mulch can be added to maintain soil moisture and supply some nutrients for in-ground plantings. Keep planting sites moist. Blood lilies need a light feeding once in March, May, and August. Use a general landscape fertilizer or slow-release product. For container-grown plants, use a water-soluble fertilizer.

Regional Advice and Care

Blood lilies grow well in all areas of Florida. In northern regions, add some extra mulch to the soil for cold protection. Blood lilies may be affected by caterpillars and slugs. Handpick pests from the plants, or treat them with a pest-control product recommended by the University of Florida.

Companion Planting and Design

Add them to the perennial or bulb garden, or mix among shrubs in full sun to light shade. Blood lily combines well with amaryllis, crinum, impatiens, gingers, and African iris.

Try These

Only the species is available in Florida.

Blue Flag Iris

Iris virginica var. virginica

Botanical Pronunciation
EYE-ris ver-JIN-ee-kah

Other Name Southern blue flag

Bloom Period and Seasonal Color
Spring blooms in lavender, purple, blue, or white

Mature Height x Spread
To 3 feet x 12 inches; will form clumps

Zones 8–10b

Among the prettiest plants of the wetlands or margins of the wetlands are the blue flags. These ephemeral flowers appear in the spring, and if you're lucky, you'll venture into a park at just the right time. The flowers are a light lavender-purple with long, yellow-and-white-marked sepals and three narrow upright petals. The flags are rhizomatous plants, not true bulbs, yet they are capable of growing in wet soil, in pots barely submerged beneath the surface of ponds. Accustomed to growing in muck, these plants are acid lovers. *Iris virginica* is basically an aquatic plant, so it really likes wet feet. The blue-purple iris, when planted strategically around a pond edge, is quite lovely. (GBT)

When, Where, and How to Plant

Plant in the late summer or fall, spacing rhizomes 8 inches apart. Plant in low-lying swales, in pots submerged in ponds, or in bog conditions. (Bogs can be created by removing soil to a depth of several inches, lining the area with plastic, then a layer of rocks, and then a highly organic mix of peat moss, muck, and sand. Muck in Florida is really a decomposed peat of sawgrass and other aquatics. On the edges of freshwater marshes and swamps, muck has some rocky and sandy components mixed in with it. When dry, it tends to blow away, particle by particle, and so a lawn or yard built on a 50-50 mix of sand and muck will eventually become just sand, with no nutrient-holding capacity at all.) In pots, keep the rhizome within 2 inches of the surface, using a regular garden potting soil. Cover the surface with rocks before submerging so the soil won't float off and fish won't dig up the plants. Mix 6-6-6 or 10-10-10 into the soil when planting.

Growing Tips

To fertilize later, wrap an appropriate amount of fertilizer in newspaper and wedge it into the pot to get it close to the roots. Fertilizer plugs are available for aquatic use. Dig the rhizomes yearly, in fall or late winter. Separate the rhizomes, clean, and repot. Use plugs or fertilizer pellets if planting in containers to be submerged, or scatter fertilizer on top of the bog as you would for any other landscape plant. Propagate by cutting the rhizome into sections, each containing a bud.

Regional Advice and Care

Blue flag iris grows well throughout Florida, except in the Keys. Make it a practice to remove yellow leaves that form as the plant expands.

Companion Planting and Design

For ponds, the upright iris looks elegant when seen against the flat, round leaves of water lilies and the superlative lotus. Keep it visually removed from other upright plants.

Try These

A white version, *Iris virginica alba*, is simply gorgeous, and I grow it in my pond.

Caladium

Caladium hortulanum

Botanical Pronunciation
ka-LAY-dee-um hort-u-LAN-um

Other Name Fancy leafed caladium

Bloom Period and Seasonal Color
Summer foliage in red, rose, pink, white, silver, bronze, and green

Mature Height x Spread
18 inches to 2 feet x 18 inches to 2 feet

Zones 9–11

Rosy pink with dark pink spots; white with wine-colored spots; green veins on white; rosy red outlined in white, separating into little islands of red against a sea of green...these are the caladiums. Aroids by birthright, charmers by God, these plants are far more durable than they look, taking the heat and humidity of summer as if to the station born. In South and Central Florida, they are magical sources of summer color, planted in beds beneath trees, which provide protection from the midday sun. For flower arrangers, the leaves offer a good source of color and will last a long time. Some old favorites include 'Candidum', 'Florida Cardinal', 'Freida Hemple', 'Gypsy Rose', 'Pink Beauty', 'Pink Gem', 'Aaron Nehrling', 'White Christmas', and 'White Wing'. (GBT)

When, Where, and How to Plant
Plant in the late winter or spring. Plant in enriched soil in the shade or sun. Set tubers 1 to 2 inches below the soil surface and 10 to 12 inches apart. Use a peat or another type of soil amendment if you wish, and mulch bulbs with pine bark. Water sparingly until the leaves emerge, which may take longer than you think. In a pot, use a regular sterile potting soil or soilless mix, and add a small amount of slow-release fertilizer, following the directions below.

Growing Tips
Water two or three times a week. Fertilize them once a month with a balanced fertilizer, such as 6-6-6, or use a slow-release fertilizer. You may want to add more slow-release fertilizer at least once during the warm growing season to keep them performing well. Although their soil should drain well, it also should remain moist. Notice that caladiums look quite wonderful after two or three days of rain. Beginning in late September through October, caladiums will die back, shed their leaves, and disappear. Reduce water and allow them to stay in the ground, or dig them up, clean them, and separate the bulbs. Dust the cleaned bulbs with a fungicide and put them in a paper bag in a cool place. You can replant in April in place of winter annuals. After about three years, you may wish to replace the tubers, which tend to get smaller.

Regional Advice and Care
In the fall, the leaves die back naturally, and the bulbs can be dug, dried, and saved in a dry place (never the refrigerator because they're tropical) for the following year. See instructions in "Growing Tips."

Companion Planting and Design
Their marvelously complex color forms mean most caladiums look best when seen in masses. Several can be used at the ends of beds or around the base of trees to replace impatiens or wax begonias.

Try These
'Florida Cardinal', 'Galaxy', and 'Aaron Nehrling' are vigorous and beautiful.

Calla Lily

Zantedeschia spp.

Botanical Pronunciation
ZAN-the-des-key-ah

Other Name Common calla

Bloom Period and Seasonal Color
Spring blooms in white, pink, yellow, cream, lavender, and purple

Mature Height x Spread
2 feet x 18 inches

Most Florida gardeners can enjoy the springtime blooms of callas for years without transplanting. Callas call attention to themselves with their large 4- to 6-inch blooms. The white, pink, or yellow blossoms are borne on tall stems that can be left in the garden or cut as bouquets. Add the plantings to a perennial garden, or spot them throughout the landscape in front of other greenery. They can also be grown in containers. After flowering, the foliage gradually declines, and the plants go dormant for the fall and winter months. A number of calla species and varieties may be planted in Florida. The large, white flowering selections appear to grow best. Every year, check for new introductions that might be suitable for planting in your landscape. (TM)

When, Where, and How to Plant
Callas are best planted from September through January. Some gardeners prefer to dig the rhizomes after the flowers and foliage decline. They will grow best in areas with six to eight hours of sun and bright light for the remaining portions of the day. The plantings like a moist soil with good drainage. Select areas that do not flood during the rainy seasons. Callas grow well in sandy soils as long as they are given plenty of water and all the nutrients needed for growth. Plants are easier to maintain if the soil is improved with organic matter before planting. Work liberal quantities of compost or peat moss and manure into the planting site. Calla rhizomes should be planted 1 to 2 inches deep and 12 to 24 inches apart. After planting, provide adequate water to moisten the soil thoroughly. When planting in containers, use large containers and a loose potting mix.

Growing Tips
A light mulch can be added to maintain the soil moisture and supply some nutrients. Keep planting sites moist by watering whenever the surface soil feels dry to the touch. Pay attention to water needs during the hotter, drier months of spring. Callas should be given a light feeding once in March, May, and August. Gardeners can use a general landscape fertilizer or slow-release product, following label instructions. After the plants have flowered, cut the old stalks back to near the ground.

Regional Advice and Care
Callas grow best in North and Central Florida. Container culture is best in South Florida. Callas may be affected by spider mites and thrips. Treat plants with a pest-control product recommended by the University of Florida.

Companion Planting and Design
Help create the tropical look with clusters of calla lilies among plantings that like the warmer climate. Some good companions include philodendrons, caladiums, anthurium, gingers, canna, and bananas.

Try These
The new calla hybrids appear to have more vigor and flower more quickly than do the older selections. One good performer is the hybrid calla 'Dwarf Pink'.

Canna

Canna hybrids

Botanical Pronunciation
CAN-uh

Bloom Period and Seasonal Color
Spring and summer blooms in red, orange, yellow, pink, cream, white, and bicolors

Mature Height x Spread
2 feet to 4 feet x 18 inches or so, depending on cultivar

Zones 9–11; *C. flaccida* to Zone 8

In 1846, according to *Flowers of the World*, a French consular agent in Chile, one M. Annee, collected cannas from South America and took them home to Paris to hybridize them. According to *Gardening in the Tropics* by R. E. Holttum and Ivan Enoch, the plants were then further hybridized in Italy, where the first to become a modern canna appeared in 1890. *C. flaccida*, the aquatic, yellow-flowering species, is a Florida native. Hybridization among species has given us bold cannas, but it has also made them difficult to maintain. They require a good deal of attention and are subject to such leaf mutilation by the canna leaf roller, a moth larva, that they are very carefully grown in South Florida. (GBT)

When, Where, and How to Plant
Plant in the late winter to spring. Plant the rhizomes in an area that can be irrigated regularly. Cannas like a rich soil, so a planting hole can have organic material (peat moss, compost, aged manure) added to it, or a whole bed can be dug and soil replaced with those ingredients. Plant about 1 to 2 feet apart and 2 inches deep. Dig and divide, then replant every year to keep cannas flowering well.

Growing Tips
Given their marshy origins and even aquatic components, cannas love moist soil and, to be vigorous, require frequent fertilizing. Use a low-nitrogen granular, such as 4-7-5, a small amount monthly, and supplement that with a weekly spray of 20-20-20. Water two or three times weekly, early in the morning, so any wet foliage will dry by nightfall to avoid fungal diseases. Because cannas like moist soil and are heavy feeders, they are not candidates for water-saving gardens unless used in an area around the house where other water-thirsty plants grow. Thin the rhizomes periodically to give plants a rejuvenating boost.

Regional Advice and Care
In South and Central Florida, the plants can be grown in the ground all year. As far south as Palm Beach, they will die down in winter. Use as an annual in North Florida and as a perennial in Central Florida, except for *C. flaccida*, the aquatic. Regularly inspect for leaf rollers and fungus. Spider mites can be a problem in the dry season. Like the frangipani, the canna is subject to rust, a fungus that looks like its name. This can be controlled by sulfur spray or a copper fungicide. Contact your local extension service office for a recommendation.

Companion Planting and Design
Tropical leaves that are broad and sometimes striped mean this tropical bulb may best be seen by itself or with other broad-leafed tropicals, such as bananas or gingers.

Try These
Canna 'Tropicana', with wine-and-orange-striped leaves, is wildly tropical and eye-catching when used with discrimination.

Daylily

Hemerocallis hybrids

Botanical Pronunciation
hem-erh-oh-CAL-lis

Bloom Period and Seasonal Color
Spring through summer blooms in yellow, orange, pink, red, lavender, and blends

Mature Height x Spread
2 feet x 18 inches

Florida boasts of some of the most popular breeders, growers, and varieties of daylilies in the nation. Daylilies sold at plant stores represent just a small portion of selections available from daylily nurseries. As the name implies, most daylily blossoms last only a day, but the buds along the stems are numerous and each stalk can continue to open blossoms for weeks. Some may bloom sporadically throughout the year. Use daylilies in large beds, rock gardens, perennial borders, and pots. These versatile plants can fit into just about any landscape situation. The best daylilies for Florida are the evergreen and semievergreen types. Deciduous varieties have been poorer performers in most Florida landscapes. (TM)

When, Where, and How to Plant

Daylilies can be added to the landscape at any time of the year as bare-root transplants or container-grown plants. They grow best in an area with six to eight hours of sun and bright light for the remaining portions of the day. The plantings like an enriched soil with good drainage. Select areas that do not flood during the rainy seasons. All bulbs should be planted in well-drained soil. Daylilies grow well in sandy soils as long as they are given plenty of water and all the nutrients needed for growth. Plants are easier to maintain if the soil is improved with organic matter before planting. Work liberal quantities of compost or peat moss and manure into the planting site. Daylilies should be set with the base of the foliage at soil level. It's better to plant a little above the ground than too deep.

Growing Tips

After planting, provide adequate water to moisten the soil thoroughly. A light mulch can be added to maintain soil moisture and supply some nutrients. Keep planting sites moist, watering whenever the surface soil feels dry to the touch. Daylilies need a light feeding once in March, May, and September. Gardeners can use a general landscape or slow-release fertilizer, following label instructions for bulbs or perennial plantings.

Regional Advice and Care

South Florida growers should check with local garden centers for the best adapted selections. Not all grow well in the hotter sections of the state. They may be affected by caterpillars, aphids, thrips, and grasshoppers. Handpick insect pests from the plants, or treat them with a natural pest-control product. Daylily rust has become a major disease. Use a fungicide labeled for rust when first noted. Remove old flower stalks as needed to keep plants attractive.

Companion Planting and Design

Gardeners often like to create entire beds of daylilies, but the plants also mix well with annuals, perennials, and shrubs. They are especially attractive with African iris, crinums, and cannas.

Try These

Some flowers just catch your eye with their great color. You really have to pick daylilies for the garden in person. My advice is to select ones in bloom with the color and form you like.

Ginger

Several genera

Botanical Pronunciation
Varies as to genus and species

Bloom Period and Seasonal Color
Mainly April through November in assorted colors plus white

Mature Height x Spread
Plants vary from a foot to over 8 feet tall and clumps forming to 6 feet wide

One Florida ginger enthusiast touted a collection of over two hundred species and varieties in his home landscape. Since gingers grow throughout the state, think how many you might grow in the warm regions, where plantings remain active year-round. Mention ginger and the edible ginger found in grocery stores often comes to mind. It has a thick, edible rhizome that grows well in a container or moist garden site, but it is not a very showy plant. What's found in most landscapes are the ornamental gingers with colorful, usually prominent blooms. Gingers form great accents, space dividers, and sometimes groundcovers. It's best to give them plenty of room to grow. Do note that some gingers like only the shady spots so select species for light requirements. (TM)

When, Where, and How to Plant
Start gingers from thick rhizomes or plants often sold at garden centers. These can be added to the garden year-round, but in the colder spots plantings might be delayed until spring. Divide clumps of matted rhizomes as needed to expand the collection or share with friends. Set the rhizomes at or slightly below ground level.

Growing Tips
Most ginger plantings prefer a moist soil but can tolerate short periods of drought. They seem to like the filtered sun best, but a majority survive and flower well in full sun when given adequate moisture. Feed with a slow-release landscape fertilizer during the warmer months. Taller cane-type gingers can grow out of control. Periodically thin out or divide the plantings. Out of bounds stalks can be removed any time. Some gardeners like to keep containers of gingers for deck or patio plantings. Fill the containers with a good potting soil, add the rhizomes, keep them moist, and feed with a slow-release fertilizer.

Regional Advice and Care
Some gingers go dormant for the winter, surviving as underground rhizomes. Cut the tops off as these plants decline. Prune all as needed when they grow thick or out of bounds or become damaged by cold. All gingers like a light mulch. Pests are a minor problem with most gingers. Lower-growing types may be attacked by slugs; natural slug baits should give control. Taller types may suffer some chewed leaves from caterpillars and grasshoppers, but control is seldom needed.

Companion Planting and Design
Combine with sun to light shade lovers as accent features or groundcovers. Taller selections can be used as backdrops. Mix with African lily, coleus, crinums, jacobinia, and split leaf philodendron.

Try These
The peacock ginger is a favorite reminiscent of northern hosta for the shady spots. Pinecone ginger is unique as the reddish cones offer a pine fragrance. Pinkish hidden gingers are a spring surprise, and the white butterfly ginger has a sweet fragrance. Equally interesting is the shell ginger with seashell-like flowers. Many like to grow the edible ginger from a grocery store as a start.

Gladiolus

Gladiolus hybrids

Botanical Pronunciation
GLAD-ee-ol-us

Bloom Period and Seasonal Color
Mainly spring through summer blooms in all colors and blends

Mature Height x Spread
2 feet x upright single-stemmed

Gardeners love their gladiolus for the tall spikes of color. The flowers come in most colors of the rainbow in addition to some blends. The trumpetlike blooms open from the base of the flower stalk and continue up the stem to the very tip. The flowering process often lasts a week or more. Often the stalks are not allowed to mature in the garden but are cut for bouquets. The lancelike foliage grows straight up. Plant gladiolus in perennial beds and rock gardens, or use them among shrub plantings. After a few months of growth and flowering, the plants gradually decline for a rest period before starting new growth. In addition to short and tall forms, many varieties of gladiolus are available from garden centers and mail order nurseries. (TM)

When, Where, and How to Plant
Gladiolus can be planted any time of the year. The bulblike corms are available from January through May for home planting. They grow best in an area with six to eight hours of sun and bright light for the remaining portions of the day. The plantings like an enriched soil with good drainage. Gladiolus grow well in sandy soils as long as they are given plenty of water and all the nutrients needed for growth. Work liberal quantities of compost or peat moss and manure into the planting site. Gladiolus corms should be set 2 to 3 inches deep and spaced 4 to 6 inches apart in the ground. After planting, provide adequate water to moisten the soil thoroughly. Glads may need staking when the stalks are produced to prevent wind damage. After the plants have flowered, most gardeners cut the old stalks back to near the ground to allow the plant's energy to go into corm production.

Growing Tips
A light mulch can be added to maintain soil moisture, supply some nutrients, and control weeds. Keep planting sites moist, watering whenever the surface inch of soil feels dry to the touch. Gladiolus need light feedings monthly during the growing period. Gardeners can use a general garden or slow-release fertilizer, following label instructions for bulb plantings.

Regional Advice and Care
Gladiolus grow well in all areas of Florida but may be affected by cold weather. North and Central Florida plantings are usually restricted to the spring and summer months. Many gardeners leave these bulbs in the ground for a few years before digging and dividing. They may be affected by caterpillars, grasshoppers, and thrips. Handpick pests from the plants, or treat them with a pest-control product recommended by the University of Florida.

Companion Planting and Design
Often planted in a row, gladiolus are equally attractive in clusters with other bulbs and perennials. They can be mixed with canna, crinum, society garlic, and rain lilies.

Try These
Call me sentimental, but my dad liked 'Dusty Miller'. It's still my favorite, with the dusty look that catches the eye.

Gloriosa Lily

Gloriosa spp.

Botanical Pronunciation
GLORY-oh-sah

Other Name Climbing lily

Bloom Period and Seasonal Color
Spring through summer blooms in red banded
with yellow

Mature Height x Spread
6 feet x vining 6 feet

Enjoy a spectacular, colorful flowering plant by adding a gloriosa lily near the patio or entrance to the home. The large blooms open in a downward-facing position and are often a blend of crimson and yellow colors. The plants start to grow shortly after planting the V-shaped tubers. You can plant gloriosa lilies individually, or you can train several along a wall or fence, because it is one of the few vining bulbous plants. After months of flowering, the plants die back or, in cooler regions, are killed back to the ground by cold weather. There are two species of gloriosa lilies usually planted in Florida: *Gloriosa rothschildiana* and *Gloriosa superba*. The species are similar, varying in the amount of crimson and yellow color in the blooms. (TM)

When, Where, and How to Plant

Gloriosa lilies are best planted from January through April in Florida landscapes. Tubers can be dug and separated from established plantings at any time of the year. They grow best in an area with six to eight hours of sun and bright light for the remaining portions of the day. The plantings like an enriched soil with good drainage. Gloriosa lilies grow well in sandy soils as long as they are given plenty of water and all the nutrients needed for growth. They can withstand periods of drought but die back and then resume growth when damper weather returns. Work liberal quantities of compost or peat moss and manure into the planting site. Gloriosa lilies should be planted 2 to 4 inches deep in the ground and spaced 12 to 18 inches apart. After planting, provide enough

water to moisten the soil thoroughly. Gloriosa lilies may grow out of bounds and need some trimming of the vining portions to prevent them from growing among other plantings.

Growing Tips

A light mulch can be added to maintain soil moisture and supply some nutrients. Keep planting sites moist, watering whenever the surface inch of soil feels dry. Gardeners can use a general garden or slow-release fertilizer, following label instructions for bulbs or perennial plantings.

Regional Advice and Care

Gloriosa lilies grow well in all areas of Florida. Plants go dormant in North and Central Florida when affected by cold. Trim off dead vine portions, and wait for new growth to begin. Gloriosa lilies may be affected by caterpillars. Handpick pests from the plants, or treat them with a pest-control product recommended by the University of Florida.

Companion Planting and Design

Plant as a backdrop for a garden or part of a perennial planting that declines during the winter. Use with lower-growing African iris, crinum, gingers, and society garlic.

Try These

Other than the species, there is not much from which to choose. *G. rothschildiana* has the vigor I like and good crimson and yellow color combinations in the blooms.

Rain Lily

Several genera

Botanical Pronunciation
Varies as to genus and species

Other Name Fairy lily

Bloom Period and Seasonal Color
Late spring through early fall blooms in white, yellow, pink, and red

Mature Height x Spread
Up to 8 inch foliage x upright with slightly arching leaves

Rain lilies are a pleasant summer surprise when garden color is often a bit sparse, popping up their attractive blooms throughout the rainy season. Some might think these are crocus with their pink, yellow, or white bell-shaped blossoms. Most keep foliage throughout the year, but it blends in with other greenery until the flowers push up to a foot above the ground depending on the species. Rain lilies are best planted in clusters to naturalize in flower beds and perennial gardens. They can also be used along walkways, as groundcovers, and in containers. All are drought-tolerant but grow best with adequate moisture. Bulbs are easiest to find at garden centers during the early spring season or ordered from mail order companies. (TM)

When, Where, and How to Plant
Add to the landscape any time of the year, but bulbs are usually available in late winter or spring. They grow and flower best in areas with full sun, good drainage, and moist soil. Work in liberal quantities of compost, peat moss, or garden soils with sandy sites. Bulbs should be planted 1 to 2 inches deep in the ground and spaced 3 to 4 inches apart. They can also be grown from seeds that germinate shortly after the pods mature. Old stalks can be removed after flowering to keep beds attractive. Rain lilies can form tight clusters after several years of growth. These plantings are best divided late fall through early spring.

Growing Tips
Because rain lilies like a moist soil at flowering time, it is good to add light mulch up to an inch thick of coarse compost or fine barks to maintain soil moisture and help control weeds. Keep plantings moist during the warmer times of the year by watering whenever the surface soil feels dry. Less water is needed during the winter. Give a light feeding once in March, May, and September with a garden fertilizer or use a slow-release fertilizer as labeled. Grassy weeds can be major competition, as some have similar leaf shapes. Use of an over the top herbicide to control grasses has given good results applied following label instructions.

Regional Advice and Care
Rain lilies grow well in all areas of the state. They may be affected by caterpillars and grasshoppers. Handpick from the plants or use a natural control where available.

Companion Planting and Design
Plant as a seasonal accent with perennials staged in front of taller plantings or as a border along walkways. Use as a groundcover with a backdrop of Indian hawthorn or dwarf yaupon holly.

Try These
Most species and hybrids grown in Florida are in the *Habranthus* and *Zephyranthes* genera. All are favorites, as they flower at different times during summer through early fall. The most vigorous color appears to be pink, but whites and yellows do well too.

Swamp Lily

Crinum americanum

Botanical Pronunciation
KRY-num amer-uh-CAN-um

Other Name Southern swamp crinum

Bloom Period and Seasonal Color
Spring blooms are white

Mature Height x Spread
To 2 feet x 2 feet

Zones 8–11

Crinum *americanum* and *Crinum asiaticum*, sisters beneath the skin, are spring-blooming tropical lilies with big showy flowers. *Crinum americanum*, the fragrant swamp lily, is a bulb native to Florida and Georgia. These lilies stand out against the swampy margins of freshwater marshes like stars in the night. In such vastness, they seem smaller than they are. At home in your garden, you will find they are substantial. The flowers are starbursts of white petals with showy stigmas and stamens on long stalks in the center. The swamp lily is a perfect candidate for low-lying swales or where water stands occasionally. *Crinum asiaticum*, the tree lily, rears itself up on a trunk, with straplike leaves several feet long and stalks of flowers equally large. (GBT)

When, Where, and How to Plant
Plant any time, but winter is best for spring flowers. Plants tend to look just a little nicer in high shade. A low-lying area that has occasionally wet conditions (or a homemade bog) will serve well. A basic rule of thumb for wetland plants: a wetland plant can be grown in dry conditions, but an upland plant cannot be grown in wet conditions. Enrich the planting hole with two parts peat moss, one part each sand and pine bark mulch (not large nuggets). Add some bone meal to the bottom, and plant the bulb at the same depth at which it grew in the container, making sure that the neck of the bulb is above the soil line. If planting several, dig a bed at least 6 to 8 inches deep, enrich the entire bed, and space 1 to 1½ feet apart.

Growing Tips
Irrigate regularly to keep the area evenly moist, and fertilize in spring, summer, and fall; and mulch. Keep lower leaves trimmed when fungal spots begin to detract from them.

Regional Advice and Care
These lilies can grow into Zone 9 and even into Georgia. Allow them to rest after flowering. *C. americanum* has a fungus that requires some work: every few weeks it needs a spray of fungicide. Beginning in March, lubber grasshoppers hatch, emerge from underground nests, and start eating their way through the landscape. Until, that is, they happen on a lily. They can take it to the mat in record time. Use a protozoa, *Nosema locustae*, which is a biological control for grasshoppers widely available on the Internet. Better yet, step on them when they're tiny and all in one area. The bigger they get, the messier the task.

Companion Planting and Design
Because these lilies grow in wetland conditions or on the edges of wetlands, they look most at home in a garden bog or with such plants as ferns, in a crescent design or a group of three or five.

Try These
Swamp lily, which is the only species, has starlike flowers and a sweet fragrance.

Voodoo Lily

Amorphophallus spp.

Botanical Pronunciation
ah-more-foh-FOUL-us

Other Name Snake lily

Bloom Period and Seasonal Color
Spring blooms of a cream to reddish-brown

Mature Height x Spread
Leaf 6 feet; some flowers to 8 feet or more x
6 feet

The name voodoo lily suggests the plant might have a little magic, and it does. It grows from nothing in early spring to a tall plant in just weeks. The leaves are deeply cut and up to several feet long and wide. Plants often have interesting trunks with green streaks and splotches some feel resemble snakeskin. Mature plants have spectacular reddish brown spring flowers. *A. titanium* is among the world's largest flowers, and can reach 8-plus feet high. A not-so-pleasant surprise is some species open flowers with a very foul odor, dispersed by even slight breezes, to attract pollinating flies. Some species grow only a few feet tall, and others grow large enough for a child to stand under. (TM)

When, Where, and How to Plant
Voodoo lilies are best planted late winter through spring, when the corms are beginning to grow. They grow best in areas with six to eight hours of sun and bright light for the remainder of the day. The plantings like an enriched soil with good drainage. Select areas that do not flood during the rainy seasons. Voodoo lilies grow well in sandy soils as long as they are given plenty of water and all the nutrients needed for growth. Work in liberal quantities of compost or peat moss and manure. Voodoo lily corms should be planted 3 to 4 inches deep and spaced 1 foot or more apart. After planting, provide adequate water to moisten the soil thoroughly. When flowers begin to decline, the shriveled blossoms can be removed. Plants are occasionally found at garden centers, but bulblike corms are more likely to be available during the early spring.

Growing Tips
A light mulch will maintain soil moisture and supply some nutrients. The lilies are drought-tolerant but grow best when the sites are kept moist, watering when the surface soil feels dry. Voodoo lilies need a light feeding in March, May, and August. Use a general garden or slow-release fertilizer, following label instructions.

Regional Advice and Care
Voodoo lilies vary as to their hardiness. Most can be grown throughout the state if the soil is mulched after they die back during the fall. All can be grown in containers and brought indoors during freezing weather. Voodoo lilies may be affected by caterpillars and grasshoppers. Handpick pests from the plants, or treat them with a natural pest-control product. By November the large stems of leaves begin to decline and can be removed from the gardens.

Companion Planting and Design
Plantings are best used as accents in a container for patios, featured with perennials, or mixed with shrub plantings for summer interest. Surround with African iris, bird-of-paradise, crinums, heliconias, and philodendrons.

Try These
There are a number of selections, but the one called 'Konjac' is the most popular. It has spotted stems.

Walking Iris

Neomarica spp.

Botanical Pronunciation
nee-o-MER-ee-ka

Bloom Period and Seasonal Color
Year-round blooms in white, yellow, blue, and brown

Mature Height x Spread
To 3 feet x 18 inches, before clumping

Zones 10b–11

The walking iris is so-named because the flower stalk gradually sinks to the ground forming plantlets, allowing the clump to expand, or "walk." These irises are good for a vertical effect in a planting bed. They can also be used alone, where they are tall enough to hold their flowers up for inspection. Like other bulbs, they like a moist and rich bed, although I've seen them thrive in low-lying, untended swales where weedy plants muck about in agreeable company. According to *Betrock's Reference Guide to Landscape Plants* by Timothy Broschat and Alan Meerow, *Neomarica caerulea* has blue flowers, *N. gracilis* has white flowers with blue markings, and *N. longifolia* is the commonly seen yellow flowering iris. (GBT)

When, Where, and How to Plant
Plant any time of the year in partial shade, in a foundation planter, a shrub bed, or in a Japanese garden-like setting. Enrich the planting hole with peat, pine bark mulch, and sand so it retains moisture but drains well. Make the planting hole slightly larger than the rootball in the container, and slide off the container, carefully placing the walking iris in the hole. Water in and mulch. From divisions or plantlets, plant just below the surface of the soil. To hasten and direct the rooting of small plantlets from the stolons, you can bend the stolon and use wire cut in the shape of hairpins to push them down and keep them in place.

Growing Tips
Walking iris has a low tolerance for drought conditions, so irrigate twice a week in winter and two to three times in summer if there is not enough rain. Fertilize with slow-release fertilizer in spring, midsummer, and fall. Slow-release fertilizer can last up to two or three months in South Florida, in spite of longer claims made by manufacturers, due to high heat and rain. However, allow the plant to indicate when it needs more fertilizer. Pale yellow leaves and fewer flowers can indicate lack of nutrients. Occasionally clean out the old stolons and leaves from beds of walking iris. Brown, dead leaf material can build up like thatch in turf grass and not only disguise weeds but also prevent plantlets from rooting.

Regional Advice and Care
A tender plant, this will die to the ground in Central Florida in winter but grows back from the rhizome. Walking iris can be replaced with bearded iris or grown in pots in North Florida.

Companion Planting and Design
Use this as a tallish groundcover around a tree or areca palms; or, such as in a Japanese garden, in a rocky area where the fan shape of the flat leaves can be highlighted against an inorganic substrate.

Try These
The yellow flowers of *Neomarica longifolia* seem like dots of golden light.

CYCADS **FOR FLORIDA**

Even before that matriarchal land mass called Pangaea broke into continents, cycads were here. Perhaps as long as 250 million years ago they spread over most of the earth. Today, in their remnant home territories, they are highly endangered species.

They look like curious palms; the name cycad comes from a Greek word meaning "palm." Their stems often form trunks, and spiky stiff leaves comprise the crowns. There are about 185 species of cycads around the world, primarily found where summers are hot and wet and winters are cool and dry.

How Cycads Grow

Like conifers, cycads have seed-bearing cones, and plants are either male or female. The cones produce aromas, from sweet-fruity to wintergreen, and the male cones, which are longer and thinner than the female cones, produce heat, sometimes becoming up to 20 degrees hotter than the surrounding air temperature when shedding pollen. (A few female cones do the same thing when ready for pollination.) In the genus *Zamia*, the temperature change occurs near sundown, before pollen is shed. Male

Dioon edule

Encephalartos ferox

cones of the *Dioon* (dye-OON) and *Encephalartos* (en-sef-a-LAR-tos) genera produce heat just after sundown. Heat as well as aroma attract pollinators.

The roots of most cycads, called coralloid because they grow up in coral-like shapes, are infested with blue-green algae. These roots fix atmospheric nitrogen at the soil's surface, which is used as a nutrient by the plants.

Dioon species of cycads are native to the New World, and can be found from sea level to 9,000 feet. *Dioon edule* (ED-you-lee) has 4- to 5-foot leaves, pinnately compound, and holds them elegantly up as if in a fountainlike spray. Females of the *Dioon* genus have relatively grand cones that are soft and furry, covered with a down, and may last two years on the plant. *Dioon edule* may be the slowest growing, and cycad specialists believe individual plants may reach an age approaching two thousand years.

Encephalartos horridus (HOR-a-dus) from Africa has wickedly spiny leaflets that are blue-gray once they mature and pinkish when they first flush out. *E. ferox* females add color to the landscape with brilliant red cones. In nature the seeds are dispersed by mammals, such as monkeys and hornbills.

The name *Encephalartos* is Greek and was assembled this way: *en*, or "in"; *cephale*, meaning "head"; and *artos*, meaning "bread." The inner part of the upper trunk is edible.

The plants in South Africa are fire-tolerant and have thick trunks, suckering from the base. Gardeners in South Florida have found it may take 15 to 20 years for one of these to produce a cone, so patience is a must.

Zamia (ZAY-me-ah) is a West Indies and Latin American group of cycads in the same tribe as *Dioon*. Zamia cones are upright, and those of *Z. furfuraceae* (fur-fur-A-see-ee) break open to release brilliant red seeds. *Z. furfuraceae* is called the cardboard palm by landscapers because of the texture of its flat, roundish leaves. Its stems are armed with short nodules that make pruning tricky. Florida's only native cycad, *Zamia integrifolia*, was endangered by overcollecting in the nineteenth and early twentieth centuries, when its tuber was made into starch. It is the larval host plant of the Atala butterfly, which also disappeared. When coontie made a comeback as a popular ornamental plant for gardens, the Atala was rediscovered. The butterfly, with its brilliant red abdomen and black wings, remains endangered. (GBT)

Mature Height x Spread
18 inches to 20 feet × 24 inches to 8 feet

Zones
10–11

When, Where, and How to Plant
Plant in late spring or early summer before the annual flush of new leaves. Leaves form a rosette at the top of the stem. Before new leaves flush, cataphylls, or protective scale-leaves, will appear. When you see these thorny growths, you know it is time to plant or transplant. The most important condition for cycads is excellent soil drainage. The plants can grow in sun to partial shade, but they will rot in wet soil. A rule of thumb on light is this: blue leaves tolerate sun, blue-green leaves need some shade, green leaves prefer more shade. Treat a cycad like a palm, and provide a wide hole as deep as the rootball. Backfill without enriching with compost or peat moss. If your soil does not drain especially fast, you may want to build up a mound, incorporating sand into a good potting soil to ensure good drainage.

Growing Tips
A fertilizer formulated for palms can be used on cycads—try 8-4-12-4 that has slow-release nitrogen and potassium in addition to micronutrients. When new leaves are still soft, apply a foliar micronutrient spray.

Regional Advice and Care
Yellowing old leaves signal magnesium deficiency; yellowing new leaves are a sign of manganese deficiency and possibly iron deficiency. Scale and mealybugs can be problems on cycads. Combat pests with insecticidal soap or systemic insecticide sprayed

alternately with light horticultural oil. Do not spray oil in summer; oil can damage leaves in heat above 85 degrees Fahrenheit.

Companion Planting and Design

Gardens benefit from cycads because these plants are so architectural. They can be used as specimens, as regal guardians of the entryway, and as accents. Two are small enough to be groundcovers—notably *Zamia integrifolia* and *Z. fischeri* (this last one has copper-colored new leaves).

Try These

There are several species, but *Encephalartos horridus* is a lovely blue-gray color. It has unusually shaped, armed leaves.

Zamia integrifolia

GROUNDCOVERS
FOR FLORIDA

Could there be lawn chairs or lawn bowling without a lawn? Croquet without grass? Chinch bugs without St. Augustine? No. Could there be happier gardeners without mowing, raking, edging, sweeping, irrigating, and fixing the sprinkler heads? Assuredly.

Give yourself this challenge: enlarge your planting beds 5 to 10 percent each year for the next five years and see if you don't love your garden more. This is where groundcovers come in: ferns instead of zoysia, bromeliads instead of chinch bugs, and kalanchoe instead of dollar spot. Serendipity instead of a national obsession. Furthermore, and this is not breaking news, groundcovers can reduce the amount of fuel we waste on lawn mowers and fertilizers, the amount of noise we must suffer with leaf blowers.

Groundcovers serve many purposes, such as softening the edges of paths and walkways.

We are not completely pro-groundcover, anti-grass. We have dogs that need a place to run. We have parts of the yard we like to visit and that require walking across a lawn to get there. We even like the nice contrast grass provides against the groundcovers. But we also like our lives to be our own.

Considering Groundcovers

The concept of groundcover may be the most variable in landscaping. A garden with small agaves as accents may have pea rock as a groundcover, whereas another garden may feature the agaves themselves as the groundcover.

In the name of creativity, small shrubs can be roped into service. Mexican heather, which is a dwarf shrub, and coontie, a dwarf native cycad, are often often used as groundcovers.

Where is the best place to put groundcovers? Around and beneath trees where grass won't grow; around shrub beds and palms; around the edges of the garden in curving beds to soften the geometry; at the base of shrubs so the plants can serve as a visual link between the flat, floorlike grass and the elevated shrub level; on slopes or grading to keep soil from

Creeping Fig

eroding; on lake fronts; in swales; next to hard surfaces such as patios or decks, again to soften the hard lines of nonliving elements and connect them with living elements.

First Things First

To successfully prepare an area for groundcovers, first get rid of the grass. There are a couple of ways to do this. One involves covering the area with clear plastic, weighting it down, and allowing the heat to kill the grass. You may not want to wait that long. In that case, you can use Roundup, an herbicide that breaks down quickly. Wait for the grass to die, remove it, and till the soil, adding compost or peat moss to enrich it. You can add a light application of a slow-release fertilizer at this time, plant the groundcovers, add mulch, and then water well.

The goal is to have the edges of the plants overlap to shade out any weeds. It may take a full growing season or two. In the interim, you'll have to weed and fertilize at appropriate times, keep the soil irrigated, and be patient.

Thinking Ahead

As the water supply becomes critical, groundcovers will become more important elements in Florida gardens. In many scenarios of climate change, rain patterns are going to change and rising seas are going to change the topography. Rain "events" will replace the rainy season and droughts will increase as well, as South Florida already has experienced.

Even without dramatic change, the water picture is critical. Drinking water, water for agriculture, and water for natural areas must all be obtained from the same source: the aquifers.

Groundcovers are the gardener's best friend, and the sponge that is the lawn may be not only a liability but a misdemeanor in the future.

Asiatic Jasmine

Trachelospermum asiaticum

Botanical Pronunciation
tray-kell-O-spir-mum A-ze-ATIC-cum

Other Name Small leaf Confederate jasmine

Bloom Period and Seasonal Color
Year-round foliage, white warm-season blooms

Mature Height x Spread
1 foot x trailing

Zones 8–10

Many landscape architects choose the small leaf confederate jasmine as their favorite groundcover due to its versatility. Only a few plants with their vining shoots are needed to fill in relatively large areas of the landscape; the plants are not particular about soil type. This species grows low and is not quite as rampant as the common confederate jasmine. Small leaf confederate jasmine is best used in larger areas where you need a reliable dense mat of greenery, for example, under trees where other ornamentals fail to take root, on slopes, and in median strips. It can be used to hang over walls and to cascade from planters. If you plant it near trees, keep it from climbing the trunks. (TM)

When, Where, and How to Plant

Small leaf confederate jasmine can be planted at any time of the year. The most stress-free time to add this jasmine to the landscape is the late fall through early spring. Plantings need well-drained soil to prevent root rot problems. Work in several inches of compost or peat moss and manure with the existing soil. Space plants 24 to 36 inches apart. Set the plant at the same depth as it was growing or a little higher. After planting, water the entire planting site thoroughly. Add a 2- to 3-inch mulch layer to keep the soil moist and control weeds. The first feeding may be provided four to six weeks after planting. Continue watering to keep the soil moist until the plants are established and send roots out into the surrounding soil.

Growing Tips

Small leaf confederate jasmine plantings are drought-tolerant but make the best growth with a moist soil. Where extra growth is needed and during periods of severe drought, water weekly with ½ to ¾ inch of water. Feed this jasmine once in spring, summer, and early fall. Use general landscape fertilizer or a slow-release product following label instructions.

Regional Advice and Care

This plant is easy to grow, but its vining nature calls for periodic trimming to keep it in bounds. Small leaf confederate jasmine grows well in all but the most southern region of Florida. It does not need special winter protection. Small leaf confederate jasmine may be affected by scale insects and white flies. Where necessary, apply an insecticide recommended by the University of Florida Cooperative Extension Service.

Companion Planting and Design

Here is a landscaper's dream for use in the more difficult areas as a lawn substitute and wall covering. Combine with shrubs and trees to fill beds and planters to complete the landscape.

Try These

You can make this groundcover planting a bit zestier by using 'Variegatum'. The cream and green foliage is eye-catching. Other good landscape selections include 'Bronze Beauty', with reddish foliage, and 'Minima', a dwarf variety.

Beach Sunflower

Helianthus debilis

Botanical Pronunciation
hell-E-an-thus DEE-bill-us

Bloom Period and Seasonal Color
Bright yellow flowers with brown centers bloom year-round except during very cold weather

Mature Height x Spread
24 inches x 48 inches

Zones 8–10

Beach sunflower plantings may be one of the most ideal groundcovers for Florida landscapes. Plantings tolerate the sandy and salty coastal conditions plus most other soils throughout Florida except wet sites. This is a long-lived annual vine that after time declines but rapidly reseeds to again fill in barren spots. Use this vine in your hard-to-grow spots, near sidewalks and on banks. It is especially useful as a planting for dunes near beaches. The leaves are bright green, glossy, and triangular in shape. Gardeners love the bright yellow blooms with brown centers that open throughout the year except during winter in the coldest portions of the state. They also appreciate its pest-free rating. (TM)

When, Where, and How to Plant
Native plant nurseries often have plants in containers to add to the landscape year-round. Give them a spacing of 3 to 4 feet apart. Otherwise they can be started from collected seeds or cuttings to propagate as needed. Plantings grow in the sandy, well-drained soils, but feel free to add organic matter to the planting sites. Set plants in the ground at their original depth if transplanted from containers. Up to a 1-inch layer of mulch can be added to help conserve water. New plantings need to be kept moist until new roots grow into the surrounding soil.

Growing Tips
Special feedings are normally not needed as plants seem to be able to obtain nutrients from decomposing leaves, mulch, and rainwater. A light sprinkling of a general garden fertilizer could be added if more growth is needed in April, June, and September. Once established, seasonal rains seem to provide adequate moisture, but you can water weekly during the really dry times if needed.

Regional Advice and Care
Plants are susceptible to cold in some central and most northern portions of the state. Freezes can severely damage the plantings, but they grow back from stems near the ground or seeds. Keep plants in-bounds throughout the year by pruning vigorous shoots. Pruning is also needed to remove plants that have completed their life cycles. Insects are seldom a problem, but plantings in too wet a soil due to overwatering or poor drainage often suffer from root rot. Plant in raised beds if needed in poorly drained soils.

Companion Planting and Design
Beach sunflowers are ideal for the dryland gardens that receive only natural rainfall and few feedings. Use beach sunflower as a groundcover with taller plants in the background or the center of beds. You might consider using these plants in the hard-to-grow areas between sidewalks and the roadside. Consider combining with African iris, century plants, false heather, firecracker plant, fire bush, lantana, and plumbago.

Try These
Only the native species is available.

Beach Verbena

Glandularia maritima

Botanical Pronunciation
gland-you-LAIR-ee-uh mari-TEE-ma

Other Name Coastal mock vervain

Bloom Period and Seasonal Color
All year

Mature Height x Spread
3 to 12 inches x 36 to 60 inches

Zones 9–10

An endangered native of South Florida dunes, this tough plant likes full sun and plenty of room in which to roam. In the warm growing season, beach verbena produces umbels of pretty lavender flowers that rise above their delicately lobed leaves. Beach verbena (syn. *Verbena maritima*) is a wonderful addition to any butterfly garden, as its flowers are tiny cups of nectar. As it comes from the sandy dunes and pinelands, it likes excellent drainage. It spreads to cover anywhere from 3 to 6 feet. When found growing naturally on dunes, it helps stabilize them as sand collects around the stems. However, because of coastal development, beach verbena is on Florida's endangered plant list. (GBT)

When, Where and How to Plant
Plant in limestone or sandy soils, in full sun. Water well and keep soil moist for the first few days after planting. Once established, this wildflower becomes drought-tolerant. If it crawls into shade, it will not flower well. Take cuttings and reestablish in a sunny spot. Flowers may decline in winter, but the plants will last. Some verbenas are used as annuals, others as three-year groundcovers.

Growing Tips
Allow 2½ feet between plantings, and don't overcrowd with other wildflowers as it will spread.

Regional Advice and Care
Beach verbena grows from Miami-Dade County to St. Johns County and in Collier and Hendry Counties, according to the Institute for Regional Conservation. It has been found once in Monroe County. Beach verbena has been replaced in the coastal areas by exotics such as Brazilian pepper and Australian pine. Beach verbena makes a beautiful hanging basket or container plant.

Companion Planting and Design
Lizard's tail, pineland lantana, and milkweed are at home in the same kinds of locations, and these are great nectar plants for a variety of butterflies and skippers. Find a south or east location that still gets direct sun when the sun sinks lower in the sky in winter to keep the blooms year-round.

Try These
Many hybrids of exotic verbena are on the market, including one called 'Imagination' with blue-violet flowers and 'Aztec', with red, orange, or pink flowers and violet eyes, with deep purple centers. Most of the hybrids will serve as groundcovers or in hanging baskets, flowering from spring through summer. The 'Aztec' verbenas are hardy in Zones 7 through 10.

Blue Daze

Evolvulus glomeratus 'Blue Daze'

Botanical Pronunciation
EE-volv-you-lus glom-er-A-tus

Other Name Hawaiian blue eyes

Bloom Period and Seasonal Color
Year-round blooms in cornflower blue

Mature Height x Spread
12 inches x 10 inches

Zones 10–11

There was a good deal of excitement a few years ago when blue daze was new to the area, primarily because of the blue color. But blue daze folds up its flowers around midday, so you have to get excited about this first thing in the morning. It can be utilized in planters or containers (where its long branches may drape over the sides), in borders, and in beds as a groundcover. Blue daze gives its best color in full sun. The plant is in the Convolvulaceae family. The term *convolvo* means to "twine around," and the family is full of vines, such as morning glories. (*Evolvulus* is from the term *evolve*, meaning "untwist or unravel.") *Evolvulus purpureo-coeruleus* has ultramarine flowers with white centers and purple lines. (GBT)

When, Where, and How to Plant
Plant any time in South Florida. Blue daze is salt-tolerant, so it could serve well in seaside gardens or oceanfront condo balconies. Space plants about 1½ to 2 feet apart. If mulching, try to keep the mulch away from plant stalks to reduce the threat of fungus. Blue daze is a moderately fast grower and can cover an area with fuzzy, silver-green foliage in a matter of weeks.

Growing Tips
Use a slow-release fertilizer, following package directions. A site that drains well is best to avoid the too-wet conditions that result in disease. Water faithfully after planting in order to help the small morning glories become established.

Regional Advice and Care
Prof. Ed Gilman, in a fact sheet for the University of Florida, says blue daze survives "on almost any soil in full sun to partial shade, with light fertilizations.... This is almost a no-maintenance plant." When too wet, however, *Rhizoctonia* fungus may set in. This fungus causes damping-off and other diseases of roots and stems. Check with the University of Florida Extension Service for an appropriate fungicide. Cut back the foliage in spring for a fresh start. Protect from cold, or use as an annual in areas where frost regularly occurs. For Central and North Florida, blue daze may best be kept in containers, using a soilless potting mix. For assurance that the pots drain well, put a layer of terracotta shards or Styrofoam packing peanuts in the bottom and add extra perlite to the mix.

Companion Planting and Design
This tiny morning glory is wonderful in a pot that accents a shady corner of the patio or as a groundcover for yellow allamanda, Carolina jasmine, or yellow shrimp plant.

Try These
If blue daze cannot be found in your garden center, you may want to try *Jacquemontia violacea*, a native plant with wonderfully blue flowers.

Cast Iron Plant

Aspidistra elatior

Botanical Pronunciation
AS-peh-DIS-trah E-lay-TEE-or

Bloom Period and Seasonal Color
Year-round foliage

Mature Height x Spread
2 to 3 feet x 2 feet

Zones 9–11

Need a groundcover just for shade? Then you might like the cast iron plant. The name probably says it all. It's durable, takes most soil conditions, and needs limited care. The cast iron plant can beat out most weeds, so once it's established you won't have to eliminate unwanted vegetation. Because it cannot take direct sun, it may be the ideal plant for gardeners asking for something for the shade. It produces dark green foliage that has a tropical and exotic look. Each wide leaf grows to 2 feet long, and there are plenty of them. Use the cast iron plant near the patio, along walkways, in containers, or wherever greenery is desired. One variety, 'Variegata', has green-and-white-striped foliage and grows well in local landscapes. (TM)

When, Where, and How to Plant
Cast iron plants can be added at any time of the year. The most stress-free time to plant is the late fall through early spring. Plant in spring and early summer in South Florida. Outdoors it's impossible to find a light level that's too low for these plants. They like a well-drained soil. Work in several inches of compost or peat moss and manure with the existing soil. Space cast iron plants 12 to 18 inches apart. After planting, water the entire planting site thoroughly. Plantings grow slowly but eventually fill in the bed with a dense stand of foliage. Control is needed to keep the shoots from invading nearby plantings. Add a 2- to 3-inch mulch layer to keep the soil moist and control weeds. Provide the first feeding four to six weeks after planting.

Growing Tips
Cast iron plants are drought-tolerant but make the best growth with a moist soil. During periods of severe drought, provide weekly watering with ½ to ¾ inch of water. Feed cast iron plantings once in spring, summer, and early fall. Use a general landscape fertilizer or slow-release product following label instructions.

Regional Advice and Care
Cast iron plants may be affected by caterpillars and slugs. Handpick the pests from the plantings, or treat them with a pesticide recommended by the University of Florida Cooperative Extension Service. The cast iron plant is cold-sensitive and is frequently damaged in Central Florida by freezing weather. It cannot be grown as a groundcover in the more northern portions of the state but can be established in containers and given winter protection. When the plant is damaged by cold, prune off the brown leaves before spring growth begins.

Companion Planting and Design
Plant with other shade lovers jacobinia, ivy, Asiatic jasmine, begonias, eucharis lily, and peacock gingers. Use as a backdrop for smaller plants or as a groundcover.

Try These
Plain green is fine, but when you can add a little color, go for the more interesting selections. 'Variegata' adds this extra interest with its white-striped foliage.

Creeping Fig

Ficus pumila

Botanical Pronunciation
FI-cuss POO-mill-AH

Bloom Period and Seasonal Color
Year-round foliage

Mature Height x Spread
6 to 8 inches x 3 feet

Creeping fig is a groundcover that hugs the soil. Its bright green leaves vary with the stage of plant maturity. When the plants are young and said to be in a juvenile stage of growth, the leaves are small, oval, and up to 1 inch long. When the plants get older and mature, the leaves are oblong and 2 to 4 inches long. Creeping fig does flower and produce a fig, but the fruit is inedible. The fruits are hard and usually only seen on the older plantings. Use creeping fig as a groundcover leading up to the turf and walkways, as a wall covering, in hanging baskets, or to cover stuffed topiaries. Be aware the roots hold fast to walls and may be hard to remove. (TM)

When, Where, and How to Plant
Creeping fig can be planted at any time of the year. The most stress-free time to add creeping fig to the landscape is the late fall through early spring season. The plant likes a well-drained soil. Work in several inches of compost or peat moss and manure with the existing soil. Space plants 12 to 18 inches apart. Dig the hole wider than the rootball but not deeper. Set the plant at the same planting depth as it was growing or a little higher out of the ground. Add soil and water to the hole to make good root-to-soil contact. After planting, water the entire planting site thoroughly. Add a 2- to 3-inch mulch layer to keep the soil moist and control weeds.

Growing Tips
Provide the first feeding four to six weeks after planting. Creeping fig plantings are drought-tolerant but make the best growth with a moist soil. During periods of severe drought, provide moisture weekly with ½ to ¾ inch of water. Feed creeping fig once in spring, summer, and early fall. Use general landscape fertilizer or a slow-release product following label instructions.

Regional Advice and Care
Creeping fig grows well in all areas of the state. No special care is needed for the different regions. Plant during the rainy season in South Florida. Creeping fig is an aggressive plant that can climb trees, shrubs, and nearby buildings. Periodic trimming is needed to keep the plantings in bounds. Pests are usually few, but creeping fig may be affected by caterpillars. Handpick the pests from the plantings, or treat them with a pesticide recommended by the University of Florida Cooperative Extension Service.

Companion Planting and Design
Use it to disguise a wall or use as a groundcover. It forms an excellent backdrop for sunny annuals of marigolds and salvia or shade-loving perennials such as jacobinia and begonias.

Try These
Numerous selections of creeping fig have been made for use in the landscape, including varieties 'Minima' with all-juvenile foliage, 'Quercifolia' with lobed leaves, and 'Variegata' with cream-and-green leaves.

Dwarf Carissa

Carissa macrocarpa

Botanical Pronunciation
ka-RISS-ah mac-roe-CARP-ah

Other Name Natal plum

Bloom Period and Seasonal Color
Year-round blooms in white, followed by red plums

Mature Height x Spread
1 to 2 feet x 2 to 4 feet

Zones 10B–11

The Atlantic Ocean and Gulf of Mexico are reasons many of us live in Florida. On the East Coast, we boast of summer's southeasterly breezes, yet people who live next to the shore often are at a loss for salt-tolerant plants in their gardens. Natal plum, or carissa, comes in two sizes: the shrub size, which can reach 10 feet but usually doesn't, and the dwarf form, which can be used as a groundcover. Originally from South Africa, the plant was introduced to this country by David Fairchild. Carissa thrives in sandy and alkaline soils, and its thick, waxy leaves won't be torn by wind. The thorny little shrubs are also good for containers on balconies facing the sea. (GBT)

When, Where, and How to Plant
Plant dwarf carissa in spring if you can provide irrigation or at the beginning of the rainy season or throughout the warm months. Carissa is tolerant of many soil types. Plant in full sun. To use as a groundcover, plant on 2-foot centers in staggered rows. Enrich the soil with peat, compost, or well-aged manure so that no more than one-third of the backfill is organic. Dig a hole as deep as the container and slightly wider; slip the container off the rootball, and position the shrub in the planting hole; water in the backfill. Mulch, keeping the mulch from direct contact with the shrub trunks to prevent disease.

Growing Tips
Water so that the plant's roots stay moderately moist. If in a windy location, dwarf carissa may require watering every other day because wind pulls moisture out of soil and leaves. Three times a year, fertilize with slow-release 8-4-12 containing micronutrients. Slow-release provides nutrients on a steady basis and helps keep a rush of fertilizer out of the water supply.

Regional Advice and Care
Carissa's white flowers are fragrant and produced throughout the warm season. Then, in the fall, small, edible fruit ripen to red, making a good addition to yards that aspire to areas of wildlife habitat. Spider mites, scale, and sucking pests such as mealybugs and thrips can infest carissa. These can be controlled with a soap and water spray (1 teaspoon of liquid Ivory per gallon of water), with alcohol on cotton, or Malathion. Because the shrub is thorny, use care when working with alcohol and cotton. Carissa may be grown in protected areas in Central Florida.

Companion Planting and Design
As a low-lying shrub, dwarf carissa, such as 'Bonsai', 'Horizontalis', 'Nana', and 'Prostrata', are for little niches in a patio or around a pool, especially in gardens near the ocean. The plants will do well for condo balconies that receive ocean breezes.

Try These
Garden cultivars include 'Horizontalis', 'Green Carpet', 'Emerald Beauty', and 'Boxwood Beauty'. The last is a thornless dwarf form that is easy to handle.

English Ivy

Hedera helix

Botanical Pronunciation
head-ER-ah heal-EX

Bloom Period and Seasonal Color
Year-round foliage

Mature Height x Spread
10 to 12 inches x trailing

Zones 8–9

For many gardeners relocated to Florida, the English ivy is the little bit of home they can bring with them. It can fill the problem spots in the landscapes where some quick-growing greenery is needed. Use it in low-light areas, dry spots, and poor soils. Many gardeners have replaced turf in shady areas with ivy. It's also good on banks and areas along walkways too small for turf. English ivy can be trained to walls and fences, and used in hanging baskets. Another species worth planting in most areas is *Hedera canariensis*; its leaves are usually three-lobed, and it grows larger than English ivy. It is used as a groundcover but must be protected from cold in the more northern portions of the state. (TM)

When, Where, and How to Plant
English ivy can be planted at any time of the year. The most stress-free time to plant English ivy is the late fall through early spring. It likes a well-drained soil. Work in several inches of compost or peat moss and manure with the existing soil. Space plants 18 to 24 inches apart. Set the plant at the same depth as it was growing or a little higher. After planting, water the entire planting site thoroughly. Add a 2- to 3-inch mulch layer to keep the soil moist and control weeds.

Growing Tips
Apply first feeding four to six weeks after planting. Continue watering to keep the soil moist until the plants are established. Air circulation is required to prevent root and stem rot during the rainy season. English ivy plantings are drought-tolerant but make the best growth with a moist soil. During periods of severe drought, provide weekly watering with ½ to ¾ inches of water. Feed English ivy once in spring, summer, and early fall. Use a general landscape or slow-release fertilizer following label instructions.

Regional Advice and Care
English ivy can grow rather rapidly to fill beds. It needs periodic pruning to keep it in-bounds and off trees and buildings. English ivy grows well in the northern and central areas of the state. In Central Florida it is best grown in partially shady to shady areas, but tolerates full sun, too. English ivy does not grow well in South Florida. English ivy may be affected by scale insects and mites. Handpick, or treat them with a pesticide recommended by the University of Florida Cooperative Extension Service. Leaf spots and rot problems affect plantings that stay too moist.

Companion Planting and Design
Plant in shady spots as a lawn substitute or in landscape beds. Combine with a backdrop of shade-loving perennials like jacobinia, cast iron plant, begonias, bromeliads, and ferns.

Try These
You are going to have to search out the better landscape varieties. Ironically they are simply sold as old English ivy selections and tend to have large simple leaves. Most growers have their favorites for the landscape.

Ferns

Many genera

Botanical Pronunciation
Varies with the genus

Bloom Period and Seasonal Color
Most with year-round foliage

Mature Height x Spread
Varies with the species

Zones Varies with the species

Add more than flowers to the landscape by planting attractive greenery from the family of great ferns. One of Florida's own native sword ferns made history, according to folklore, when a shipment north was noticed to have a little different leaf and was later designated the "Boston Fern." But this is just one of many ferns that have attractive leaf forms and sizes that make them great landscape accents, groundcovers and container plantings. Many can be grown in planters and hanging baskets to display individually or mixed with other foliage plants for the patio or balcony or set throughout the landscape. Ferns add the airy look to the landscape and are ideal for shady, high-humidity areas. Gardeners often get concerned about brown spores on the back of the leaves, but they are normal. (TM)

When, Where, and How to Plant

Ferns can be added to the landscape year-round, but the warmer months are best. Most like to grow in humid locations and out of the drying breezes. Some produce surface or underground shoots that can be divided but all can be found in containers at garden centers. Many can be grown in sands, but it is best to improve these soils with organic matter to increase their moisture-holding ability. Set the plants in the soil so the top of the rootball is even or slightly above the soil surface. Then add a light mulch to help keep the soil moist.

Growing Tips

Some ferns are drought-tolerant, but most grow best when kept moist. Sword ferns and staghorn ferns hung in trees can survive periods of drought, but the tree ferns like frequent watering. Best growth is produced when ferns are kept moist by watering twice a week during the hot, dry weather. Keep ferns growing with feedings two to three times a year. Many like to use liquid fertilizers at half the normal rate, but a slow-release product can feed them more uniformly following label instructions.

Regional Advice and Care

Select your fern by the area of the state where it is to grow. Consult your local extension office or garden center for the selections that do best in your area. Ferns can be trimmed as needed. Some, such as the native sword and leather-leaf ferns, spread rapidly and must be kept in bounds. Winter may damage the cold-sensitive selections. These are sure to need trimming in late February before new growths begin.

Companion Planting and Design

Grow in combination with other shade-loving selections of cast iron plants, azaleas, Amazon lilies, gingers, camellias, impatiens, and begonias. Use the ferns to fill voids or give contrasting greenery with the flowering plants.

Try These

Gardeners who want an exotic fern look are going to love the tree and staghorn ferns. Obtain information as to their exact care. Other good groundcover ferns are the native sword or Boston fern, autumn fern, holly fern, and broad sword fern.

Flax Lily

Dianella tasmanica

Botanical Pronunciation
die-AH-nell-ah taz-MAN-E-ka

Bloom Period and Seasonal Color
May through November small blue
starlike flowers

Mature Height x Spread
2 feet x 2 feet

New plants are always welcome additions to the Florida landscape, especially when they are tough and durable. A native of Australia, the flax lily has quickly become popular with gardeners, especially in the poor and dry soils. Foliage can be bright green, but the most popular selection seems to be with leaves that have white margins and grow to 2 feet in length. It makes a great accent when staged with other greenery. Plantings are usually clustered to form a groundcover, but they can also be added to containers for patio, balcony, and entrance displays. Flax lily can also be planted along walkways or as a low space divider. Gardeners find this a good plant for minimal-maintenance landscape. (TM)

When, Where, and How to Plant
Add the flax lily to the landscape year-round, but the warmer months are best. Plantings do grow in the poorer sandy soils, but adding organic matter makes for better plant growth. Divide older clusters or obtain plants from your local garden center to plant in sun to shade. Set the plants in the ground so the top of the rootball is even with or slightly above the soil line. Then water and add a 1- to 2-inch layer of mulch.

Growing Tips
Although this is a drought-tolerant plant, it still grows best in a moist soil. Watering once or twice a week during the hot dry times is best. Plants in the full sun may stay a bit on the yellowing green side. Part sun to part shade locations are the better sites. Plantings in too much shade tend to develop more insect problems. When adequate moisture is available, feed once in March, June, and September with a general landscape fertilizer or use a slow-release product as instructed on the label.

Regional Advice and Care
Plantings in the colder areas of the state are likely to suffer freeze damage. Often this is just the browning of the edges of the leaves. Give plants needed pruning during the end of February before spring growth begins. Remove out of bounds leaves or shoots at any time. A rust fungus can cause brown streaks and spots in the leaves that are usually ignored, and scale insects may be noted. Apply a fungicide and natural insecticide as needed for these pests.

Companion Planting and Design
Flax lily plantings blend in with most other landscape greenery and flowers. They are often used as a groundcover with pittosporum, Indian hawthorn, yaupon holly, and similar shrubs. Add them to perennial gardens to fill voids with gingers, bush daisy, roses, cannas, and similar flowering plants.

Try These
Green leaf forms are available, but most gardeners prefer the variegated selection with white margins along the bright green, lancelike leaves.

Kalanchoe

Kalanchoe blossfeldiana

Botanical Pronunciation
kal-en-KOE-ee bloss-feld-EE-ana

Other Name Flaming Katie

Bloom Period and Seasonal Color
Winter and spring blooms in red, yellow, orange, white, and salmon

Mature Height x Spread
1 foot x 1 foot

Zones 10–11

Kalanchoes add winter color to those far reaches of your garden where you either don't want to water or water infrequently. The succulent leaves store water and are waxy to the touch. The plants are upright when young and somewhat sprawling when full grown. Their size and color make them good candidates for garden edges, where they look pretty against gravel or mulch as well as against greener and more upright plants behind them. Many cultivars of kalanchoe are sold, and their flowers come in several colors. A related species called *K. tomentosa*, the panda plant, with silver-gray, fuzzy leaves makes a nice houseplant, patio plant, or rock garden specimen. *K. pumila* has silver leaves with stalks of pink flowers; use as a houseplant. (GBT)

When, Where, and How to Plant
Plant any time in full sun to partial shade. Choose well-draining, sandy soil. The standard nursery topsoil, a 50-50 mix of sand and muck, can be used. Even a mix of 70 percent sand and 30 percent muck will do. Space 6 to 10 inches apart. At the time of planting, use 2 teaspoons of slow-release fertilizer with micronutrients either in the planting hole or on top of the root zones, and water in. Cut back the flower heads, called racemes, after the bloom period stops to remove seeds, make the plants neater, and avoid fungus. Kalanchoes are easy to start from cuttings in the spring. Snip off 4 or 5 inches, remove the bottom leaves, and root in a peat moss-perlite mix that is kept moist and in the shade. Roots should form in four to six weeks; or remove plantlets that form along the stems.

Growing Tips
Use slow-release fertilizer, applying in spring and fall. Although somewhat succulent, these plants from Africa and Madagascar are wonderfully drought-tolerant when established. However, you will find that regular irrigation during the spring growing season, and even during the summer if rain is sparse, makes them much more attractive and robust. Protect from midday sun in summer.

Regional Advice and Care
Plant in part shade and protect from freezing. Kalanchoes are excellent indoor houseplants, and thrive in an east or west window in well-draining potting mix.

Companion Planting and Design
Kalanchoe is an excellent groundcover for use around palms, with dusty miller as a fine contrast, with taller and spikier plants, such as agave or some cycads, and among bromeliads.

Try These
Red-flowering kalanchoe appears around the winter holidays and adds to the seasonal color. Yellow kalanchoes brighten a partially shady area of the winter garden.

Lantana

Lantana spp.

Botanical Pronunciation
lan-TAN-ah

Bloom Period and Seasonal Color
Year-round in white, orange, yellow, and lavender

Mature Height x Spread
3 to 4 feet x spreading

Planting lantana has often sparked controversy due the ease with which at least one introduced species has spread by seeds in the plants. New varieties are different and much more unlikely to become a nuisance due to sterile flower features. It's hard to bypass the fact the plant is very drought-tolerant, grows in poor soils, and resists most pests. It is a good survivor for low-water-use gardens as well as moist and well-fed perennial plantings. Use as a groundcover, in flower beds, or as a backdrop for other gardens. They make good container plants and may be trained to topiaries. Lantana comes in an array of bright colors and varying heights. It does have one sometimes objectionable feature, as many have a pungent leaf odor. (TM)

When, Where, and How to Plant
Lantana is best added to the landscape during the warmer months starting in March throughout much of the state. Plants are available in various-sized containers. The larger the container, the greater the distance that can be between the plants, but a spacing of 24 to 36 inches would be best. Plantings can grow in poorer but well-drained soils. Still, it is best to improve the sandy planting sites to obtain the best plant growth. Keep moist after planting and until the new roots grow into the surrounding soil.

Growing Tips
Lantana has a drought-tolerant reputation and can usually go a week or more between watering during the hot, dry times. Best growth is usually obtained when the soil is moist but not overly so. Plants can grow with nutrients derived from mulches and decomposing plant portions but keep their good green color and flower best when fed with a slow-release fertilizer two to three times a year. Whitefly and leaf miner insects can affect the plants. Control as needed with one of the new systemic insecticides found at local garden centers.

Regional Advice and Care
Plantings are vigorous and tend to grow out of bounds in time. Feel free to prune errant shoots back as needed. Most plantings are damaged by frost or freezes in the colder portions of the state. These need pruning back, normally in late February. Lantana are robust plants, so don't feel bad about trimming back to the main stems.

Companion Planting and Design
Some grow lantana as individual plants, but most grow them in clusters with room to spread. Other good drought-tolerant perennials, including African iris, blackberry lily, bush daisy, firebush, Porter-weed, and shrimp plants, make good companions. Add other seasonal flowers, if used in containers.

Try These
Many selections of lantana are available with new ones arriving each year. Some selections of the common lantana to plant include 'Bandana Red', 'Gold Mound', 'Luscious Citrus Blend', 'New Gold', and 'Purple'. Also popular is the trailing lantana species of a purple color, but white and yellow are also available.

Liriope

Liriope muscari

Botanical Pronunciation
lu-RYE-oh-pee muss-CARE-ee

Other Name Lilyturf

Bloom Period and Seasonal Color
Summer and late-summer blooms in white, pink, blue, lavender, or violet

Mature Height x Spread
1 foot x 1 foot

Zones 7–11

This may be one of the most popular ground-covers of recent years. The dark color and slender leaves that spike up and arch over in a small clump make it a nice contrast to St. Augustine, mulch, shrubs, and trees. The drawback is that you cannot walk on it. But many groundcovers share that characteristic, so most of us bipeds are well trained not to step on it. Lilyturf takes a wide range of conditions, from sun to shade, well watered to dry. A number of cultivars of liriope are now sold, including those with silver or gold variegation, and pink, white, blue, or lavender flowers. 'Big Blue' and 'Evergreen Giant' are the tallest, but there also are 'Monroe White', 'Silvery Sunproof', 'Variegata', and 'Variegated Giant'. (GBT)

When, Where, and How to Plant

Plant in the early summer. Liriope is slow growing, and early summer planting will give it a full growing season to take hold. Shade is preferable, although cultivars for sun are available. Specify where it will be used, and ask your nursery or garden center expert for sun-tolerant cultivars if your site is sunny. For covering or edging, plant these 8 to 10 inches apart. The dwarf types can be more closely spaced. Sometimes, if containers are quite full in the nursery, you can simply divide them when planting.

Growing Tips

Fertilize annually in spring. Keep moist for the first month or so to allow the plant to become established. Water in extremely dry weather. In shade, when given too much water from rain or over-irrigation, the plants can succumb to fungus. A broad-spectrum fungicide can be used according to directions on the label.

Regional Advice and Care

In Central and North Florida, protect from freezes. The large, arching tufts of liriope leaves are favorite hatching spots for lubber grasshoppers in South Florida. Lubbers hatch in the early spring, about March, and sometimes can be found by the dozens on just a couple of blades of liriope. When newly hatched, they don't move for a few hours, and if you spot them, you can step on them—without hurting the liriope. Lilyturf does get scale; insecticidal soaps and horticultural oils (in winter) can be used to combat them. 'Webster Wide Leaf' is susceptible to leaf spot, a fungal disease.

Companion Planting and Design

Liriope is one of the great all-purpose groundcovers. It is useful as a border plant and when planted with shrubs such as crotons, *Brunfelsia*, *Brugmansia*, or even planted with nonliving elements in the garden, such as boulders, decks, or steps.

Try These

The 'Big Blue' cultivar is a sturdy plant where a swath of dark green is needed.

Mexican Bluebell

Ruellia brittoniana

Botanical Pronunciation
rue-ELL-ee-ah brit-TONE-ee-ah-nah

Other Name Mexican petunia

Bloom Period and Seasonal Color
Throughout the warm season, blooms in blue, white, pink, and lavender

Mature Height x Spread
2 feet x 1½ feet to 2 feet

Zones 10–11

Blue flowers are an acquired taste, and some plants shouldn't be forced to produce them—roses, for instance, or daisies. The blue flowers of Mexican bluebells are gloriously blue. This indeed is the blue of the West, a fierce blue, potent and capable, which, when it darkens on its way into the flower's throat, becomes the purple-blue of mesas. The delicately textured flowers open one or two at a time on stalks that develop in the axils of the terminal leaves. They last but one day, so that each morning flowers are fresh again—providing they have been watered and fed sufficiently. A compact line of Mexican bluebells has been developed, and it is ideal for groundcovers. The dark green, linear leaves form little mounds. (GBT)

When, Where, and How to Plant
Plant Mexican bluebells any time from spring through fall. Plant in partial shade (the color will be deeper) to mostly sun. In too much shade, however, the plants will not flower. Select a sandy mix with a peat moss component that drains well but can retain some moisture. For groundcovers, plant 12 inches apart in staggered rows. With compact types, plant closer to 6 inches on center. Water well to establish, and provide with a time-release fertilizer at the time of planting, either in the planting hole or scattered around the root zones. Cut them back a couple of times a year if you're using the tall variety.

Growing Tips
Water a couple of times weekly in winter, every two or three days in summer if rain is light. Reapply fertilizer in midsummer and in October. The plants will become light green if they are hungry.

Regional Advice and Care
Snails are fond of the foliage and tend to collect on these groundcovers. Inspect for them early in the morning after a rain or on a cloudy day. Use a snail bait that lasts several days in South Florida's rainy season. Use only a small amount; snail bait is toxic to pets. Experienced growers in Central Florida say bluebells are weedy, reseeding everywhere. Use care when planting, and pull unwanted seedlings, lest they escape. In North and Central Florida, Mexican bluebells can be taken back to the ground in winter weather, but usually they resprout from basal buds.

Companion Planting and Design
Plant them in beds, to accent yellow-flowering hibiscus or walking iris, use around green and yellow *Schefflera arboricola*, yellow-flowering shrimp plant, or beneath *Cordia lutea*, a small yellow-flowering tree.

Try These
The dwarf varieties produce low-growing plants with comparatively large flowers. The cultivar *Ruellia brittoniana* (syn. *Ruellia tweediana*) 'Katie' is blue and a morning bloomer.

Mexican Heather

Cuphea hyssopifolia

Botanical Pronunciation
coo-PHEE-ah hiss-op-a-FO-lee-ah

Other Name False heather

Bloom Period and Seasonal Color
Spring and summer blooms in white, pink, and purple

Mature Height x Spread
1 feet x 2½ feet

Zones 10–11

Mexican heather is such a little guy that it almost cries to be used as a groundcover or in a raised pot, close to the eye. As a groundcover, its power is lost if you fail to take care of it. The better care it receives, the larger the leaves and the more flowers it will produce. The size of this dwarf shrub, combined with the cooler color, should tell you that it must be positioned somewhere within a few feet of the viewer or it won't be noticed. Several cultivars are carried by nurseries, including one called 'Georgia Scarlet', which has flowers shaped like Mickey Mouse. *Cuphea ignea* has tubular flowers that are red with a black ring, hence the common name, cigar plant. (GBT)

When, Where, and How to Plant
Plant in the spring in South Florida or year-round in Central Florida. Plant in full sun to light shade. In part shade, the fernlike leaves will stay darker green. To the planting soil add compost, peat moss, or aged manure so the ratio is about 1:3 amendment to original soil. Then, in this enriched soil, place plants about 18 inches apart.

Growing Tips
Keep Mexican heather, from Guatemala as well as Mexico, well irrigated and fertilized. The plants don't like to dry out completely or they will die. Mulching can moderate soil moisture. Fertilize three times a year, or use a slow-release fertilizer, such as 13-13-13 or 14-14-14 with micronutrients.

Regional Advice and Care
Freezing weather will kill branchlets on these little shrubs, but you can prune them back in spring to remove the dead twigs and let them resprout. In Central and North Florida, use them in containers, either alone or as edging for a larger plant. Or, consider them as annuals, planting in the summer. The plants are susceptible to nematodes that attack their roots. Nematodes are microscopic worms that can reduce the vigor of plants and ultimately cause their demise by invading the roots, stems, or leaves. Root knot nematodes interfere with the water and nutrient uptake of plants. Look for round nodules, almost like underground galls, on roots. Nematodes are kept somewhat at bay by keeping plants growing vigorously so root hairs form frequently, and by mulching.

Companion Planting and Design
Use this sturdy miniature shrub in 3-foot urns at the front door or massed as a groundcover, toward the front of the planting bed, where readily visible.

Try These
Purple-flowering Mexican heather is a good container plant.

Mondo Grass

Ophiopogon japonicus

Botanical Pronunciation
O-fee-O-poe-gon JA-pon-EH-cuss

Other Name Dwarf lilyturf

Bloom Period and Seasonal Color
Year-round foliage

Mature Height x Spread
3 to 4 inches x 6 to 8 inches

Zones 8–10

Florida gardeners rely upon mondo grass as a groundcover for shady areas. It's not a true grass, but the leaves are linear and give a turf-like look to landscapes. As with most groundcovers, it cannot take foot traffic but can be used among steppingstones for a pathway through the planted areas. The dark green leaves are about ¼ inch wide. Use mondo grass on hard-to-mow slopes and along walkways. It can fill in an area near the home, under trees, or in front of shrubs. Mondo grass often appears in Oriental gardens. This durable groundcover grows where other plants cannot take the poorer, drier soils. It also needs minimal care and has few pests, making it an excellent plant for the carefree landscape. (TM)

When, Where, and How to Plant
Mondo grass can be planted at any time of the year. The most stress-free time to add mondo grass to the landscape in Central and North Florida is the late fall through early spring. At that time of the year it is possible to dig and divide clumps. It's hard to find an area in the landscape that has too low a light level for mondo grass. The plants like a well-drained soil. Work in several inches of compost or peat moss and manure with the existing soil. Space plants 8 to 10 inches apart. Set the plant at the same planting depth as it was growing in the container. After planting, water the entire planting site thoroughly. A 2- to 3-inch layer of mulch can be added to keep the soil moist and control weeds. Mondo grass slowly fills in the bed sites. After several years of growth, it may invade nearby areas. Dig out the plants to fill in bare areas.

Growing Tips
Provide the first feeding four to six weeks after planting. Continue watering to keep the soil moist until the plants are established. Mondo grass plantings are drought-tolerant but make the best growth with a moist soil. During periods of severe drought, provide weekly watering with ½ to ¾ inch of water. Feed mondo grass once in spring, summer, and early fall. Use a general landscape or slow-release fertilizer, following label instructions.

Regional Advice and Care
Mondo grass grows well throughout all but the most southern portions of Florida. Mondo grass may be affected by scale insects. Apply an insecticide recommended by the University of Florida Cooperative Extension Service.

Companion Planting and Design
A filler for use along walkways, in large beds, or where you need just a little greenery, it's often planted with shrubs of pittosporum, dwarf yaupon holly, and Indian hawthorn.

Try These
The more dwarf the form, the better. There are a number of selections, but 'Nana' is a good dwarf mondo grass that does well in our landscapes. A dark leaf form often sold as black mondo is attractive in container gardens.

Pineland Lantana

Lantana depressa var. *depressa*

Botanical Pronunciation
lan-TAN-ah de-PRESS-ah

Other Name Rockland shrub verbena

Bloom Period and Seasonal Color
Year-round, unless in cold or drought; yellow

Mature Height x Spread
6 inches to 3 or 4 feet x spreading

Zones 9–11

Bright yellow clusters of flowers and aromatic leaves are hallmarks of this native ground-cover that hails from South Florida's pine rocklands. It is found in many butterfly gardens, as butterflies and skippers love nothing more than to sip from many small cups of nectar at one sitting. The pink and yellow *Lantana camara* is a weedy exotic that has invaded natural areas, and it is wise to avoid buying it. It is, in fact, a pan-tropical weed. There are cultivars of lantana sold in garden centers, some of which are sterile and therefore useful in a garden; 'Gold Mound', 'New Gold', and 'Samantha' are three of these. Try growing *Lantana depressa* as a cascading plant over a boulder; it's beautiful. (GBT)

When, Where, and How to Plant
Lantana loves full sun and soil that drains well. It will spread across several feet, so keep that in mind when planning. It takes poor soils, therefore there is no need to amend your planting area, but mulch will be of benefit and help reduce soil nematodes. Water daily for a week after planting, and gradually reduce watering when you see new growth.

Growing Tips
Pineland lantana appreciates some irrigation to look its best. Prune to shape or to reduce height. If in shade, lantana can come down with powdery mildew, especially in the dry season. Leaves will become yellow and then dry to a grayish brown. Cut away affected parts, and either prune away shade or relocate to a sunny area. *Lantana involucratea* also is susceptible to powdery mildew when in too much shade. This species, however, is a magnet for the small butterflies called skippers.

Regional Advice and Care
Grow in protected areas in Central Florida. A selection of sterile lantana may have more cold hardiness than the species, which is endemic to South Florida.

Companion Planting and Design
For a native planting with lantana, use salvia (*Salvia coccinea*), milkweed (*Asclepias* species), Indian blanket (*Gaillardia pulchella*), pineland jacquemontia (*Jacquemontia curtissii*), and pineland heliotrope (*Heliotropium polyphyllum*). This is an excellent plant for a butterfly garden or as a groundcover beneath pines.

Try These
Wild sage, *Lantana involucrate*, also is a Florida native and magnet for butterflies. It is found inland on sandy dunes. This can become a large shrub and has white flowers with yellow throats. There are other forms of *Lantana depressa*: *Lantana depressa* var. *floridana*, endemic to the eastern peninsula and *L. depressa* var. *sanibelensis*. The Sanibel lantana grows to several feet on the west coast of Florida.

Wax Jasmine

Jasminum volubile

Botanical Pronunciation
jazz-MY-num voh-LEW-buh-lee

Bloom Period and Seasonal Color
Spring and summer blooms in white

Mature Height x Spread
2 feet x 3 feet

Zones 10B–11

Once you know the fragrance of jasmine, you'll always recognize it. Wax jasmine is fragrant and sweetly pretty with its starry flowers against the green. It grows as a vining groundcover or shrub and may be aggressive. It is a hardy plant that's able to endure without irrigation or with little supplemental irrigation. Flowers occur in the warm months, April to September. It takes full sun without turning yellow. As the state's population continues to climb, house lots are smaller and water supplies are becoming more unreliable. Smaller landscape plants such as this can be doubly useful—as a groundcover, it can reduce the area of your garden devoted to thirsty St. Augustinegrass. (GBT)

When, Where, and How to Plant
Plant in the spring or at the beginning of the rainy season. Choose a location in full sun or partial shade. Prepare a large area with the addition of peat or compost. Once the bed components have been mixed to a depth of about 6 to 10 inches, you can place the plants (in their containers) 24 to 48 inches apart to determine how they look. Dig the hole, slip the container off the plant, and position the plant, backfilling and watering in as you do so. Mulch all the plants once you have finished planting.

Growing Tips
Water daily for one or two weeks, reduce watering to every other day for another two weeks, and then go to two times a week if rain is scarce, which

sometimes happens in midsummer. By summer's end, the plants should be growing well. Apply slow-release fertilizer at the time of planting and again in the fall, or a general-purpose 6-6-6 with micronutrients two to three times a year. Cut back the jasmine quite hard once a year to keep this under control. Or, if using this in a formal way, you can keep the plants clipped to a hedge. In this case, plant individuals on 4-foot centers. By hedging or close clipping, sparse flowers will be even sparser, but it may be a desirable, low hedge for a property line barrier, a formal walk, or green edge around a patio area.

Regional Advice and Care
This is not a plant for Florida's cold regions.

Companion Planting and Design
Wax jasmine is a versatile plant that can serve well in a foundation planting or in a more formal setting because of its ability to be pruned. It can climb or form a mound.

Try These
Jasminum sambac, Arabian jasmine, is recommended for Florida's Gulf Coast; *J. grandiflorum* produces clusters of large flowers in the summer.

ORCHIDS FOR FLORIDA

The splendor of orchids is almost impossible to resist if you live in a climate where they can be grown easily. They are among the most romantic of flowers and comprise the largest plant family known, with more than 25,000 species and untold numbers of man-made hybrids.

The Many Faces of Orchids

There are orchids that look like the back ends of female bees, orchids that are moon-faced, orchids that are spiderlike, and orchids that seem to be playing dead. There are some that are leafless and some with minute flowers that develop right on the leaves. Some flowers are hairy, others are covered with warts, some have tails, and others hold up spiraling horns.

Orchids have become hugely popular in recent decades, with *Phalaenopsis* orchids topping the charts. One reason is the long-lasting spray of flowers, which can remain pretty for two months. Commercial orchid growers have developed highly colored *Phalaenopsis* blooms, with stripes, spots, and splotches vying for attention in colors ranging from tangerine to deep mahogany. *Cattleya* flowers and plants have been hybridized as windowsill plants, shrinking in size but also becoming more colorful. And *Vanda* species and their relatives are able to produce flowers three or four times a year, rather than once, with smaller but more boldly colored blossoms.

Enticing perfume is a characteristic of many orchids. Cattleyas and encyclicas, for example, may give off rich chocolate or vanilla aromas. Others possess fragrances that remind you of grapefruit, cloves, or coconut.

Because of recent DNA analysis, many orchids are being renamed. Many of the orchids we have known as *Cattleya*, such as *C. skinneri*, the national flower of Costa Rica, are now classified as belonging to the genus *Guarianthe*. (gwar-AN-they). *Guaria* is the Costa Rican word for orchid; *anthe* is Greek for flower. The new genus includes *Guarianthe aurantiaca*, *Gur. bowringiana*, *Gur. skinneri*, and *Gur. patinii* (also formerly *C. skinneri* var. *autumnalis*, *C. skinneri* var. *patinii*).

Oncidium

Cattleya

How Orchids Grow

Many orchids, such as cattleyas, are air plants, or epiphytes (*epi* means "upon"; *phyte* means "plant"). They grow on other plants, most often tree branches, expanding into clumps by means of a rhizome, or a stem from which roots grow downward and shoots grow up. They are not parasites—they take no nutrients away from the trees on which they grow.

Some orchids grow in the ground. These "terrestrials" include *Phaius*, or the nun's orchid; *Spathoglottis* orchids, now widely used for mass plantings and as groundcovers in South Florida; and a few Florida natives such as *Bletia* and ladies tresses, *Spiranthes*.

The epiphytic orchids most easily grown in South Florida are the cattleyas and relatives and hybrids, vandas and several relatives and hybrids, oncidiums, phalaenopsis, and dendrobiums. Cattleyas are sympodial, meaning new growth arises at the base of a parent after the parent has flowered, forming a series of stems. Vandas, phalaenopsis, and other orchids are monopodial, meaning they grow on a single stem. Growing in trees, epiphytic orchids have developed special roots that are photosynthetic, yet covered with a silver-gray coating of cells that absorbs water and protects against desiccation. These roots cling tightly to tree bark or clay pots. Pseudobulbs are water-storage organs. Orchids with pseudobulbs, such as cattleyas and oncidiums, require less water than do those without.

Examining Orchid Flowers

Orchid flowers, although wildly dissimilar, have several things in common: the pollen is found in masses that look like round golden drops of resin, and these are attached to a stalk or column. Also in the column is the female stigma, or the reproductive surface. Insects—bees, flies, and moths—move the pollen mass (pollinia) of one orchid to the reproductive surface of another, where the pollen germinates.

Seeds develop in pods and are produced by the millions. They have no endosperm, or the starchy tissue that normally feeds embryos; rather, they depend on fungi for food and germination. A specific fungus invades the tiny seed, grows into it, and absorbs minerals and water, whereas the orchid offers a safe haven in return.

Cattleya

Cattleya spp.

Botanical Pronunciation
CAT-lee-uh

Other Name Corsage orchid

Bloom Period and Seasonal Color
Fall blooms in white, lavender, and purple

Mature Height x Spread
20 to 40 inches x 20 to 40 inches

Zones 10B–11 outdoors

This is the queen of orchids. Once called the corsage orchid, *Cattleya* species really started the orchid craze in Victorian England that has not ended yet. There are two types of these plants: a unifoliate type, meaning it has one leaf per pseudobulb and a bifoliate type, with two leaves. The unifoliate cattleyas produce one or two large flowers; bifoliate cats produce many smaller flowers. Buds are called "eyes" and break at the base of the newest pseudobulb. They may develop before new roots or after roots form. New roots are a signal to repot if needed. On either bifoliate or unifoliate types, when flower bulbs poke through the protective sheath, they seem like newborn butterflies, free at last from the confines of their fetal enclosure. (GBT)

When, Where, and How to Plant

Planting in the case of cattleyas means potting or repotting, and that usually should be done in late February or early March or when new roots first appear. (Be aware that some cattleyas will produce a bulb first and then roots.) Soak a clean terracotta orchid pot in water until air bubbles cease rising to the water's surface. Fill to within an inch or two of the top, using a fast-draining orchid mix. A cattleya with four or five "back" bulbs should be positioned on a tall mound of mix. The oldest bulb should rest against one side of the pot, whereas new growth should be headed toward the center. Use a pot clip to anchor the rhizome; remember to remove it after roots develop.

Growing Tips

Water every three or so days, depending on weather. The object is to allow the medium to become almost dry. Use a high-nitrogen (30-10-10) fertilizer if the medium is primarily bark. Otherwise, use 15-5-15 every week throughout the growing season in a medium-coarse orchid mix containing charcoal, bark, fern, and perlite, or in clay pebbles. Peel away papery sheaths on the pseudobulbs to avoid scale. Cattleyas like a relatively high humidity, 50 to 80 percent. A plant that doesn't bloom usually isn't getting enough light.

Regional Advice and Care

North and Central Florida gardeners can keep orchids outdoors in trees or shade houses during the warm months. Protection is necessary for cattleya orchids when temperatures approach freezing. To prevent fungus, don't overcrowd your plants. They can take a wide range of temperatures, from the upper 90s to lower 40 degrees Fahrenheit.

Companion Planting and Design

Attach cattleyas to trees with rough bark in 50 percent light. Wire or tie your cattleya to an oak or tabebuia trunk or limb. Or plant in pots that can be brought inside when the flowers are glorious.

Try These

Laeliocattleya Irene Finney 'Chicago' is a sentimental favorite because it was the first I bought as a bare-root plant, and it required many years to flower. *Lc.* 'Mildred Rives' is a gorgeous white with purple lip.

Dendrobium

Dendrobium spp.

Botanical Pronunciation
en-DROW-bee-um

Bloom Period and Seasonal Color
Fall, spring, and summer blooms in white, yellow, lavender, rose, and maroon

Mature Height x Spread
6 inches to 4 feet, depending on species

Zones 10–11 outdoors

One of my favorite dendrobium sights is a white-flowering *Den. bigibbum* var. *phalaenopsis* hybrid. Every fall, it sends out a long and lovely stalk of blossoms that poke their noses out from among tree branches and palm fronds. Although there are thousands of species of *Dendrobium*, many are cool-growing, meaning Florida may be too warm for them. Most of the species that do well in South Florida like to rest in winter, so reduce watering to two or three times a month from December through February. Many species bloom on canes without leaves; if you water them during the rest phase, the buds may not set. The exception to the winter rest is the "antelope" group, with twisted, upright sepals, and the evergreen *nobile* (no-BUH-lee) group. (GBT)

When, Where, and How to Plant
Attach orchids onto pieces of cork; in pots in quick-draining medium, such as Hydroton and charcoal; or on trees or in 50 to 70 percent shade in shade houses. As with cattleyas, when planting dendrobiums in clay pots, put the oldest back canes against the sides of the pot so new growth heads toward the center. On cork, use florist's tape or thin wire to secure the plant. Attach *Den. aphyllum* and *Den. anosmum* to palms and watch the flowers cascade down in the later winter. Allow the tape or wire to remain on the plant until roots securely anchor it to the substrate and then remove.

Growing Tips
With deciduous plants, withhold most water in winter; water two or three times a month and your plants should be fine. When a dendrobium is overwatered, it may produce offshoots on the cane instead of flowers. To remove the baby plants, called keikis, use a straightedge razor to cut away a portion of the mother cane with the plantlet, then repot. With evergreen or persistent-leafed plants, reduce the amount of water and stop fertilizing in winter. When spring arrives, feed and water generously. You can use a 15-5-15 weekly during the growing season. Make sure the sun is shining when spraying liquid fertilizer so the plants can absorb it right away. A few slow-release pellets are fine if growing dendrobiums or cattleyas in clay pots, but apply only once in the spring. By the time fall arrives, the pellets will be depleted and the plants ready to quit growing and begin the process of setting buds.

Regional Advice and Care
North and Central Florida orchid growers can keep dendrobiums outside in trees or shade houses during the warm months, but protection is needed when temperatures drop below 50 degrees Fahrenheit.

Try These
Dendrobium spectabile produces yellow and brown flowers that look like curly fries, all twisted and kinked but wonderfully bizarre in their own right.

Epidendrum

Epidendrum

Botanical Pronunciation
epi-DEN-drum

Bloom Period and Seasonal Color
Spring and summer blooms in greenish white, red, yellow, lavender, and pink

Mature Height x Spread
2 to 3 feet x 2 to 6 inches

Zones 10B–11 outdoors

As orchid names change thanks to DNA research, it becomes difficult to remember which is or was what. Many epidendrums recently have been moved to the genus *Encyclia*. Here's one way to differentiate between them: encyclias have small pseudobulbs, whereas epidendrums usually have thin, upright stems. The flowers of epidendrum species have lips that are fused to the column; encyclias have free-floating columns. One orchid that was an oddball encyclia, the clamshell orchid, now is *Prosthechea* (pros-the-KAY-uh) *cochleata*. The lip has inverted to the upright position and resembles a clam's shell. Florida is home to several small epidendrum/encyclia orchids, and you can spot them in the Everglades. (GBT)

When, Where, and How to Plant

Epidendrums are good candidates for growing on trees because many grow that way naturally in South Florida. If using a terracotta pot, plant so that slender roots are embedded in a loose, fast-draining mix, such as charcoal and redwood chips. *Epidendrum ibaguense*, nicknamed a reed-stem orchid because of its round stems, is excellent for using as a groundcover in a mulched bed that drains well. The reed stems have been hybridized to come in many colors. They can take morning sun and even some afternoon sun.

Growing Tips

Water as you would cattleyas, allowing the plants to almost dry before watering again. Use a soluble 15-5-15 fertilizer every week in the growing season. In winter, reduce water and fertilizer. Repot in the spring when new growth begins. For epis in the ground, try mixing several colors in individual clumps. The soil must contain sand, perlite, or another material that allows for rapid run-off. A layer of mulch on the surface of the soil will help retain moisture and give the roots ample room for roaming. You may want to stake some of the larger cultivars. To get your epidendrum garden started, water every day or every other. Fertilize "weakly weekly" at one-quarter strength, using water-soluble fertilizer. The orange-flowering *Epi. ibaguense* will develop fairly quickly; others may take longer.

Regional Advice and Care

Central and North Florida orchid growers can keep orchids outside beneath trees or in a shade house during warm months. However, these orchids require some protection when temperatures drop below 50 degrees Fahrenheit.

Companion Planting and Design

The reed stem types—*Epidendrum ibaguense* (formerly *Epidendrum radicans*) and *Epidendrum cinnabarinum*—can be grown in the ground, and together they make an interesting garden of their own.

Try These

Epidendrum pseudoepidendrum combines lime green with tangerine orange in a delicate flower that swoops into your field of vision and stays there.

Oncidium

Oncidium spp.

Botanical Pronunciation
on-SID-ee-um

Other Name Dancing lady orchids

Bloom Period and Seasonal Color
Primarily spring blooms in yellow with brown,
maroon, or olive sepals

Mature Height x Spread
3 inches to 3 feet x 3 inches to 3 feet

Zones 10–11 outdoors

Oncidiums, from the Caribbean, Mexico, and Central and South America, are often called dancing ladies because the long stems hold lots of little flowers with big skirt-like lips that seem to dance in the breeze. The plants have round pseudobulbs with long, narrow leaves. Every orchid lover should have a clump of *Oncidium sphacelatum*, which blooms with hundreds of flowers if allowed to get large enough in a tree crotch or big basket. This ideal species performs consistently with just basic care and little fuss. Mule-ear oncidiums have thick, stiff leaves that look like what their name suggests. They like to dry thoroughly between watering. These plants are superior for growing outside on trees in full or partial shade. Miniature oncidiums now are in the genus *Tolumnia*. (GBT)

When, Where, and How to Plant
Attach these orchids to tree crotches, limbs, or the trunks of trees and palms. Use plastic-coated wire, florists' tape, or pantyhose to tie them in place. Full-sized oncidiums can be acclimated to tolerate morning sun. Plant in a fast-draining mix, such as gravel developed for orchids or a rock-like medium, chunks of tree fern with horticultural charcoal, or a general orchid mix over a layer of polystyrene peanuts. If using a general mix that contains wood chips, be alert to snow mold, a type of fungus that can form when chips stay wet. It develops fuzzy white hyphae in the mix and eventually suffocate the roots.

Growing Tips
Oncidiums like to stay evenly moist, except for the tolumnias and the mule-ears. The large, soft-leaved types, such as the famous chocolate-smelling *Oncidium* 'Sharry Baby', grow in medium to bright light and good air circulation. They like weekly fertilizing during the warm growing season with 15-5-15; every other week in cool weather. Reduce watering in winter.

Regional Advice and Care
North and Central Florida orchid lovers can grow oncidiums outside during warm months, but bring them in or provide protection when temperatures drop below 50 degrees Fahrenheit. Set pots in a tray of pebbles that has water to the pebble tops to keep up humidity.

Companion Planting and Design
Oncidiums are star performers in trees in South Florida. Four or five bulbs of an oncidium will multiply into a large clump in just a few years and produce long, arching sprays of yellowish flowers.

Try These
Oncidium sphacelatum 'Sweet Sugar' is a version of an old favorite that produces flowers with large, bright yellow lips. The common name of *O. sphacelatum* is golden shower orchid, and it is a reliable and easy plant to grow.

Phalaenopsis

Phalaenopsis spp.

Botanical Pronunciation
fail-en-OP-sis

Other Name Moth orchid

Bloom Period and Seasonal Color
Winter to spring blooms in an array of colors, spots, and stripes

Mature Height x Spread
8 to 16 inches x 8 to 16 inches

Zones 10–11

For pure grace of line, phals are the best. With beautifully shaped sepals and petals and intricately lobed and whiskered lips, phals are the essence of sophistication and elegance. Their wide, dark green, and succulent leaves can span 1 foot or more; their flowers can stay unblemished for weeks when kept inside. In addition, the number of flowers per spike is increasing, due to breeding efforts around the world. More than 100 small flowers may hang from many-branched spikes like the daintiest of ornaments. The French introduced spots into the flowers; Californians added stripes; Taiwanese hybridizers created the harlequins or flowers with color blotches. Deep red and deep blue to violet flowers have been created by American orchid breeders, and they are lovely. (GBT)

When, Where, and How to Plant
Phals like more shade than do cattleyas or vandas, but they won't flower if you keep them in too much darkness. Shade cloth that screens out 70 percent of the light is recommended, though you can grow them with 50 percent. Phals like to have their roots moist but not wet, drying slowly although never completely. Use a large-grade, loose-draining mix, containing perlite, redwood chips or bark, and tree fern, but add sphagnum to retain moisture. Or grow them in straight sphagnum moss if growing in a covered orchid house.

Growing Tips
Leaves develop from the center of the plant, pushing out and to the side. As new leaves form, a resulting cup in the crown can hold water, leading to crown rot. Plant them so they lean to one side, or use a basket that you suspend sideways. Feed 15-5-15 every week during growing season. As winter approaches, nighttime temperatures drop into the 60s, and days grow shorter, the plants will begin to set buds. In the waning weeks of October, you may add 1 tablespoon of Epsom salts to a gallon of water to strengthen the flower spike. Epsom salts mixed with potassium nitrate (1½ tablespoons each per gallon of water) can be used as a fertilizer every third or fourth watering on all orchids to strengthen cells and roots.

Regional Advice and Care
In North and Central Florida, grow phals outside in shade structures during warm months. Protect plants when temperatures drop below 55 degrees Fahrenheit. If crown rot occurs, sprinkle a healthy dose of cinnamon into the crown. The crown will die, but the plant will produce keikis (babies).

Companion Planting and Design
Many florists use *Phalaenopsis* orchids in arrangements combined with small *Tillandsia* bromeliads, dendrobiums, or just by themselves, with an addition of Spanish moss. You can try this when you bring flowering phals inside.

Try These
The light pink phals are lovely plants (*Phal. sanderiana* is a glorious pink species), and there are many from which to choose. Hot pink and raspberry colors are often too harsh; deep reds tend to be smaller flowers.

Vanda

Vanda spp.

Botanical Pronunciation
VAN-duh

Bloom Period and Seasonal Color
Blooms throughout the year

Mature Height x Spread
10 inches to 5 feet

Zones 10–11

A wonderful thing has happened to the vandas on the way to the orchid show. They have taken on the color of the late summer sky just after sundown, the royal inclinations of amethyst, the sheen of golden Buddhas. Vandas are grouped by their leaf structure, which determines how much sun they require. 'Miss Joaquim' is a terete type, meaning her leaves are as round as soda straws, a reduction in leaf surface that allows teretes to survive in full sun. These plants, though, have been shifted to the genus *Papilionanthe*. Semiterete vandas have hard, V-shaped leaves. They can stand full sun in South Florida when gradually acclimated to it. Flat-leaved vandas need shade. Vandas require daily watering unless it is cool. (GBT)

When, Where, and How to Plant
Use wooden slatted baskets, with or without a medium, or simply attach to an S-hook with wire or twisties. Teak baskets last the longest, but teak is hard to find. If a plant needs a larger basket, soak the plant's roots in water until they become pliable, and then carefully work them into the larger basket. To remove keikis (the small offshoots) snip the base of the keiki away from the mother plant when it has several small roots and wire into a small basket to keep it steady as roots develop.

Growing Tips
Vandas like to be warm and well watered. Water in the morning to allow water to dry on the leaves. (In July and August, even September, mist the plants at midday to cool them.) Commercial growers use a very weak fertilizer solution whenever they water. You can use soluble 15-5-15 weekly in the warm months, every two weeks in winter. Should the long roots become unsightly, trim them slightly between May and August and they will branch into new roots. Move vandas into more light in winter.

Regional Advice and Care
Bring vandaceous orchids inside when temperatures reach 55 to 50 degrees Fahrenheit. In Central and North Florida, they can be grown outside in warm months. Use Dithane M-45 mixed with Captan (1 tablespoon each per gallon) or copper fungicide when you see black spots surrounded by a yellow halo. Viral infections cause black spots and streaking on leaves and can affect flowers. Little can be done for viruses other than destroying the infected plant and using sterile tools. Never use clippers on more than one orchid without sterilizing them in a flame between cuts. Dirty tools spread disease.

Companion Planting and Design
Attach to the east side of a palm trunk, fasten to the slender stems of *Dracaena marginata*, or hang in wooden baskets or even on an S-hook to allow vandas roots to hang free in the air.

Try These
There are many gorgeous hybrids in this group. The related *Rhyncostylis gigantea* is wonderfully citrus scented, and half a dozen cultivars have found their way into my collection.

ORNAMENTAL GRASSES **FOR FLORIDA**

Almost everyone has some turf, but it's not the only grass that grows in the landscape. You can also use grasses as ornamental plants. Most are native types, plus there are a few species from other countries. Like lawn grasses, the ornamental types are tough—but none makes a good lawn. For one thing, they grow too tall and they form clumps that spread out very slowly. Actually this makes them the ideal landscape plantings, as they won't take over the garden with unwanted greenery. Most of the year they have attractive foliage, and each offers some unique garden color.

Planning for Ornamental Grasses

Ornamental grasses double for other ornamental plantings. Taller types can act as view barriers and form space dividers between areas of the landscape. Others serve as groundcovers just a foot or two in height. Ornamental grasses can be used as border plantings and make a great backdrop for annual, perennial, and vegetable gardens.

Their Unique Features

Perhaps where ornamental grasses really shine is as accent features. The foliage alone is different, being long and thin bladed and easily blown by the winds to add some interest. Most stems of foliage grow upright with the ends of the leaf blades gracefully turning downward. Some have arching stems with leaves that reach out to touch one another. Most are in bloom when other plantings have stopped providing good seasonal color from midsummer through fall. The inflorescence is unique, usually creating a feathery plume of color that can range from silver to pink, red, purple, and brown. Many of the flowers and seedheads yield feed and nesting materials for wildlife.

Pampas Grass

Planting Considerations

Ornamental grasses should be planted in well-drained areas of the landscape. Most are accustomed to the drier soils and may decline with wet feet. They also need sunny sites, so find an open area with six to eight hours of direct light. Plantings can be made in Florida's infertile sands, but care is often better if the soil is improved with organic matter. Give the grasses plenty of room to grow. It is a good rule to leave a distance equal to the expected height of the plants between neighboring grasses. Remember most are going to reach out and intertwine with one another.

Fountain Grass

Plant ornamental grasses at the same depth as they were growing in their containers. Those already growing in the landscape can also be divided and set at the same level in the ground. Water the plants well to make good soil-to-root contact. Then keep the soil moist to help the roots grow out into the ground. Apply a 2- to 3-inch mulch to help prevent weeds. During early growth keep broadleaf weeds and other grasses from competing with the plantings. Most can be hand pulled from the beds, but a nonselective herbicide made for spot weed control among ornamental plantings can also be utilized.

A Little Care

Once the root system is established in the surrounding soil most ornamental grass can exist with minimal care. Native types are especially adapted to surviving with moisture from rain. They also make needed growth using nutrients found in the rainwater plus decaying organic matter deposited on the soil surface. Growth is slow under these conditions, and most gardeners prefer to give the plantings a little better care: watering, especially during periods of drought, or as needed to encourage growth. Applications of lawn fertilizer can be made in February, June, or September.

Grasses make lots of growth spring through summer and by fall start to decline. Maturing portions of many types turn brown, bronze, and reddish—colors often associated with the fall season. These should be removed before spring growth begins.

Ornamental grasses are perennials and after a period of time become crowded. Some types or varieties die out, leaving an open center with shoots around the outer edges. Every three to five years the beds may need rejuvenation. At this time it's best to dig the clumps and divide them into new sections for plantings.

Florida Gama Grass

Tripsacum floridana

Botanical Pronunciation
trip-SAH-come flor-EH-dana

Bloom Period and Seasonal Color
Fall blooms in golden brown

Mature Height x Spread
1 to 2 feet x 2 feet

If you need a low-growing, clumping grass for sun or light shade, consider Florida gama grass. Plantings grow between 1 and 2 feet tall and are as wide as they are tall. The grass blades are narrow and bright green in color. In most areas of the state the grass remains evergreen until frosts and freezes arrive. The arching leaves add a light, airy feeling to landscapes. Flowering stems are produced above the foliage during the fall and provide golden-brown color. Use this grass as a groundcover. Its tolerance of most soil types makes it versatile in the landscape. This is a plant for difficult moist conditions, when other ornamentals are not suitable. It can be clustered among shrub plantings as a small accent. (TM)

When, Where, and How to Plant

Florida gama grass can be planted at any time of the year. The best planting time is between March and August when the grass is making good growth. Prepare a bed by working in liberal quantities of compost and peat moss plus manure. Space plants 24 to 36 inches apart. If the rootballs are tightly intertwined with roots, they should be lightly loosened to encourage new growth into the surrounding soil. Dig the holes wider but not deeper than the rootball, and set the plants in the ground at the original planting depth. After planting moisten the entire planting site, and add a 2- to 3-inch mulch layer.

Growing Tips

Once established the grass can exist with moisture from the rains and nutrients from decaying organic matter. Water weekly during the drier times of the year. Florida gama grass can be fed with a general garden or lawn fertilizer once in February, June, and September. Follow recommended lawn rates, or just apply a light scattering of fertilizer.

Regional Advice and Care

Florida gama grass is evergreen in the milder portions of the state. Where frost and freezes are common, it turns brown during the winter months. Schedule a pruning to rejuvenate plantings during late winter. Florida gama grass can be cut back to within 6 inches of the ground. Grooming can be performed at any time to keep plantings in bounds or remove browning portions. After pruning apply a late winter feeding to encourage new growth. Caterpillars may feed on the foliage during the growing season but are seldom a serious problem.

Companion Planting and Design

Cluster plants together to create a fall accent or use them as a groundcover for native plant settings with asters, gaillardia, liatris, coreopsis, iris, bush daisies, and other grasses.

Try These

Only the species is available in Florida. Another common name for it is dwarf fakahatchee grass.

Fountain Grass

Pennisetum setaceum

Botanical Pronunciation
pen-NEH-see-tum set-A-see-um

Bloom Period and Seasonal Color
August to October blooms in pink to purple

Mature Height x Spread
3 feet x 3 feet

Fountain grass is one of the more popular ornamental landscape grasses for home landscapes. The foliage is bright green and about ¼ inch wide. Leaves are arching, often with the outermost rows touching the soil. Fountain grass is added to perennial beds for an accent and often used as a groundcover. Plantings remain green late into the fall but start to brown with the first hint of winter. Fountain grass can be used in natural plant settings with a Florida look. A number of varieties of fountain grass are available, including dwarf forms that are ideal for containers and other types with colorful foliage. Like most ornamental grasses clumps are going to need renewal pruning in late winter to look their best in the season ahead. (TM)

When, Where, and How to Plant

Fountain grass can be planted any time of the year. The best planting time is between March and August. Plantings should be made in sites that receive six to eight hours of full sun and are bright throughout the remaining portions of the day. Prepare a bed for planting by working liberal quantities of compost or peat moss and manure into the soil. Space plants 24 to 30 inches apart. If the rootballs are tightly intertwined, loosen the roots a little to encourage new growth. Dig the holes wider but not deeper than the rootballs, and set the plants in the ground at the original planting depth. After planting, moisten the entire planting site and add a 2- to 3-inch mulch layer. When the first real cold weather arrives, the grass begins to decline and finally turns totally brown.

Growing Tips

Grasses take minimal care. Once established they can exist with moisture from rains and nutrients from decaying organic matter. Fountain grass makes the best growth if watered during periods of drought. As a general rule, water weekly during the drier times of the year. Fountain grass can be fed with a general garden or lawn fertilizer once in February, June, and September. Follow lawn rates, or just apply a light scattering of fertilizer.

Regional Advice and Care

Throughout the warmer portions of the state, fountain grass may remain semievergreen for most of the winter. In Northern and Central Florida, it turns brown with the first frosts and freezes. It needs rejuvenation pruning by late winter. Caterpillars may feed on the foliage during the growing season but are seldom a serious problem.

Companion Planting and Design

Plant as a groundcover or colorful accent for the landscape. Plants can also be used as standalone view barriers or a backdrop for annual and perennial flowers or shrubs.

Try These

The most popular is purple-leaf fountain grass, which grows to 5 feet tall. Reddish and copper-leaved forms are also available. Add lots of interest to the plantings by growing variety 'Rubrum', which has a good reddish color.

Lopsided Indiangrass

Sorghastrum secundum

Botanical Pronunciation
sor-GHAS-trum sah-COME-dumb

Bloom Period and Seasonal Color
Fall blooms in golden brown

Mature Height x Spread
2 feet (foliage) to 6 feet (flowers) x 2 feet

Lopsided Indiangrass grows foliage to only 2 feet tall but can send up flower spikes that grow to 6 feet in height. This is a native clump-forming grass that ranchers refer to as "wild oats." It has a large seedhead with flowers and seeds borne on one side of the stalk, similar to oats. The leaves are light to medium green. They are about ½ inch wide and 24 inches long. During the fall the plant declines to a golden brown color that matches the maturing seed stalks. Seed stalks may be used in dried flower arrangements. Gardeners may also want to plant a similar species known as Indiangrass, *Sorghastrum nutans*. Plantings turn yellow to orange during fall and grow to about 5 feet tall. (TM)

When, Where, and How to Plant
Lopsided Indiangrass can be planted at any time of the year. The best planting time is between March and August. Lopsided Indiangrass tolerates light shade. Plantings are best made in landscapes that receive six to eight hours of full sun and are bright throughout the remaining portions of the day. Lopsided Indiangrass is tolerant of varying growing conditions including damp soils. Prepare a bed by adding liberal quantities of compost or peat moss and manure. Space plants 18 to 24 inches apart. If the rootballs are tightly intertwined at planting, loosen them a little to encourage new growth out into the surrounding soil. Dig the holes wider but not deeper than the rootball, and set the plants in the ground at the original planting depth. After planting moisten the entire planting site, and

add a 2- to 3-inch mulch layer. During fall the grass turns golden brown and begins to decline after producing flowers and seedheads.

Growing Tips
Grasses take minimal care. Once established they can exist with moisture from rains and nutrients from decaying organic matter. Lopsided Indiangrass makes the best growth if watered during periods of drought. Water weekly during the drier times of the year. Lopsided Indiangrass can be fed with a general garden or lawn fertilizer once in February, June, and September. Follow lawn rates, or just apply a light scattering of fertilizer.

Regional Advice and Care
Northern and Central Florida plantings may mature earlier than Southern plantings. All need rejuvenation pruning by late winter. Caterpillars may feed on the foliage during the growing season but are seldom a serious problem.

Companion Planting and Design
Plant clusters to create a groundcover for a golden fall accent, or mix with perennials, including gaillardia, black-eyed Susans, showy primrose, goldenrod, and asters, for a native Florida look.

Try These
Only the species is available in Florida.

Muhly Grass

Muhlenbergia capillaris

Botanical Pronunciation
MOO-len-BER-gee-ah cap-ILL-air-is

Other Name Pink muhly

Bloom Period and Seasonal Color
Fall blooms in pink to purple

Mature Height x Spread
3 feet x 3 feet

It's easy to tell when fall arrives by the coloration of the attractive muhly grass in Florida landscapes. Pink to purple flower clusters form high above the foliage to create an accent planting any gardener would love. The leaf blades are thin, arching, and bright green during the spring and summer months to create mounds of foliage. Use muhly grass in border plantings where some fine, delicate foliage is needed. Add it to perennial gardens and natural settings. It's a great groundcover for drier areas. During late fall the plantings turn brown with the onset of colder weather. Muhly grass is best planted where there is room to add clusters of plants to get the best effect from the fall color. (TM)

When, Where, and How to Plant
Muhly grass can be planted at any time of the year. The best planting time is between March and August. For best flowering, muhly grass plantings should be made in landscape sites that receive six to eight hours of full sun and are bright throughout the remaining portions of the day. Gardeners can improve sandy soils with organic matter before planting. Space plants 12 to 18 inches apart. If the rootballs are intertwined at planting they can be loosened a little to encourage new growth. Dig the holes wider but not deeper than the rootball, and set the plants in the ground at the original planting depth. After planting, moisten the entire planting site and add a 2- to 3-inch mulch layer. During the fall muhly grass begins to decline after producing colorful flowers and seedheads.

Growing Tips
Grasses take minimal care. Once established they can exist with just moisture from rains and nutrients from decaying organic matter. Muhly grass makes the best growth if watered during periods of drought. Water weekly during the drier times of the year. Muhly can be fed with a general garden or lawn fertilizer once in February, June, and September. Use at one-half the lawn rates, or just apply a light scattering of fertilizer.

Regional Advice and Care
North and Central Florida plantings may brown earlier during the fall due to the arrival of cool weather. Muhly grass growing in all areas of the state does need late winter rejuvenation to produce attractive spring growth. Caterpillars may feed on the foliage during the growing season but are seldom a serious problem.

Companion Planting and Design
Plant a large bed as a groundcover or just small patches among other natural plantings. Enjoy the fall color when mixed with other grasses, asters, goldenrod, and daisies.

Try These
Only the species is available in Florida.

Pampas Grass

Cortaderia selloana

Botanical Pronunciation
coor-tah-DARE-e-ah sell-low-A-nah

Bloom Period and Seasonal Color
Late summer and fall blooms in white to pink

Mature Height x Spread
8 feet x 8 feet

One of the most sensational ornamentals for the Florida landscape is pampas grass, introduced from South America. It's a good grass to use in coastal areas due to its salt tolerance. The foliage is bright green, up to an inch in width, and quite sharp. Keep pampas grass away from pedestrian traffic to prevent injuries from brushing against the foliage. In warmer areas of the state it may remain evergreen throughout the cooler months, but it usually turns brown after the first periods of cold. Plantings are often used as view barriers, space dividers, and accent plants. The late summer through fall inflorescences are very showy, being white or sometimes pinkish. It's a favorite to cut and add to dried arrangements. (TM)

When, Where, and How to Plant

Pampas grass can be planted at any time of the year. The best time to plant is between March and August. For best flowers plant in landscape sites that receive six to eight hours of full sun and are bright throughout the remaining portions of the day. Pampas grass forms large clumps and needs plenty of room. It's not well suited to small landscapes. Prepare a bed by adding compost or peat moss and manure. Space plants 36 to 48 inches apart. If the rootballs are intertwined at planting, loosen the roots a little to encourage new growth. Dig the holes wider but not deeper than the rootballs, and set the plants in the ground at the original planting depth. After planting moisten the entire planting site, and add a 2- to 3-inch mulch layer. During the fall, pampas grass begins to decline after producing flowers and seedheads.

Growing Tips

Grasses take minimal care. Once established they can exist with just moisture from rains and nutrients from decaying organic matter. Pampas grass makes the best growth if watered during periods of drought. Water weekly during the drier times of the year. Pampas grass can be fed with a general garden or lawn fertilizer once in February, June, and September. Follow lawn rates, or just apply a light scattering of fertilizer.

Regional Advice and Care

Northern Florida growers can expect winter damage to their plantings. Keep the plants well mulched to prevent plant loss. All pampas grass needs pruning prior to spring growth. Caterpillars may feed on the foliage during the growing season but are seldom a serious problem.

Companion Planting and Design

Form an eye-catching accent, view barrier, or backdrop for gardens with groupings of pampas grass in the landscape. Add other grasses or contrasting native shrubs, perennials, and annual flowers for accents.

Try These

Some selections with unique variegated foliage include 'Gold Band', 'Silver Stripe', 'Silver Comet', and 'Sun Stripe'. Gardeners can also look for varieties like 'Rosea', with pink plumes, and 'Pumila', a dwarf for perennial beds and containers.

Purple Lovegrass

Eragrostis spectabilis

Botanical Pronunciation
air-ah-GRAH-tiss SPEC-tah-bill-is

Bloom Period and Seasonal Color
Fall blooms in reddish purple

Mature Height x Spread
2 feet x 2 feet

Catching the wind a foot or more above the foliage, the reddish purple flowers of purple lovegrass create a cloud of color and an excellent accent for the fall landscape. Plant large beds of this native clumping ornamental to enjoy what may be Florida's most attractive grass. Leaves of the grass are thin and offer good green growing compact mounds of foliage. During fall the foliage turns a reddish color that adds extra interest to the landscape. Use purple lovegrass as a replacement for one of your not-so-colorful groundcovers, or add it to natural landscape areas for a real Florida look. Many gardeners also like to use its colorful inflorescence in dried arrangements. See 'Elliott' lovegrass for another species to add to the landscape. (TM)

When, Where, and How to Plant
Purple lovegrass can be planted at any time of the year. The best planting time is between March and August. Plantings of purple lovegrass should be made in landscape sites that receive at least six to eight hours of full sun and are bright throughout the remaining portions of the day. Prepare a planting bed with compost or peat moss and manure. Space plants 12 to 18 inches apart. If the rootballs are tightly intertwined at planting, loosen the roots a little to encourage new growth out into the surrounding soil. Dig the holes wider but not deeper than the rootball, and set the plants in the ground at the original planting depth. After planting moisten the entire planting site, and add a 2- to 3-inch mulch layer. During the fall, purple lovegrass begins to decline after producing flowers and seedheads.

Growing Tips
Grasses take minimal care. Once established they can exist with just moisture from rains and nutrients from decaying organic matter. Purple lovegrass makes the best growth if watered during periods of drought. Water weekly during the drier times of the year. Purple lovegrass can be fed with a general garden or lawn fertilizer once in February, June, and September. Follow lawn rates, or just apply a light scattering of fertilizer.

Regional Advice and Care
North and Central Florida plantings may decline sooner than will South Florida plantings due to early frosts and freezes. All do need trimming by late winter to renew the foliage during spring. Caterpillars may feed on the foliage during the growing season but are seldom a serious problem.

Companion Planting and Design
Use this pinkish flowering grass in clusters as a groundcover or late summer accent. Mix with native shrubs or wildflowers of gaillardia, asters, daisies, goldenrod, and black-eyed Susans.

Try These
Only the species is available in Florida.

Sand Cordgrass

Spartina bakeri

Botanical Pronunciation
spar-TIN-ah baker-I

Other Name Switchgrass

Bloom Period and Seasonal Color
May through June blooms in brown

Mature Height x Spread
5 feet x 5 feet

Sand cordgrass is one of Florida's wetland grasses for use lakeside and in marshlands. Plantings grow upright with a slight curve to the ends of the foliage. Leaf blades are about a quarter-inch wide, light green on the surface, and dark green below. Florida ranchers refer to the clumps in the wetlands as switchgrass, perhaps due to the long flexible stems. Flower heads arise above the foliage. Some gardeners cut the flower heads for use in dried arrangements. Plant sand cordgrass in wetland gardens and natural settings where the soil can be kept moist until the plants are established. Lake and canal-side gardeners can consider sand cordgrass for use as a space divider, view barrier, and accent plantings. (TM)

When, Where, and How to Plant

Plant any time of the year. The best planting time is between March and August. Plantings should be made in landscape sites that receive six to eight hours of full sun and are bright throughout the remaining portions of the day. Sand cordgrass is a native bunch grass that prefers moist soil but once established can tolerate dry conditions. It also needs plenty of room to grow and may not be suitable for small landscapes. Select only sites that can be kept moist. Prepare a bed by tilling in compost and peat moss plus manure. Space plants 48 to 60 inches apart. If the rootballs are tightly intertwined, loosen the roots a little to encourage new growth. Dig the holes wider but not deeper than the rootball, and set the plants in the ground at the original planting depth. After planting moisten the entire planting site, and add a 2- to 3-inch

mulch layer. During the fall, sand cordgrass begins to decline, turning a brownish color.

Growing Tips

Once established sand cordgrass can exist with just moisture from the wetlands and nutrients from decaying organic matter. Growth is best when watered weekly during the drier times of the year. Sand cordgrass can be fed with a general garden or lawn fertilizer once in February, June, and September. Use at one-half the lawn rates, or just apply a light scattering.

Regional Advice and Care

Expect sand cordgrass to turn completely brown in the colder areas of the state. Some green may remain in the base of the plantings in warmer locations. Caterpillars may feed on the foliage during the growing season but are seldom a serious problem.

Companion Planting and Design

Create a view barrier or backdrop for a garden with seasonal flowers as accents. Also use as a groundcover grouped with dwarf yaupon holly, Indian hawthorn, and junipers.

Try These

Only the species is available in Florida.

Wiregrass

Aristida stricta var. *beyrichiana*

Botanical Pronunciation
ah-RIST-id-ah strict-ah by-ree-KEY-ana

Bloom Period and Seasonal Color
Summer through fall blooms in yellow

Mature Height x Spread
1 ½ feet x 1 ½ feet

Wiregrass creates the natural Florida look many gardeners are trying to develop in large areas of the landscape. It needs full sun to produce summer-through-fall fields of golden flower heads. This plant is a natural for wildflower plantings, seeming to give protection to the growing broadleaf plantings. This is a bunch-type grass that is best used in wide-open spaces with other wildflowers or used alone as a groundcover. The leaves are wiry, quite thin, and upright to arching. With time plants grow to a mounded shape and to 1 and 1½ feet tall. Perhaps wiregrass's greatest asset is its ability to grow in poorer soils. It's ideal for use in site restoration plantings. (TM)

When, Where, and How to Plant
The best planting time is between March and August. Wiregrass plantings should be made in landscape sites that receive six to eight hours of full sun and are bright throughout the remaining portions of the day. Wiregrass grows well in sandy landscape sites where it gets minimal maintenance. This actually helps prevent weeds of unwanted greenery from becoming established with the grass. Space plants 12 to 18 inches apart. When using transplants dig the holes wider but not deeper than the rootball, and set the plants in the ground at the original planting depth. After planting moisten the entire planting site and add a 2- to 3-inch mulch layer. Wiregrass seed can also be sown in early winter. During the fall, wiregrass begins to decline after producing flowers and seedheads.

Growing Tips
Once established wiregrass can exist with just moisture from rains and nutrients from decaying organic matter. It makes the best growth if watered during periods of drought. Water weekly during the drier times of the year. Fertilizer is not needed but can be used to speed growth with light feedings of a general garden or lawn fertilizer once in February, June, and September. Use at one-half the lawn rates, or just apply a light scattering.

Regional Advice and Care
Culture of wiregrass is similar throughout the state. It may start the winter decline earlier in North and Central Florida due to cool weather. It should be given a rejuvenation pruning each winter in all areas of the state. Caterpillars may feed on the foliage during the growing season but are seldom a serious problem.

Companion Planting and Design
Create the Florida look with clusters or beds of wiregrass as a groundcover among other native plantings of wax myrtle, local hollies, asters, goldenrod, pines, palmettos, and liatris.

Try These
Only the species is available in Florida.

PALMS FOR FLORIDA

P alms can be more diverse than one might think initially. Their trunks display an array of lean, sway, or uprightness, stoutness, and thinness. Fronds or leaves of palms can be blue-gray or olive-green, yellow-green or deep green. The new leaves may emerge red or wine-colored. The fronds are either pinnate (feather-shaped) or palmate (shaped something like the palm of your hand). But within these two forms are variations on a theme: long and graceful pinnae (individual leaflets) or short, stubby ones; great, round, and stiff palmate fronds or deeply incised and graceful ones.

The flowers are tiny when seen individually but often form pretty sprays when viewed as a whole branching stalk. Fruit is scarlet to deep purple, blue-green or white, yellow or black, and it ranges from coconuts to dates to inedible berries.

To Know Them Is to Love Them

Palms are like cats in many ways; you have to get to know them to see the gradations in character, from sober to puckish, from aloof to endearing. And one cat by itself will never do; cats must come in multiples. Unless it is a massive and handsome specimen, such as a talipot palm or a Bismark, a palm by itself is a lonely character indeed. Use

Miniature Date Palm

them in groups. Make them taller and shorter within the group. Let them mingle like company at a cookout. To regiment them militarily is unnatural—they grow in groups and clusters, not in straight rows and long lines. Royal palms, however, were used in South Florida along property lines of early settlers, and these rows are part of the historical look of the place.

Cabbage Palm

Some palm trunks are attractively marked, like those of cabada palms, which are green with distinct white rings rather like bamboo. Some palm trunks are clothed in fibers. The lady palms are wrapped in dark-brown to black fibers along their slim trunks. *Coccothrinax miraguama*, a relative of the Florida silver palm, has matting that appears to be handwoven on a loom. And the old man palm, *Coccothrinax crinite*, is loved for the thick, full beard of strawlike hair that clings to the trunk.

In the wild, you find all kinds of things growing in the old leaf stems. I've seen a snake curled in the boot of a cabbage palm, dozing in contentment. Ferns love to germinate there, and bromeliads and orchids can lodge themselves into a boot as naturally as can be. In your South Florida garden, you can train vanilla orchids or philodendrons up the trunk of a palm for a tropical look.

One of my favorite sights is palm fronds in moonlight. We are accustomed to our plants' shapes and colors in daylight, but at night they take on an ethereal quality. If there is the slightest breeze on a night of the full moon, the fronds (particularly the feathery or pinnate fronds) move magically and most beautifully.

My own garden is full of palms, including the quick-growing *Ptychosperma* that provide height, foxtail palms with bright red seeds, and several licualas because I love their orbicular, pleated fronds. I also have included *Coccothrinax* and *Thrinax* specimens, a clumping cabada, a sabal palm, and different species of shade-loving, small palms in the *Chamaedorea* genus. A *Kerriodoxa elegans*, with black petioles and enormous round fronds, is here, along with a Cuban petticoat palm, so-called because the old fronds stay attached and hang down around the trunk like a woman's petticoat.

Palms have the built-in ability to pull potassium from aging leaves, which is why pruning off old leaves interferes with the nutritional cycle of the plant. Wait until the entire frond has turned brown to prune it if it is not "self-cleaning"—meaning the fronds drop of their own accord.

Whereas some palms, such as the coconut, may show brown fronds after cold weather, most are quite able to recover within a growing season. And they are champion survivors of hurricanes.

Areca Palm

Dypsis lutescens

Botanical Pronunciation
DIP-sis loo-TESS-cens

Other Name Butterfly palm

Bloom Period and Seasonal Color
Throughout the year; golden bloom spikes

Mature Height x Spread
About 20 feet x 15 feet plus, depending
on pruning

Zones 10–11

One of the most frequently used palms in South Florida, areca palm still is one of the most graceful. The arching fronds are featherlike (pinnate) and light green. The tips of the individual leaflets curve forward, adding to the arching effect. The crown shaft from which new spears emerge is golden with a powdery, waxy coating, and leaf bases are golden. The palm forms a thick clump and, for that reason, it is widely used for screening or hedging. However, when kept pruned to allow light and air to flow through the clump, this is a beautiful specimen plant. Originally from Madagascar, these palms love water and often are found on riverbanks. When cared for properly, they are exquisite. (GBT)

When, Where, and How to Plant
Areca palms are tolerant of many soil types and conditions. When buying them, notice that some have been adapted to shade, making them appear darker green with longer fronds than those grown for sun. Ask about early growing conditions when purchasing your plant. In South Florida, avoid the addition of compost, aged manure, or other soil additives when planting in rocky soil to avoid creating a containerlike condition that discourages roots from penetrating into poor surrounding soils. When planting in sandy soils, you can help retain moisture by adding some organic matter.

Growing Tips
Fertilize with 8-4-12 slow-release fertilizer with micronutrients. Arecas are susceptible to potassium deficiency. Yellow spots on older fronds may reflect potassium shortage, not age; older leaves also yellow due to magnesium deficiency. These two elements can be given together. Use magnesium and coated potassium sulfate 2 to 4 pounds per tree four times a year. Water the area around the root zone the day prior to applying the supplements, and then water them in. Keep roots moist the first year, then irrigate once or twice a week, depending on rain. I have a clump of arecas next to a pond that regularly overflows; they love it.

Regional Advice and Care
Remove small suckers from the interior of the clump to keep air flowing through the stand. Open trunks are less vulnerable to fungus, scale, and mealybugs, as well as adventitious suckering. If palms in your garden contract ganoderma, or butt rot, do not cut out individuals from overcrowded stands, as spores from the fungus spread through the stumps. Conchs on the base of the trunks are symptomatic of the disease. Remove the clump.

Companion Planting and Design
Arecas can be used as a large specimen clump, background planting, or screen. They are compatible with many tropical flowering shrubs, serving as a backdrop against which to display blooms. *Dendrobium anosmum* is a beautiful orchid that resides resplendently on the trunks of areca palms and in the spring shows off scores of cascading flowers in purple or white.

Try These
You'll be glad you planted the species.

Bailey Palm

Copernicia baileyana

Botanical Pronunciation
cope-pre-NEE-sha bay-LEE-ana

Bloom Period and Seasonal Color
Flowers are on long stalks that grow among the leaves; flowers are creamy white and appear from February to April; fruit from August to October

Mature Height x Spread
40 to 50 feet x crowns 15-plus feet across

Zones 10–11

Cuba is home to many *Copernicia* palms, including this most handsome one. Fronds are palmate and blue-gray, and the leaf stems are armed with recurving thorns. The genus is named for Copernicus, while the species remembers Liberty Hyde Bailey, botanist and horticulturist from Cornell University who created the largest palm herbarium. The palms are slow growing but monumental in stature and effect. Seedling palms take many years to establish their roots, but when they do, and once top growth is underway, these palms seem to transform rapidly into big specimens. Leaf stems stay attached to the whitish trunks for years until you remove them. Fronds can be 5 feet across; flower stalks emerge between the leaves. (GBT)

When, Where, and How to Plant
Baileys are similar to other palms in planting requirements. Plant so the crown is at the same level in the ground as it was in the container. Provide good drainage and plenty of room for the palm's ultimate size. Keep the root zone moist throughout the first growing season. Fertilize lightly every couple of months until December or cool weather. Resume fertilizing after cold weather passes. Because the palms take a long time to emerge from the ground, fertilize three or four times a year once a young plant has enough fronds to form a vase.

Growing Tips
Many palms are drought-tolerant once established. However, provide moisture frequently and regularly when the palms are young. Water weekly in the dry season. Also, fertilizer is a must for these robust palms as they produce giant leaves and trunks. Use palm-special fertilizer (formulated for alkaline soils of South Florida) according to rates on the bag. The latest fertilizer recommendation is 8-4-12 with 4 percent magnesium and a full complement of micronutrients. A waxy coating on *Copernicia* leaves prevents absorption of foliar sprays.

Regional Advice and Care
The heavy fronds will collapse with their own weight. However, the old leaf stem bases, called boots, often are left attached to the gray-white trunk. Use a handsaw to remove the boots after palms are large enough to begin bringing their trunks out of the ground. Never tear these away and rip tissue. If under stress, the palms are susceptible to palm leaf skeletonizer, the larvae of a moth. These caterpillars chew leaf tissue on the undersides of the fronds, build protective tunnels of frass (insect droppings), and disfigure the fronds. Treat with a systemic insecticide according to package directions. Air circulation is vital.

Companion Planting and Design
Stately Bailey palms planted in a lawn are without compare.

Try These
You will be glad you planted this palm species.

Blue Latania Palm
Latania loddigesii

Botanical Pronunciation
la-TAIN-ee-a low-duh-JEEZ-e-eye

Other Name Latan palm

Bloom Period and Seasonal Color
Summer bloom stalks with large leaves; blue-gray fruits, turning brown from August to November

Mature Height x Spread
30 feet tall x crown of 20-plus feet

Zones 10–11

This plant's stately bearing gives it appeal as a specimen or when used as a pair at the entrance to a driveway. The big leaves are costapalmate, meaning palmate with a distinct midrib extending into the blade, which gives the frond a characteristic fold in the center. This palm is from the Mascarene Islands, which have wet-dry seasons similar to South Florida's. The *Latania* is not nearly as big as the blue Bismarck palms, with which it sometimes is confused. It only reaches 30 to 40 feet, compared with the Bismarck's 40-plus. Its leaves are less monumental as well. The *Latania* is slow growing but speeds up its growth after the trunk has been established. Male and female flowers are on different plants. (GBT)

When, Where, and How to Plant
An adaptable palm that does well in a range of soils, *Latania* is suitable for yards where it has space to grow. Young palms adapt readily to being transplanted at the start of the rainy season and are more easily handled by homeowners than are big specimens, which have to be root pruned over a period of time before transplanting. Placing the top of the rootball at the soil level is key. Palms planted too deep (as a method of stabilizing them) often die within several years. Mulch around the base, being careful to keep mulch from crowding the trunk so you don't create conditions for fungus disease. Allow for air movement around the crown.

Growing Tips
Broadcast 8-4-12 fertilizer with 4 percent magnesium and micronutrients three times a year, beginning in late February/early March, June/July, and October. Follow the directions on the bag. Use ½ pound on newly planted specimens, gradually increasing the amount. Latania palms are highly drought-tolerant; after keeping the roots moist during the first growing season, allow nature to take over. Only during drought will a blue latania palm need supplemental water.

Regional Advice and Care
Avoid pruning all palms until the leaf stalk is brown. Palms can translocate nutrients, especially potassium and magnesium, from old leaves to new. By pruning away old leaves, you remove a source of nutrients. Palm leaf skeletonizers can take up residence on the undersides of the big leaves, especially if the palm is under some stress. These moth larvae rasp away leaf tissue, build protective tunnels of frass (their droppings molded with saliva), and remain protected from the elements. Use a systemic insecticide or a hard spray of water to dislodge them. For heavy infestations, remove the frond. Although aesthetically undesirable, skeletonizers seldom kill palms.

Companion Planting and Design
The blue-green color of a *Latania* invites use of opposite or complementary colors nearby. They stand out against the small, dark green leaves of stoppers. Or they may be complemented with plumbago, ruellia, or purple queen as perennials.

Try These
A triad of latania palms is quite handsome.

Butia Palm

Butia capitata

Botanical Pronunciation
BEW-tee-ah CAP-eh-TAT-ah

Other Name Pindo palm

Bloom Period and Seasonal Color
Spring flowers are yellow to reddish; fruit ripens
July and August; color varies from yellow to red

Mature Height x Spread
15 feet x 15 feet

Zones 8–10

Found naturally in South America, butia palms are one of the state's finest landscape plants. Butias grow ever so slowly, and they need room to spread, growing about as wide as they are tall. Most gardeners know this palm by a few other names, including pindo and jelly palm. The latter comes from the edible fruits; the sweeter types make tasty jelly. Better selections have leaves a blue-green color, and most twist a little toward the tip. The fronds have an arching habit with the end curling toward the ground. Here is a very hardy and versatile palm that is often planted as a focal point throughout the landscape or to line streets. Use it in the minimal-maintenance landscape with limited watering. (TM)

When, Where, and How to Plant
Palms make limited root growth during the fall through early spring. For this reason butia palms dug from fields are best moved during the warmer spring through summer months. Well-established container specimens of the butia palm can be added to the landscape at any time of the year. Butia palms should be kept at least 10 feet from sidewalks, driveways, and buildings. Transplant the butia palm by digging a hole two to three times wider but not deeper than the rootball. Create a berm at the edge of the rootball to help thoroughly wet the root system at each watering. After planting, add a 2- to 3-inch mulch layer over the root system. Periodically, butia fronds decline and need removal. Prune them back as close to the trunk of the palm as possible. Older bases that have loosened can be pulled from the plant as needed.

Growing Tips
Newly planted butia palms should be kept moist until the roots begin to grow out. Make sure the soil does not thoroughly dry for several growing seasons. Once established the butia palm is very drought-tolerant and rarely needs special watering. Encourage growth and maintain the best color by applying a fertilizer once in March, June, and October. Palms are very specific as to their nutrient needs, so use an 8-2-12 palm fertilizer that contains the minor nutrients as formulated by the University of Florida.

Regional Advice and Care
Butia palms grow throughout most of Florida except for the most southern portion. They are susceptible to leaf spots and trunk rots that commonly affect palms. Remove declining shoots and old flower- or fruit-producing stems as needed. Keep as much green foliage on the palms as possible.

Companion Planting and Design
There is plenty of room for groundcover plantings beneath this large palm. Some good ornamentals that repeat their needlelike look include junipers, liriope, mondo grass, and African iris.

Try These
Only the species is available in Florida, but a cross with the queen palm is available; it's called the mule palm.

Cabbage Palm

Sabal palmetto

Botanical Pronunciation
SAY-ball PAHL-met-toe

Other Name Sabal palm

Bloom Period and Seasonal Color
Summer; white flowers and black fruit

Mature Height x Spread
40 feet x 10 feet

The Florida cabbage palm is our official "state tree." It's a bit confusing, but palms are not true trees, though they resemble them often with straight, tall, thick trunks. This palm has been more than a towering landscape addition, finding use in making hats, baskets, and roofs for early Native American homes. As the older leaves mature and drop, the bases, called boots, remain on the trunks for added interest. Cabbage palms are good tree replacements in the landscape and are especially useful in small locations where there is limited room for lateral growth. They can also be used where you want the tree look but limited shade. This tall-growing palm makes a good complement for taller buildings. Often the palms are set in clusters of three or more. (TM)

When, Where, and How to Plant
Cabbage palms are best moved during the warmer months. Container specimens can be added to the landscape at any time. Plant at least 10 feet from sidewalks, driveways, and most buildings. Cabbage palms are drought-tolerant but also tolerate moist soils. They are dug and moved with very little root system at the base of the palm. Cabbage palms transplant best if all the fronds are removed after planting. All roots die back to the base of the palm trunk after digging. Transplant the cabbage palm by digging a hole two to three times wider but not deeper than the rootball. Create a berm at the edge of the rootball to wet the root system thoroughly at each watering. After planting, add a 2- to 3-inch mulch layer over the root system. Larger specimens need bracing to prevent wind damage.

Growing Tips
Newly planted cabbage palms should be kept moist until the roots begin growing into the surrounding soil. Make sure the soil does not dry for several growing seasons. Once established the cabbage palm needs special watering only during extreme periods of drought. Encourage growth and maintain the best color by applying a fertilizer once in March, June, and October. Palms are very specific as to their nutrient needs so it is important to use an 8-2-12 palm fertilizer that contains the minor nutrients as formulated by the University of Florida.

Regional Advice and Care
Cabbage palms grow well throughout the entire state. Remove declining shoots and old flower- or fruit-producing stems as needed. Keep as much green foliage on the palms as possible.

Companion Planting and Design
Cabbage palms may be used as a single specimen, but they look best in clusters of three or more. Use with plantings of junipers, Indian hawthorn, dwarf yaupon hollies, and liriope.

Try These
Only the species is available in Florida. A native relative, the dwarf palmetto, *Sabal minor*, is found throughout Florida growing mainly as an understory plant to 6 feet tall. Another relative, the Puerto Rico hat palm, *Sabal causiarum*, should be considered for larger home sites.

Chinese Fan Palm

Livistona chinensis

Botanical Pronunciation
liv-a-STONE-a chai-NEN-sis

Bloom Period and Seasonal Color
Warm season, late winter/spring; seeds ripen summer through fall

Mature Height x Spread
20 to 30 feet x 15 feet; fronds 3 to 6 feet wide

Zones 9–11

Sturdy and moderately fast growing, the Chinese fan palm has palmate fronds that are divided into slender segments, with the ends of the segments gracefully drooping like delicate ribbons. The trunk turns a corky brown-gray with age. The fruits are among the most beautiful in the palm family, a unique blue-green. The Chinese fan palm's cold hardiness and ease of growth makes this a good landscape plant, but the petioles are armed with sharp spines and great care must be taken when pruning or mulching. (GBT)

When, Where, and How to Plant
Plant with plenty of room around the palm, because the crown is large. Dig a hole as deep as the rootball and two or three times as wide. Water in as you backfill, and mulch around the root zone. Keep the planting area moist throughout the first growing season, irrigating if rain is insufficient. By planting at the beginning of the rainy season, you reduce irrigation requirements. Plant several together, but include varying heights.

Growing Tips
A palm for the armchair gardener, the Chinese fan palm is not fussy and doesn't require babying. If fertilized a couple of times a year, it does quite nicely. You may be motivated to remove yellowing fronds when the palms are small; however, the longer you can tolerate a yellow or brown frond, the better off the palm will be, because these plants can pull back potassium from the old leaves as

they age. Many palm experts recommend trimming palms only when the leaf stems are as brown as the fronds.

Regional Advice and Care
Grow these palms in containers in areas of Central Florida where freezing temperatures are likely, but be careful if you have to move them indoors for winter protection. This is not a palm for North Florida. *Livistona chinensis* is susceptible to lethal yellowing disease as well as ganoderma or butt rot, a fungal disease found in older palms. To prevent ganoderma, keep the area around the base of the palm open so air circulation is unhindered.

Companion Planting and Design
Melaleuca mulch around the base will allow for air circulation, but keep mulch 2 inches away from the trunk to avoid fungus. William Lyman Phillips designed the Bailey palm glade at Fairchild Tropical Botanic Garden and used Chinese fan palms to tie together two sides of the vista that runs through it. The palms create a harmonious sight and direct the eye to the lakes and sky beyond.

Try These
The unique blue-green color of this species makes it an extra-special palm for your yard.

Date Palm

Phoenix spp.

Botanical Pronunciation
FEE-nex

Bloom Period and Seasonal Color
Flowers during spring producing cream
colored blooms

Mature Height x Spread
10 to 50 feet x 30 feet

Zones 9–11

Date palms make up a large collection of stately, feather-leaf, mostly tree form additions to Florida landscapes. Most grow quite tall and wide spreading like the very popular Canary Island date palm, but a few are patio size as the pygmy date palm often called by its species name roebelenii palm. Typically they form single trunks, but pygmy dates are commonly marketed as clusters with up to three trunks of individual palms for accent features. This later palm may be used in a container or in the ground. Taller growing selections are very formal looking and often planted as street tree replacements, and used to line driveways and form accents near the home, off patios and along walkways. Note the size when deciding which of these palms fits your landscape needs. (TM)

When, Where, and How to Plant
Palms are best added to the landscapes during the warmer months but container plants can be planted at any time. All grow best in a well-drained soil. Give these palms room to grow. Position the rootball so the top is at or slightly above the soil line. Then form a berm of soil around the edge of the rootball to hold water that can be directed through the ball and out into the surrounding soil. Keep the rootball moist until the plantings begin to make new growth and send roots out into the surrounding soil. Then provide normal watering. If the fronds were tied up at planting time, the ties can be removed in 30 or so days. Give the first feeding when new growth is noted.

Growing Tips
Once established palms are very drought-tolerant. The best growth is produced when they are watered weekly during the very hot dry weather. Encourage growth and maintain the best color by applying a fertilizer once in March, June, and October. Phoenix palms are especially sensitive to nutrient deficiencies, so it is important to use an 8-2-12 palm fertilizer that contains the minor nutrients as formulated by the University of Florida.

Regional Advice and Care
Palms in this genus are best grown in the warmer portions of the state. In border zones they may suffer frond damage that is removed in late February before new growth begins. Remove old inflorescences and fronds, but leave the green fronds. Beetles are a problem at transplant time, and fusarium wilt disease has been a problem in many areas. Check with your local Extension office before planting in your area and for available controls.

Companion Planting and Design
Most gardeners like the pygmy date palms for poolside and patio displays. Combine with other palms or landscape shrubs. They grow well with waterwise plantings like Asiatic jasmine, bromeliads, junipers, dwarf yaupon holly, and liriope.

Try These
Taller specimen palms for landscape features in this group include the Canary Island date, edible date palm, Senegal date, and wild date palms.

European Fan Palm

Chamaerops humillis

Botanical Pronunciation
CAM-mer-ops hoo-MILL- lis

Bloom Period and Seasonal Color
Spring blooms of a yellow color

Mature Height x Spread
10 feet x 10 feet

Gardeners throughout Florida can enjoy this small fan leaf palm in their landscapes in a container or in ground. The fronds are very attractive with the leaf portions a bright to blue-green color often deeply divided. This is one very hardy clump-forming palm that seems to have few pest problems. Plantings produce multiple trunks that are usually kept to three to five in number. It can be left to grow as a mounded plant, or the lower fronds can be removed to expose the attractive trunks. European fan palms are often set to the side near the entrance of the home, in flower gardens as an accent, near patios, and along walkways. Do set them back far enough so not to affect visitors with their spiny fronds. (TM)

When, Where, and How to Plant

Palms are best added to the landscapes during the warmer months, but container plants can be added at any time. Position the rootball so the top is at or slightly above the soil line. Then form a berm of soil around the edge of the rootball to hold and direct water through the ball and out into the surrounding soil. Keep the rootball moist until the plantings begin to make new growth and send roots out into the surrounding soil. Then provide normal watering. Give the first feeding when new growth is noted.

Growing Tips

Once established palms are very drought-tolerant. Still, the best growth is produced when they are watered weekly during the very hot, dry weather. Add a 2- to 3-inch mulch layer over the root system but back from the trunk 6 inches or so. Encourage growth and maintain the best color by applying fertilizer once in March, June, and October. Palms are very specific as to their nutrient needs, so it is important to use an 8-2-12 palm fertilizer that contains the minor nutrients as formulated by the University of Florida.

Regional Advice and Care

European fan palms grow throughout the state with minimal care. Keep shoots from the base pruned back unless needed for a new trunk. Prune declining shoots to keep the plants attractive and create open plant forms as desired. Better wear leather gloves with this one, as the spines are plentiful. Scale insects are occasional pests but can be controlled with a natural horticultural oil spray.

Companion Planting and Design

Plant alone as an accent feature, or combine with other annual and perennial plantings. Some to consider include the yaupon holly, juniper, bush daisy, Mexican heather, Indian hawthorn, coontie, and Asiatic jasmine. Also include fan palms as a container plant for patio displays.

Try These

Garden center offerings can be quite variable as to growth features. Most produce the multiple trunk palms enjoyed in landscape settings. Single trunk selections are also available. Ones with silvery leaves are marketed as the variety *cerifera*, and there is a green leaf mounding form too.

Florida Silver Palm

Coccothrinax argentata

Botanical Pronunciation
coco-THRI-nax ar-JEN-ta-ta

Other Name Silver palm

Bloom Period and Seasonal Color
White flowers in spring; black fruit

Mature Height x Spread
20 feet x 5 feet

Zones 10B–11

A single-trunked palm with delicate, softly drooping fronds that are very silvery on the undersides, *Coccothrinax argentata* is slow growing and hardy. This graceful Florida native may reach 20 feet eventually. Although fragile-looking, Florida silver palm is extraordinarily tough. In preserves and natural areas you can sometimes find blackened trunks caused by rainy-season lightning strikes that attest to their durability. This palm is good for seaside homes, because it is highly salt-tolerant. Its drought-tolerance makes it an excellent candidate for native gardens. Its size makes it suitable for patio and townhouse gardens where space is limited. *Coccothrinax argentata* should never be collected from the wild. Bees love the flowers. (GBT)

When, Where, and How to Plant
Plant in an area with excellent drainage. Because it grows naturally in fast-draining, dry conditions, this palm may become diseased if overwatered. Hopefully drainage will be excellent around your entryway, because this palm can serve as a specimen plant to greet visitors. A crescent of them near the front door is an outstanding sight. Water as with any newly planted palm, shrub, or tree; daily for a week, every other day for two weeks, every third day for two weeks, and then just to keep the root zone moist during the first growing season. Eventually this palm can withstand growing on its own without any supplemental irrigation.

Growing Tips
Use a palm fertilizer such as 8-4-12—with 4 percent magnesium and micronutrients—in March, June, and October when the palm is young. As it matures, you can allow it to get along on its own. However, if you notice the leaves becoming off color, then apply nutrients again. If you wait long enough, the fronds on the *Coccothrinax* will fall, leaving the bottom stubs of leaf stems sticking up or out through the trunk fiber. Fiber does not stay attached to the trunk very long, however.

Regional Advice and Care
Grow the Florida silver palm in a container, and protect it from freezing in Central and North Florida.

Companion Planting and Design
This small, beautiful palm grows so heroically on Big Pine Key that some of that other tough native flora seem to beg to go with it, such as locustberry, palmettos, and dwarf Fakahatchee grass among them.

Try These
In times of water restrictions, it's nice to have a native species like the Florida silver palm as a great landscape option.

Hurricane Palm

Dictyosperma album

Botanical Pronunciation
dick-tee-o-SPERM-a AL-bum

Other Name Princess palm

Bloom Period and Seasonal Color
Spring/summer; reddish flowers followed by
purple-black fruit

Mature Height x Spread
Up to 30 feet x crown of 12 feet or so

Zones 10–11

As much as the University of Miami Hurricanes would hope, this palm was not named for them. It garnered its common name because of its ability to withstand tropical cyclones—hurricanes. Its long fronds have a distinctively long-lasting "rein" of tissue that runs along the edge of the leaflets, holding individual young leaflets perfectly in place on the arching fronds. Trunks are light brown and more barklike than those of many other palms, and the crown shaft has a distinct bulge at the base. Originally from the Mascarene Islands in the Pacific, *Dictyosperma* is cut for its edible heart on Reunion, has disappeared in the wild from Mauritius, and is threatened by hybridization on Rodrigues. The World Conservation Union lists this palm as endangered. (GBT)

When, Where, and How to Plant
As a solitary palm, this strong and handsome specimen can be given star placement or used in groups of three, five, or seven, as is true of other single trunk palms. The magical three, five, and seven are more pleasing to the eye than trees planted in even numbers. Allow for excellent drainage but rich soil. If it has been planted in an area where fill has been dredged from grass prairies to get above the water table, create a mound that drains well and can keep the palm's roots out of water. The crown of this palm is quite handsome, and if you plant it where it will be seen against palmate palms or big-leafed trees, the crown will be more distinguishable. There is a

purple crownshaft form, which is rare; a red form, with reddish new leaves and a yellow form, with golden cast to the undersides of the leaves.

Growing Tips
Use 8-4-12 with 4 percent magnesium and a full complement of micronutrients to counter the poor soils in South Florida that are often leached of nitrogen and potassium. Keep weeds away from the base of this and every palm trunk for maximum growth. Grass and weeds compete with palm roots for nutrients and water. Use composted mulch to refurbish organic matter to the roots. This palm is moderately susceptible to lethal yellowing disease, which remains active in South Florida, and may be damaged by cold.

Regional Advice and Care
Keep your hurricane palm well fertilized and watered, and it can withstand full sun (as well as wind). It likes adequate water but is drought-tolerant when it's mature. This is a wonderfully hardy palm.

Companion Planting and Design
Grasses, such as dwarf Fakahatchee grass or muhly grass, are complementary to palms, as are bromeliads.

Try These
The variety with red leaf edges is an especially desirable landscape addition. It's called *Dictyosperma album* var. *rubrum*.

Key Thatch Palm

Leucothrinax morrisii

Botanical Pronunciation
loo-ko-THRI-nax mor-RIS-ee-eye

Other Name Brittle thatch palm

Bloom Period and Seasonal Color
Long, arching inflorescences of yellow flowers
in spring and summer; clusters of fruit are white

Mature Height x Spread
25 feet x 8 feet

Zones 10–11

Found in the Florida Keys, the Bahamas, and the Antilles, this sturdy and handsome palm has palmate fronds that are green above and whitish below. For many years it was called *Thrinax morrisii*. Its name was changed after a DNA analysis. Its leaves are divided into segments, and the very tips are split in two. The petioles are split in two at the base; the fruit are white. This solitary palm will reach about 25 feet. The palm blooms in the spring. Its rough bark turns gray with age. It is closely related to the genus *Coccothrinax*, but is distinguished by small white dots on the undersides of the leaves. It is well behaved and tolerant of many conditions, but not full shade. (GBT)

When, Where, and How to Plant
Spring through midsummer is the best time to plant. The key thatch palm will be happy in an area that can retain moisture but drains well. The limestone and sandy soils of South Florida are more than adequate. Do not add organic material to the planting hole. The key thatch palm may be planted in coastal areas, as it is salt-tolerant, growing naturally in coastal habitats.

Growing Tips
Given plenty of sun and good drainage, this palm still is considered to be slow growing. But in small yards, this is a desirable trait. Drought-tolerant once established, it can benefit from an occasional helping of palm fertilizer. Thatch

palms generally do not show damage from cold fronts that come through South Florida, but all palms can benefit from a mix of copper fungicide with Dithane M-45 after cold weather or hurricanes. Hurricanes may not down palms, but they can shake them, and the hearts of the palm may be bruised as a result, making them susceptible to rot. Because the palm has but a single growing point, unlike trees, the quick application of the fungicide can help prevent heart rot. Simply pour the solution into the heart of the palm, where the single spear is emerging.

Regional Advice and Care
Protect from cold in Central and North Florida.

Companion Planting and Design
Key thatch palm can be planted in groups or with native pineland crotons (*Croton linearis*), muhly grass, or Elliot's love grass.

Try These
A close relative to the *Coccothrinax*, *Leucothrinax* also is related to the critically endangered *Hemithrinax ekmanianai* from Cuba and *Zombia antillarium*, a palm from Hispaniola noted for its thorny trunk. A grouping of these would create a family album and save rare germplasm.

Lady Palm

Rhapis spp.

Botanical Pronunciation
RAY-pis

Other Name Tall lady palm

Bloom Period and Seasonal Color
Small orange inflorescences appear from time to time, followed by black fruit

Mature Height x Spread
6 to 15 feet x 15 feet

Zones 10–11

Perhaps it is the slender form or the comeliness of the divided leaves; perhaps it is the pliable and forgiving nature. Perhaps it is the sense of grace she brings to a landscape. Perhaps it is none of these, but this is indeed a lady palm. *Rhapis* means "needle," for the narrow and often pointed segments of the palmately divided fronds. Two species work well in Florida, *R. excela* and *R. humilis*. *R. excela* is the large lady palm; she slowly grows to 12 or 14 feet on slender stems wrapped in black fibers. *Rhapis humilis* is the slender lady palm, taller than *R. excela* but with delicate leaf segments that are more graceful and drooping. *Rhapis humilis* takes more cold than does *Rhapsis excela*. (GBT)

When, Where, and How to Plant

If transplanting a large clump, root prune four to six weeks before the moving date; fill in the trench around the rootball with soil or mulch, and keep moist until you transplant the palm. Dig a planting hole three times as wide and just as deep as the rootball. Then, dig beyond the inside of the trench to gather new roots that have developed and can keep on growing when in their new home. Be diligent about watering so the rootball doesn't dry until the palms put out new growth. Once established lady palms may be watered and allowed to become slightly dry before watering again. Plant as a hedge or a specimen in a well-draining area. These palms spread on underground stems or rhizomes.

Growing Tips

Use a fertilizer formulated for palms two or three times a year. When the palm is hungry, the leaves will begin to turn yellow. When sited in full sun, the leaves also yellow. Once through the first growing season, lady palms are able to withstand fairly dry conditions, and watering can be reduced to a minimum except in periods of drought. When old fronds turn brown, snap the delicate petioles to remove them.

Regional Advice and Care

Grow in protected areas of Central Florida; in colder northern areas of the state, grow in a container.

Companion Planting and Design

Lady palms serve as a screen and hedge when grown as a middle layer between a groundcover, such as a small *Philodendron* 'Burle Marx' and taller pinnate palms; or use in containers.

Try These

The Japanese have developed variegated and dwarf forms of *Rhapis*. Some of these are grown as bonsai. Cream variegation is usually a genetic sport. *Rhapis excela* 'Zuikonishiki' is one of the most popular, and it was developed in 1958; 'Kobannoshima' was developed in 1988. There are many cultivars, but basically they all are from *Rhapis excela*.

Old Man Palm

Coccothrinax crinita

Botanical Pronunciation
ko-ko-THRI-nax crin-NEET-a

Bloom Period and Seasonal Color
White inflorescences appear among the leaves in spring and summer; fruit is purple-black

Mature Height x Spread
25 to 30 feet x 8 feet

Zones 10–11

A Cuban native, the old man palm is one of the must-haves for palm nuts. Its slender trunk is covered with woolly, light brown fiber that may—if you are lucky—remain attached for years. Probably because the hairs seem rather beardlike, the palm got the moniker old man. The leaves are round and stiff. According to *Palms Throughout the World* by David Jones, there are two subspecies of the old man: *Coccothrinax crinita* ssp. *crinita* from Western Cuba that grows in seasonally flooded, low-lying areas and *C. crinita* ssp. *brevicrinis*, with short hairs, from southern Cuba's montane areas. (GBT)

When, Where, and How to Plant
Plant any time during the warm season, without soil amendments, in full sun to partial shade. The old man palm takes a wide range of soils and is moderately drought-tolerant once established. However, make your site selection carefully, because if you attempt to transplant it later, the beard could become unattached. Apply a palm fertilizer (8-4-12) two or three times a year.

Growing Tips
The old man palm likes South Florida's limestone soils, which drain well and still retain moisture. It can be faster growing than it is given credit for if it's given consistent fertilizer and water. These can be quite hardy.

Regional Advice and Care
For Central Florida, try to find the subspecies *brevicrinis*, from the mountainous areas of Cuba. One of my old man palms developed crown rot after a cold spell, and I treated it with a dose of an intensely strong fungicide. An unsightly crust formed in the crown of the small palm, which I picked out. Gradually the palm recovered, sending out deformed, tiny fronds at first, then larger and larger, until today it is growing full-sized fronds once more.

Companion Planting and Design
Give this palm a prominent spot in your garden where it can be seen and appreciated, perhaps near the entry. *Coccothrinax crinita* makes an excellent single specimen, underplanted with wildflowers or grasses; or a handsome set of three is equally appealing.

Try These
Coccothrinax borhidiana and *C. miraguama* are two wonderful relatives of the old man palm. Both are from Cuba, and an interesting grouping can be made by flanking the old man with these. *Coccoghrinax borhidiana* is a dwarf palm with palmate fronds that are held close to the trunk and close together, giving the appearance of growing in a circle.

Pacaya Palm

Chamaedorea tepejilote

Botanical Pronunciation
kam-a-dor-REE-a tep-ee-hee-LOW-tay

Bloom Period and Seasonal Color
Warm-season flower spikes are yellow to green;
fruit are black on red or orange rachis

Mature Height x Spread
To 8 or 9 feet x crown 3 to 4 feet on solitary
palms (x 7 feet on clumping types)

Zones 10B–11

Of the numerous *Chamaedorea* species, pacaya, or *C. tepejilote*, is among the nicest for home landscapes. This is an understory rainforest palm from areas that are seasonally dry. The relatively broad leaflets are pointed on the ends; fronds are long and graceful in an uncluttered crown. The trunk is slender and straight and bears white rings where old leaves were attached. Some are solitary in habit, whereas others cluster. *C. tepejilote* flower stalks appear below the crown (there are male and female inflorescences on separate plants). When fruits appear, the short branches of the infructescence turn bright orange-red. Several solitary pacayas together make a handsome group beneath large, tropical trees, transporting a little of tropical America to a South Florida garden. (GBT)

When, Where, and How to Plant
Similar to other palms, the best season for planting is at the onset of the rainy season (late May or June). Plant in a shady area, beneath large trees, or within their shade zone, where early morning or late afternoon sun can hit the leaves. *C. tepejilote* can form "adventitious roots" at or just above the ground and occasionally at nodes along the stem in much older specimens. These roots help the palm balance itself—whether in the rainforest on slippery slopes or among tree roots in your yard. Though not as prone to nutrient deficiencies as other palms, *C. tepejilote* still needs palm fertilizer in South Florida's soils.

Growing Tips
The palms are used to seasonally dry conditions, which makes them right at home in South Florida's seasonally wet/dry cycle. When the palm is happy, the fronds are deep green. South Florida's rainy season can wash away the effect of regular granular fertilizers, causing yellow leaves. Slow-release fertilizers don't lose their nutrients all at once, but supply nutrients over a period of time, depending on soil moisture or, in newer versions, soil temperature.

Regional Advice and Care
This is an easy-care type of palm, with no particular insect or disease problems. It can come down with a good case of scale or mealybugs if it grows in conditions that are too wet and dark with little air movement. Use alcohol on cotton or insecticidal soap to treat. Fronds can be broken by squirrels.

Companion Planting and Design
An assortment of understory rainforest plants, from calatheas to ferns and aroids, complement this tropical palm.

Try These
Devote a shady area of your yard to a small *Chamaedorea* collection where you can compare and contrast these small palms. With an abundant canopy overhead, these rainforest plants will do well through winter.

Royal Palm

Roystonea elata

Botanical Pronunciation
ROY-stone-ee-ah EE-late-ah

Bloom Period and Seasonal Color
Summer; flowers whitish; fruit, maroon to black

Mature Height x Spread
50 feet x 30 feet

Zones 10–11

Two royal palms are often confused with each other because they look so similar and some feel they are really the same. Most still recognize a native *Roystonea elata* and introduced species *Roystonea regia*, the Cuban royal palm. Some feel the difference is in the trunks, with the Cuban royal palm having an obvious bulge in the trunk and the Florida royal palm being more uniform. Both are cold-sensitive and limited to South Florida, and both are good landscape additions. What catches the attention of many admirers is the area of long, smooth green trunk at the top. These majestic palms are best used in large landscapes. Plant them in clusters as accent features, or line them in rows along a wide street or drive. (TM)

When, Where, and How to Plant

Royal palms dug from fields or landscapes are best moved during the warmer spring months through midsummer. Well-established container specimens of royal palms can be added to the landscape at any time. This is a tall-growing palm that should be located where it has adequate overhead space. Keep it at least 10 feet away from sidewalks and driveways and 20 feet from the home. Transplant the palm by digging a hole two to three times wider but not deeper than the rootball. Create a berm at the edge of the rootball so each watering wets the root system and then moves out into the surrounding soil. After planting, add a 2- to 3-inch mulch layer over the root system. Larger specimens of royal palms need bracing to prevent wind damage. Periodically remove older leaves, where possible, to keep an attractive specimen.

Growing Tips

Newly planted royal palms should be kept moist until the roots begin to grow out. Although this is a fast-growing palm, make sure the soil does not thoroughly dry for several growing seasons. Once established the palms need watering about once a week or whenever the soil begins to dry, especially during periods of drought. Encourage growth and maintain the best color by applying a fertilizer once in March, June, and October. Royal palms are very specific as to their nutrient needs, so use an 8-2-12 palm fertilizer that contains the minor nutrients as formulated by the University of Florida.

Regional Advice and Care

Royal palms are limited to South Florida. Winter freezes make it impossible to grow the palms farther north. Royal palms can exhibit nutrient deficiencies in some South Florida soils. Apply a fertilizer with adequate potassium and minor nutrients needed for growth.

Companion Planting and Design

These are tall palms to plant alone or in clusters of three or more. Add ornamentals that complete the tropical look, including bougainvillea, crotons, ti plants, ferns, allamanda, gingers, and philodendrons.

Try These

Only the species is available in Florida.

Saw Palmetto

Serenoa repens

Botanical Pronunciation
sair-EN-oh-ah REA-pens

Other Name Palmetto

Bloom Period and Seasonal Color
Early spring and summer

Mature Height x Spread
6 feet x 6 feet

Early settlers probably viewed saw palmettos as a threat to their livelihood. The plants had sharp needles on the leaf petioles, formed almost impermeable thickets, and covered much of the desirable crop and grazing lands. Today gardeners are taking a new look at these palms that can grow in most soils, harbor wildlife, and provide an early Florida look. This clump-forming palm can grow in sandy to enriched soils. It's best used as a low view barrier, a space divider between properties, and an accent plant near patios and along walkways. Saw palmettos are usually planted in clusters of three or more. Pale green forms are most often found in the wild but a blue leaf form in also noted. This is a great palm for minimal-maintenance landscapes. (TM)

When, Where, and How to Plant
The very best planting time for the saw palmetto is the warmer spring months through midsummer, but container-grown specimens can be added to the landscape at any time of the year. This palm grows as wide as it is tall, so it needs space to spread out in all directions. Keep it at least 10 feet away from sidewalks, driveways, and the home. Transplant the palm by digging a hole two to three times wider but not deeper than the rootball. Create a berm at the edge of the rootball to ensure wetting of the root system at each watering. This palm usually does not need staking. The saw palmetto gradually increases in size and may overgrow walks and encroach upon other landscape plantings. Prune the plants back as needed.

Growing Tips
Add a 2- to 3-inch mulch layer over the root system. Newly planted saw palmettos should be kept moist until the roots begin to grow out. Although this is a very drought-tolerant palm, make sure the soil does not thoroughly dry for several growing seasons. Once established the saw palmetto does not need special watering but can be given periodic watering along with other landscape plantings. The saw palmetto needs infrequent feedings. Fertilizing other nearby plantings usually is enough to feed the palm plantings too. Where light feedings are provided in spring and summer, use an 8-2-12 palm fertilizer that contains the minor nutrients as formulated by the University of Florida.

Regional Advice and Care
Saw palmettos grow throughout the state without special care. Saw palmettos may be affected by palmetto weevils and palm leaf skeletonizers. Where needed, treat with a pesticide recommended by the University of Florida.

Companion Planting and Design
Create view barriers and space dividers with clusters or add to natural Florida settings. Mix with native hollies, ornamental grasses, beach sunflower, beautyberry, pines, coreopsis, aster, and daisies.

Try These
Gardeners often avoid the saw palmetto as a landscape plant due to its common occurrence in the wild. Many do like the blue leaf form, because it adds more interest to the native plantings.

Washington Palm

Washingtonia robusta

Botanical Pronunciation
wash-ING-toe-knee-ah row-BUST-ah

Other Name Mexican fan palm

Bloom Period and Seasonal Color
Spring with white blooms

Mature Height x Spread
80 to 90 feet x 30 to 40 feet

Very tall palms lining streets and accompanying tall buildings are likely Washington palms. Yet these are the same palms sold at garden centers and set next to homes in new developments. Many love the palm for its stately and real tropical look. It is best used where it can grow in proportion to the landscape. Several may be clustered in a gathering area to define the space and cast a little overhead shade. Use them to line a long driveway or as a streetside planting. Washington palms could be set out to define the properly line and as light overhead cover for understory plantings. It is a palm Florida gardeners often plant, but make sure there is adequate room for eventual growth. (TM)

When, Where, and How to Plant

Washington palms can be purchased as container or balled-and-burlapped plants ready for the landscape. Dug palms are best moved during the warmer spring months through midsummer. Well-established container specimens can be planted at any time. This is a tall-growing palm that should be located where it has adequate overhead space away from electrical wires. Keep it at least 10 feet from sidewalks and driveways. It is not for near-home planting. Transplant the palm by digging a hole two to three times wider but not deeper than the rootball. Create a berm at the edge of the rootball to retain water during the establishment period. After planting, add a 2- to 3-inch mulch layer over the root system. Larger specimens of Washington palms need bracing to prevent wind damage.

Growing Tips

Newly planted palms should be kept moist until the roots begin to grow out. Although this is a fast-growing palm, make sure the soil does not thoroughly dry for several growing seasons. Once established water once a week or whenever the soil begins to dry, especially during periods of drought. Encourage growth and maintain the best color by applying a fertilizer once in March, June, and October. Palms are very specific as to their nutrient needs, so it is important to use an 8-2-12 palm fertilizer that contains the minor nutrients as formulated by the University of Florida.

Regional Advice and Care

Washington palms grow throughout Florida and are hardy to about 20 degrees Fahrenheit. They often make three to four feet of growth a year. Some let them accumulate the leaves along the trunks to give them a petticoat look. Others trim off all but the full green fronds.

Companion Planting and Design

Shrubs to complement these palms include powderpuff, gingers, ligustrums, viburnums, and dwarf yaupon holly. Groundcovers might include the Asiatic jasmine, liriope, and sensitive plant.

Try These

Washington palms are normally available as the species, but there is also a California palm of the same genus that is a bit small. A hybrid of the two species is sometimes available.

Wine Palm

Pseudophoenix vinifera

Botanical Pronunciation
sue-do-FEE-nix vyn-IF-era

Other Name Cherry palm

Bloom Period and Seasonal Color
Various times; yellow flowers on stalks that grow within the leaves develop into round, red fruit

Mature Height x Spread
8 to 40 feet x a crown about 15 feet

Zones 10B–11

The wine palm is so slow growing it should be planted by young gardeners—or bought at great price by old gardeners. Native to the island of Hispaniola, this ultra-attractive palm grows a solitary trunk that develops a distinct bulge beneath the crown. The gray-green pinnate fronds arch up and out, and the overall impression is one of self-possession and dignity. A distinct swollen area in mid-trunk gives this palm a bottlelike appearance. It produces enormous branched inflorescences that arch gracefully quite far down the trunk. Once the sap was used to produce wine. It will take alkaline soils and full sun. (GBT)

When, Where, and How to Plant
The wine palm likes sun and sea air and rocky soils. Although it thrives on rocky coastlines, the difficulty is digging the hole in the rock. The wine palm is frustratingly slow growing, and it may be partly for that reason that it is not often seen in South Florida gardens. No extra soil amendments are needed for the wine palm to succeed, just patience and excellent drainage, as well as ample fertilizer to push it along a little.

Growing Tips
Use palm fertilizer, and don't worry about supplemental water once it has become established. If drought occurs when the palm is young, water once or twice a week.

Regional Advice and Care
Because this palm is so slow growing, do not prune away any of the fronds until all leaflets and the stalk are brown. Keep weeds and grass away from the root zone to better increase the palm's ability to thrive. The palm is not susceptible to lethal yellowing disease. Nor is it listed as vulnerable to ganoderma or butt rot disease. However, it is one of 32 palm species found to be susceptible to red palm mite, which feeds on cell sap. The mites spread throughout the Caribbean before being found in Florida half a dozen years ago. It also attacks bananas, heliconia, and ginger. There are known predators, such as lacewings and predatory mites.

Companion Planting and Design
Because it is such an elegant palm, this one can benefit from the addition of mulch to the base and little else. However, used among boulders in a landscape design or with dune plants, it can be striking.

Try These
Pseudophoenix eckmanii is a species from the coastal scrub of the Dominican Republic that is shaped rather like a carrot, with a swollen portion below a pinched crown.

PERENNIALS FOR FLORIDA

Perennials are longer-lived than annuals and shorter-lived than trees. In some parts of Florida, most things can be made perennial if you work at it, even coleus and impatiens.

You can expect to get a few years out of these plants, but not a few decades. You can expect many of them to be herbaceous, though some, like pentas, can become woody with age. You can expect them to be accents or groundcovers or vines too. You may expect that bulbs are sometimes included in perennial listings, because they return seasonally but must be replaced from time to time. As with life itself, you can expect the unexpected, and you will not be disappointed.

Ever-Changing Perennials

Perennials are among the elements of your garden that bring it to life, that add richness and dimension. They could just as easily not be there; if you never had them, you might never miss them. But if you add perennials, and then remove them, taking them away will make all the difference.

Bird-of-Paradise

Pentas begin life in the garden looking one way—pert is a description that comes to mind for young pentas. Over the course of two or three years or more, they become robust, big landscape plants. After a while in this stage, they must be pruned back quite hard or eliminated altogether and begun again. Or they may be replaced with another plant that will change the look according to your change of heart.

This changing aspect of the garden is important, as we all change our tastes over time. So allow a portion of the garden to be devoted to perennials that are less labor intensive than annuals but will not become permanent, plants that can repeat their performances but may be replaced should they wear out their welcome.

Gaillardias, daylilies, kalanchoes, walking iris, begonias, Mexican tarragon, milkweed, and phlox are among the plants we consider perennials, but tropicals may also be included. Consider the bromeliads that flower every year, send out pups, and then

A lush garden invites guests to linger and enjoy its ambience.

die, giving up their space to the new generation. Or the costus and calatheas, the gingers and the rest, which may die back in colder winters but linger along in mild ones to send out new and exuberant foliage and flowers in the warm months.

In South Florida many of the plants called tropicals are perennials: bananas, for instance, which flower and fruit every year to eighteen months; gingers and heliconias, which bloom reliably in the warm months; spathiphyllums, which produce their white flags of peace during the warm months; and birds-of-paradise.

Growing Tips

It is a mistake to assume that plants can be left to grow on their own just because they are perennial.

Taking care of them extends their lives. Refresh a bed; add more mulch; remove spent flowers; divide the rhizomes or tubers or bulbs; fertilize regularly; water regularly...the same good habits of good gardeners are required with these as with other plants in your care.

On a different scale, perennials may be considered the intermediate care plants in your garden. If annuals require intense fussing over to provide maximum color (think of deadheading the petunias and geraniums, of watering the impatiens), not to mention the tedium of planting and ripping out every few months, then perennials are less demanding. But perennials also are more demanding than an oak tree.

Care, however, is what gardeners give. It defines the garden and the gardener. Without it, there is no garden. That's why we garden. Perennials are those plants that define our role.

Begonia

Begonia spp.

Botanical Pronunciation
buh-GO-nya

Bloom Period and Seasonal Color
Spring and summer blooms in pink, white, and red

Mature Height x Spread
10 inches to 4 feet x 10 inches to 4 feet

Zones 10B–11

Just as impatiens have become brighter and geraniums bolder and salvias more diverse in their colors, begonias have undergone a revolution. They're coming back into the landscape. Angel-wings, which grow on woody canes, have leaves shaped as if they were plucked from the back of Gabriel. Often spotted with silver, or green on green, or metallic green, the undersides can be plain green, maroon, or pink. Rhizomatous begonias have succulent stems with sometimes grand leaves close to 1 foot across that look velvety. Other leaves are quilted, puckered, round, star-shaped, or pointed, with the points slightly off center. *Begonia popenoei* is a large plant excellent for landscape use, as is *B. nelumbifolia*. *B.* 'Wild Pony' has serrated leaves with dark brown markings on the veins. (GBT)

When, Where, and How to Plant
Plant begonias in spring to midsummer, when they are growing actively. Plant them in shade, in raised beds or in areas with excellent drainage. Build a raised bed, or add rock or even orchid potting mix to a bed. Pea rock in the bottom of a planting hole will assure good drainage. The beds have to drain perfectly, yet retain water. Begonias have delicate roots that stay in the upper 2 or 3 inches of the soil. Tim Anderson, a Miami nursery expert who has grown begonias for many years, likes to say, "They like a lot of water a little at a time." Anderson said that wet rocks provide ideal conditions so that roots, which don't like to be completely dry, can have air but stay moist.

Growing Tips
Use a potting soil with sand, pea rock, or limestone added. Don't overload it with peat moss or too much organic matter, and avoid muck. Use a slow-release fertilizer to keep a supply of nutrients available to the plants, and occasionally apply fish emulsion.

Regional Advice and Care
Cane-type begonias can be pruned to any desired height. The cuttings then may be rooted. Rhizomatous begonias can be divided by cutting a piece of rhizome large enough to have several old nodes and two or three leaves, placing this horizontally beneath mulch or on a peat-perlite mix and allowing it to root. Tuberous begonias do not do well in South Florida. Other types, such as angel-wing and rex, may best be grown in protected areas, such as southeast corners in North and Central Florida. Cover in cold weather. Otherwise, grow in containers and bring inside.

Companion Planting and Design
They make good companions for ferns, bromeliads, or aroids around a pond, in a shady garden bed, or in a covered shade house where watering is controlled and leaves protected from damage.

Try These
Iron cross begonias are beautiful additions to tropical gardens, with interesting leaves and markings.

Bird-of-Paradise

Strelitzia reginae

Botanical Pronunciation
struh-LEET-zee-uh RE-jeen-a

Bloom Period and Seasonal Color
July and August blooms in orange and white with blue

Mature Height x Spread
4 to 5 feet x 4 feet

Zones 9–11

English plant explorers discovered the bird-of-paradise at the Cape of Good Hope in 1773. When the plant was taken back to the Royal Botanic Garden, Kew, Sir Joseph Banks, King George's horticultural advisor and nobody's fool, named it to honor Queen Charlotte, Princess of Mecklenburg-Strelitz, *Strelitzia* and *reginae*, meaning "queen." Birds-of-paradise are composed of a bract within which orange sepals and blue, fused petals arise. Inside the petals are the stigma and stamens. The bird head is rather heronlike. Appropriately, birds pollinate the birds. *Strelitzia alba* has claret bracts and white flowers; *S. nicolai*, the giant bird that can grow to 30 feet, has white bracts with blue flowers. The cultivar *S. reginae* 'Kirstenbosch Gold' has yellow sepals. (GBT)

When, Where, and How to Plant
Plant in the warm season, May through midsummer, to give the plant ample growing time before winter. Plant in full sun. Birds-of-paradise have tuberous roots, and they like to clump, holding quite long gray-green leaves on stiff stems. Give them space to grow. Enrich the planting hole with peat moss or well-rotted manure, but don't sink them too deep into the ground. Tubers should be just at the surface. Mulch lightly. Good care and proper planting depth will speed up flowering.

Growing Tips
Birds like to be well fed. Fertilize monthly, using a balanced fertilizer, such as 6-6-6. A plant from a 3-gallon container should receive 3 tablespoons of fertilizer; a mature larger plant, 2 cups. Or use a slow-release fertilizer to supply the plant with a constant source of nutrients. Because they have an extensive system of tuberous roots, don't let them sit in water; provide good drainage. Birds should be well watered and then allowed to dry. If overcrowded, neglected, and unfertilized, they will not flower. As the older leaves die and bend out from the clump, cut them out to allow light into plants in the center. From seed, birds-of-paradise may take several years to mature and produce flowers. Transplanting can be difficult due to the large number of deep roots.

Regional Advice and Care
Protect from cold in Central and North Florida. Prune out damage in the spring. Scale insects may be a problem if plants do not have good air circulation. A systemic insecticide is useful against a widespread infestation of scale. Malathion is good for small populations.

Companion Planting and Design
An old, freestanding clump of birds in a sunny part of the garden is hard to beat, or use them with their plant relatives, including travelers palms and heliconias, at the back of the garden. They can be part of a foundation planting or in front of a hedge.

Try These
When well grown, *S. nicolai* can be arresting. It needs ample fertilizer and water to look its best, but provides color outside and cut flowers for inside.

Bush Daisy

Euryops pectinatus

Botanical Pronunciation
you-RHE-ops peck-tin-AH-tuss

Other Name Golden bush daisy

Bloom Period and Seasonal Color
Spring through fall with yellow blossoms

Mature Height x Spread
2 to 3 feet x 2 to 3 feet

Zones 9–10

Add bush daisy plants to the perennial garden and there is going to be just about year-round displays of sunshine. The plants are in bloom during all but the very coldest weather filled with yellow daisy-type blossoms held well above the foliage. The plantings are surprisingly hardy, withstanding frosts and light freezes. Use the plant as a central feature or backdrop in gardens or line them out along walkways. Gardeners like their rounded shape that can also be used to fill voids among shrub plantings. This is a plant for the container garden too that can be set on patios, at entrances, and on balconies. Plantings are drought-tolerant and pest free, which makes them good for the low-maintenance landscapes. (TM)

When, Where, and How to Plant

Add the bush daisy to the landscape year-round, but plantings made during the warmer months are best, as they avoid possible cold damage. The daisy plants bloom best in full sun but can give a good display in filtered sun. They tolerate most soils, but care is easier if sandy sites are enriched with organic matter to help extend the time between watering. Open a hole wider but no deeper than the rootballs. Set the plants in the ground so the top of the rootballs are even with or slightly above the soil line. Add a light mulch and water frequently to keep the soil moist.

Growing Tips

Bush daisy plantings are drought-tolerant but need frequent watering until the roots grow out into the surrounding soils. During the hot, dry times they are best watered at least weekly to keep the plants growing and flowering. Feed every six to eight weeks during the warmer weather with a general landscape fertilizer, or use a slow-release product following label instructions. Maintain a light mulch to stretch the time between watering and control weeds.

Regional Advice and Care

Plantings grow best in Central Florida where they survive the heat and cold. Some freeze damage may occur during the winter and can be removed in late February. This is also a good time to reshape the plantings. Plants may be pruned at other times of the year to keep growths in bounds and remove declining portions. Few pests affect these plants, but they do decline after a few years and must be replaced.

Companion Planting and Design

Bush daisy plantings make a good backdrop for gardens. Some like to use them as the main planting by clustering a number of plants in beds to create a burst of color. Use them with shrubs of Indian hawthorn, dwarf yaupon holly, and dwarf Walter's viburnum. Plant with other perennials, including roses, jacobinia, perennial salvias, pentas, and begonias.

Try These

Bush daisy is commonly marketed as the species, but the variety 'Viridis', often called the green leaf bush daisy, with darker green foliage, is also available.

Calathea

Calathea spp.

Botanical Pronunciation
kal-ah-THEE-ah

Other Name Rattlesnake plant

Bloom Period and Seasonal Color
Foliage in shades of green, white, pink, and combinations

Mature Height x Spread
10 inches to 5 feet x 6 inches to 4 feet

Zones 10B–11

The beautifully patterned leaves of the *Calathea* species rise from a short stem that has a sheathed base. Among the most ornate of plants, calatheas bear leaves worthy of a graphic designers' hall of fame. Markings usually follow the central vein, branching to side veins. They can be dark green on light green, silver on hunter green, bright pink on dark green, pink and white on dark green . . . the combinations seem endless. The undersides of the leaves are frequently red or wine colored. Flowers are produced inside bracts; bracts can be spikes or racemes arising among the leaves. *Calathea zebrine* is the snake plant. Another, *Calathea burle-marxii* 'Ice Blue', has unmarked, broad green leaves on long stems and a spike of pale blue to white cuplike bracts from which white flowers emerge. (GBT)

When, Where, and How to Plant
Plant in spring, especially if you are taking divisions of the tubers. The plants can be grouped in beds beneath trees, such as oaks, because they do well with bright light (or high shade) but not direct sun. Most of the calatheas form clumps over time. Place the tubers in beds that are a mix of rich organic matter, such as compost or good potting soil, with sand or perlite or another material to enhance drainage.

Growing Tips
Use a slow-release fertilizer to keep a good supply of nutrients available to the roots. The patterns will be especially bold if the plants are well fertilized and well watered. These perennials can tolerate early morning sun or late afternoon sun. *C. burle-marxii* 'Blue Ice' in the ground beneath thatch palms with a southern exposure did well during one winter's cold snaps, which sent temperatures into the upper 30s. They fare less well when they dry out, as leaf edges become brown and curl under. Other species are less tolerant of cold, particularly if the weather is cool for many days in a row and when wind is high.

Regional Advice and Care
Tender tropicals, calatheas like protection in winter beyond southern Florida. For the most part, calatheas should be used as houseplants in Central and North Florida. Plastic pots can serve to keep the potting mix moist, providing there are pot shards or Styrofoam peanuts in the bottom to aid in drainage. Potting mixes today contain a little slow-release fertilizer and are quite light, but you may want to add a little perlite to make sure they are adequately aerated. Keep the containers out of drafts and in bright, indirect light. Be on guard against snails when growing these outside in the ground.

Companion Planting and Design
Calatheas are wonderful for planting in beds beneath canopy trees, with palms, aroids, and maidenhair ferns. *C. zebrine* and *C. makoyana* are great company for each other.

Try These
Calathea ornata 'Rosea-lineata' is a pretty foliage plant that brings tidy color to the shade.

Coneflower

Echinacea purpurea

Botanical Pronunciation
ECH-ah-NAH-she-ah pur-PUR-ee-AH

Bloom Period and Seasonal Color
Flowers open late spring through fall in purple, yellow, orange, and white

Mature Height x Spread
1 to 2 feet x 1 to 2 feet (with blooms)

Zones 8–9

Maybe it's a memory from gardens past or just fascination with the big colorful blooms, but most gardeners would like to grow the coneflower. Coneflower is limited to the northern and most central portions of the state due to temperatures. In Central Florida it grows best as a short-term perennial, often living up to a year. Coneflowers make great focal points for the garden sending up the tall flower stalks with large sunflower-shaped blossoms. Purple blooms have been familiar, but there is now a wide selection of colors available. Cluster plants in perennial beds or use them in containers. The blossoms last for several weeks and can be cut for arrangements. This is a flower often added to wildflower mixtures and can reseed in gardens. (TM)

When, Where, and How to Plant

Add coneflowers to the landscape year-round, but plantings made during late winter or early spring seem to have the longest garden life. The plants bloom best in full sun but can give a good display in filtered sun. They tolerate most soils, but care is easier if sandy sites are enriched with organic matter to help extend the time between watering. This also seems to help extend their garden life. Dig holes wider, but no deeper, than the rootballs. Set the plants in the ground so the tops of the rootballs are even with or slightly above the soil line. Add a light mulch, and water frequently.

Growing Tips

Give coneflowers frequent watering until the roots grow out into the surrounding soils. During the

hot, dry times they are best watered at least weekly to keep the plants growing and flowering. Feed every six to eight weeks during the warmer weather with a general landscape fertilizer, or use a slow-release product following label instructions. Maintain a light mulch to stretch the time between watering and control weeds. Few pests affect these plants, but they often decline during the summer months, especially in Central Florida. In cooler areas they can last for several years.

Regional Advice and Care

Many consider coneflowers a short-term perennial and enjoy the blooms during the spring through early summer months. Remove the faded flower stalks to keep more blooms coming. Surviving plants die back during the winter to a rosette of foliage, and the brown portions need to be removed by February to allow for spring growth.

Companion Planting and Design

Add to the perennial flower beds as a grouping of coneflowers to give a good display of color. Some companion perennials might include perennial salvia, bush daisy, coreopsis, whirling butterflies, and yellow alder. Many annuals may also be added to the bed.

Try These

A favorite is the native purple, but in recent years many selections have been made with an assortment of colors to include varieties such as 'Sunrise', 'Pink Double Delight', 'Raspberry Truffle', 'Tangerine Dream', and 'Hot Papaya'.

Coreopsis

Coreopsis spp.

Botanical Pronunciation
core-ee-OP-sis

Other Name Tickseed

Bloom Period and Seasonal Color
Spring through fall with yellow blooms

Mature Height x Spread
12 to 24 inches x 12 to 24 inches

Those wonderful yellow flowers seen along the roadside and in natural settings are most likely coreopsis, the Florida state wildflower. Many species are native to Florida and others, plus hybrids, have been introduced. Native species have yellow flowers, but the many hybrids that have been developed and other species give us orange, red, pink, and purple selections. Plantings are best considered short-lived perennials that survive for several seasons and then decline. They often reseed to continue the color, especially in native and natural Florida settings. Use coreopsis in perennial beds for bursts of color throughout the warmer months. Plant in clusters and combine with other perennials and annuals to create colorful gardens. Plantings are drought-tolerant and need minimal care. (TM)

When, Where, and How to Plant

Add coreopsis to the landscape year-round, but plantings made during late winter or early spring seem to have the longest garden life. The plants bloom best in full sun but can give a good display in filtered sun. They grow well in most soils, but care is easier if sandy sites are enriched with organic matter to help extend the time between watering. Many like to sow the native species in prepared garden sites and natural settings during the fall to begin bloom by spring. These soils should be prepared as for any garden. Coreopsis plants ready to bloom are available at garden centers. Plant these by opening holes wider but no deeper than the rootballs. Set the plants in the ground so the tops of the rootballs are even with or slightly above the soil line. Add a light mulch, and water frequently to keep the soil moist.

Growing Tips

Coreopsis needs minimal care in natural settings. Keep the soil moist when the surface begins to dry. When adding new plants, keep them moist until the roots grow out into the surrounding soils. During the hot, dry times they are best watered at least weekly. Feed during the warmer weather with a slow-release product following label instructions. Maintain a light mulch to stretch the time between watering and control weeds.

Regional Advice and Care

Plantings need grooming to remain attractive in formal garden settings. Remove declining flowers and plant portions as needed. Established plantings can be given major pruning during winter before new growth begins.

Companion Planting and Design

Combine with other perennials, including gaillardia, coneflower, perennial salvia, pentas, bush daisy, Mexican heather, Stoke's aster, and shrimp plants in flower beds for a lasting display of color. They also combine well with seasonal annuals.

Try These

Packets of native coreopsis seeds can be used to create wildflower displays or natural garden settings. Garden centers offer many colorful selections in containers: 'Autumn Blush', 'Crème Brûlée', 'Early Sunrise', 'Moonbeam', and 'Tequila Sunrise'.

Firespike

Odontonema cuspidate

Botanical Pronunciation
oh-don-toe-Nee-ma kus-PEH-day-tah

Bloom Period and Seasonal Color
Year-round in warm locations opening spikes of red blooms

Mature Height x Spread
6 feet x 4 feet

Zones 9–11

irespike plantings are going to attract attention in the landscape, filling with upright spikes of red blooms. The insects and hummingbirds are going to like it too, coming to visit when it's added to butterfly gardens. Plantings can be standalone accents to mix with shrub features or used as a backdrop and space divider for gardens. This is a tall-growing plant that makes a good view barrier during the growing season. In the colder locations expect freeze damage, but the plants normally grow back. The tall spikes of color can be used in a bouquet alone or mixed with other blooms. Firespike is a low-maintenance plant but does need some periodic grooming to stay in bounds. Otherwise it is very carefree. (TM)

When, Where, and How to Plant
A good time to add firespike plants to the landscape is early spring in the cooler portions of the state, otherwise they can be planted year-round. They grow well in most soils, but care is easier if sandy sites are enriched with organic matter to help extend the time between watering. Give the plants plenty of room to grow with a spacing of 3 to 4 feet. Plant by opening holes wider but no deeper than the rootballs. Set the plants in the ground so the tops of the rootballs are even with or slightly above the soil line. Add a light mulch, and water frequently to keep the soil moist.

Growing Tips
Give firespike plantings frequent watering until the roots grow out into the surrounding soils. During the hot, dry times they are best watered at least weekly to keep the plants growing and flowering. Feed every six to eight weeks during the warmer weather with a general landscape fertilizer, or use a slow-release product following label instructions. Maintain a light mulch to stretch the time between watering and control weeds.

Regional Advice and Care
Plantings are often frozen in the cooler portions of Central Florida. Give these plantings a renewal pruning, often back to near the ground, during mid- to late February. All plantings grow large and wide during the warmer months. Some periodic pruning is often needed to keep them in bounds. Where winter damage is not noted, a February pruning to reduce and reshape the plantings is recommended. Pests are seldom a problem, and pesticide applications are rarely needed.

Companion Planting and Design
Combine with other shrubs in background plantings for space divider, view barrier, and flower garden plantings. The red blooms contrast well with pittosporum, Simpson stopper, Florida privet, and yaupon hollies. May also be mixed with taller-growing perennials and flowering bulbs such as cannas.

Try These
Only the species is marketed in local garden centers. A relative, *O. callistachyum*, is also available. It has a similar growth habit but has purple blooms for winter and is best used in warm locations.

Jacobinia

Justicia carnea

Botanical Pronunciation
just-TISH-see-ah car-KNEE-ah

Other Name Flamingo flower

Bloom Period and Seasonal Color
Year-round in warm locations with pink or white flowers

Mature Height x Spread
3 to 6 feet x 3 to 4 feet

Plant popularity travels in cycles and many gardeners have probably forgotten jacobinia, but it is worth rediscovering for the shady areas. These are spots where it can be hard to find good color and especially a nice pink. Also called cardinal flower and Brazilian plume for the 6-inch or larger spikes of brilliant blooms, plantings can be in bloom almost year-round. Although listed for the shady sites, some plantings have done well in part sun. Jacobinia is a great understory plant, almost a shrub, with large evergreen leaves filling in voids, creating view barriers and forming accents. It can also be grown in containers, especially in the colder locations where winter protection is desired. Jacobinia likes moist, enriched soil, but otherwise it is pretty carefree. (TM)

When, Where, and How to Plant
Shaded to partly shaded sites are best, but some plantings have tolerated almost full sun for portions of the day. Jacobinia can grow in most soils, but sands should be enriched with organic matter to give them moisture-holding abilities. Open holes wider but no deeper than the rootballs. Set the plants in the ground so the tops of the rootballs are even with or slightly above the soil line. Lightly mulch, and water frequently to keep the soil moist.

Growing Tips
Jacobinia can tolerate short periods of drought but grow best in a moist soil. During the hot, dry times they are best watered at least weekly to keep the plants growing and flowering. Water container-

grown plants when the surface soil begins to feel dry to the touch. Feed in-ground plantings every six to eight weeks during the warmer weather with a general landscape fertilizer, or use a slow-release product following label instructions. Feed container plantings with a slow-release fertilizer. Maintain a light mulch to stretch the time between watering and control weeds.

Regional Advice and Care
Plantings in the warmer locations grow and flower year-round. Major displays of flowers are produced several times a year with sporadic blooms in between. In the cold locations plants are damaged by freezes and often frozen to near the ground. Give these plants a renewal pruning in mid- to late February. In all areas when the flower clusters begin to decline remove them from the plants. Plants may also be groomed throughout the year by pinching back the tips to encourage branching and more blooms.

Companion Planting and Design
Use as an accent and space divider in shady locations. Combine with azaleas, camellias, ferns, and gingers. Also use with tropical foliage plants in warmer locations. Set in large containers to display on shady patios, at entrances, and on balconies.

Try These
Jacobina is usually offered as the species. Some dwarf selections, good whites, and intense pinks have also been propagated for sale.

Pentas

Pentas lanceolata

Botanical Pronunciation
PEN-tahs LANS-see-o-lata

Other Name Egyptian star clusters

Bloom Period and Seasonal Color
Spring through summer and possibly year-round in South Florida; blooms in pink, white, lilac, or red

Mature Height x Spread
1½ to 2½ feet x 18 inches

Zones 9–11

With the wild popularity of butterfly gardening pentas have come into their own. The tiny nectar cups beneath the five-petaled corollas are a lure for all kinds of hungry butterflies. A butterfly garden can take any shape or form but include both nectar plants and larval food plants; plan for butterflies that are locally plentiful. The nectar and pollen sources should be in the sun, protected from the wind by hedges or small trees. Include a source of water. (The butterflies are free.) Bees, too, will be plentiful. Pentas are easy to care for, and they are rapid growers. Pentas come in regular and dwarf sizes so you can use them as background shrubs or foreground flowers. (GBT)

When, Where, and How to Plant
Plant pentas in spring and early summer. Plant in full sun to partial shade where there is good drainage. Mix with other butterfly plants, like milkweed and wild petunia. Space the plants 12 to 24 inches apart, as they grow quite large and will form a wave of color. Use a trowel to dig a planting hole just larger than the rootball, add slow-release fertilizer to the bottom of the hole, backfill with soil from the planting hole, and water. Water daily for a week or two, gradually tapering off until you water once or twice weekly.

Growing Tips
Water once or twice weekly. Use slow-release fertilizer at the time of planting and again every three or four months if in South Florida. Six-month slow-release will be used up more quickly in South Florida than in cooler areas, unless it is formulated for South Florida conditions. Prune back to within 6 inches in February for new spring growth.

Regional Advice and Care
Pentas require a little care to look their best. They tend to get woody and leggy after three or four years, and you can take cuttings and replace the old plants with new ones. Cut back in the early spring to rejuvenate the plants. Keep well mulched during winter in Central Florida to help protect the basal bud from cold. Watch for spider mites in winter. Spider mites are tiny, difficult-to-see sucking insects that will suck out cell sap. They cause the upper surface of leaves to look pale or yellow. A hard spray of water will knock off these dry-season insects. Superfine oil, which is paraffin-based, can be used any time.

Companion Planting and Design
Use as a wave of a single color for best effect and to attract butterflies. Pink or white are standout colors for shade or in the evening. Or plant in a meadow with other wildflowers, such as tickseed, milkweed, and yellowtop.

Try These
White pentas shows up at night and makes the garden's enjoyment nocturnal as well as diurnal. A dwarf pink is available. Additional cultivars include 'Cranberry Punch', 'Rose', and 'Lilac Mist'.

Perennial Salvia

Salvia spp.

Botanical Pronunciation
SAL-vee-ah

Bloom Period and Seasonal Color
Year-round with best colors, of red, pink purple, lavender, or yellow during the warmer months

Mature Height x Spread
2 to 4 feet x 2 to 4 feet

Zones 8–10

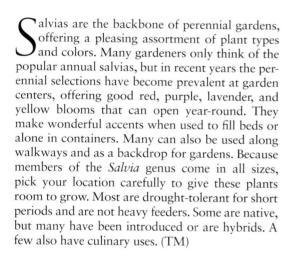

Salvias are the backbone of perennial gardens, offering a pleasing assortment of plant types and colors. Many gardeners only think of the popular annual salvias, but in recent years the perennial selections have become prevalent at garden centers, offering good red, purple, lavender, and yellow blooms that can open year-round. They make wonderful accents when used to fill beds or alone in containers. Many can also be used along walkways and as a backdrop for gardens. Because members of the *Salvia* genus come in all sizes, pick your location carefully to give these plants room to grow. Most are drought-tolerant for short periods and are not heavy feeders. Some are native, but many have been introduced or are hybrids. A few also have culinary uses. (TM)

When, Where, and How to Plant
Add salvia plantings to the landscape year-round, but during late winter and other warmer months is best to avoid possible cold damage. The plants bloom best in full sun but can give a good display in filtered sun. They tolerate most soils, but care is easier if sandy sites are enriched with organic matter to help extend the time between watering. Dig holes wider but no deeper than the rootballs. Set the plants in the ground so the tops of the rootballs are even with or slightly above the soil line. Add a light mulch, and water frequently.

Growing Tips
Salvia plantings can tolerate short periods of drought, but frequent watering is needed until the roots grow out into the surrounding soils. During the hot, dry times they are best watered at least weekly to keep the plants growing and flowering. Feed every six to eight weeks during the warmer weather with a general landscape fertilizer, or use a slow-release product following label instructions. Maintain a light mulch to stretch the time between watering and control weeds.

Regional Advice and Care
Plantings grow well throughout most of Florida but are susceptible to cold. In mid- to late February give the plantings a renewal pruning to reshape the plants and remove dead and declining portions. Also groom the plantings throughout the growing season to keep them in bounds and remove old flower heads. Few pests affect these plants but as with most perennials they do decline after a few years and must be replaced.

Companion Planting and Design
Incorporate with other perennials and annuals in flower beds and where there are voids in shrub plantings. Some good companion plants include bush daisy, coneflower, Mexican heather, and roses.

Try These
A wide selection of salvias is available. Some to try include the red autumn sage, red scarlet sage, lavender Mexican sage, blue majestic sage, blue indigo spires, and yellow forsythia sage. Varieties with assorted flower colors are available for many of these. Gardeners can also grow the herbal salvias of common sage, Greek sage, and pineapple sage.

Periwinkle

Catharanthus roseus

Botanical Pronunciation
cath-a-RAN-thus rose-ee-us

Other Name Vinca

Bloom Period and Seasonal Color
Year-round blooms in pink, white, and rose

Mature Height x Spread
12 inches x 12 inches or as tall as 24 x 24

Zones 10B–11

Bless their hearts, these naturalized bright little flowers are abandoned-lot hardy. They were among the first flowering plants the pioneers in South Florida traded and planted. Who knows how they got to Florida, but the women who longed for some tangible beauty around their rough-hewn houses knew to plant periwinkles, which needed nothing more than a smile and a splash of water. That's practically all they need still. Use periwinkles in sun and partial shade. Plant them in front of the ligustrum hedge or the podocarpus; put them over the septic tank. Periwinkles have been fancied up by breeding and come in bright new colors. And although the originals are lanky and rangy, the spiffy new ones are shorter. The long-legged originals continue to outperform the hybrids. (GBT)

When, Where, and How to Plant
Plant any time; the beginning of the rainy season is the best time. Plant in beds or in pots, in sandy, dry soil. Periwinkles can be cut back when they get too straggly. You can root cuttings in March or April, and by May they will be ready to set into beds. To transplant, simply use a trowel to lift out soil, insert the periwinkles, and refill the hole. Then water. Cuttings are easily started. Use a 50:50 mix of peat moss and perlite; wet it thoroughly. Cut periwinkles; remove several pairs of leaves and flowers; insert the cutting into the medium and place it in shade, out of wind, but where you will remember to keep the mix moist. To reduce the need to water, you can put the pots in plastic bags. Insert one or two bamboo stakes

in the pot to keep the plastic from sagging onto the plants, and then tie the bag closed. Wait three or four weeks before checking to see if there are sufficient roots to allow planting.

Growing Tips
Water to keep the roots moist for a month or so, and then gradually taper off, allowing the plant to reduce its water needs. A teaspoon of slow-release fertilizer at planting time is sufficient. Too much pampering is not for these rugged perennials. When small, these bright plants look their best, if you like upright and neat gardens. When they age, they will sprawl and lean, and eventually you will have to cut them back. Use them where a certain unkemptness is desirable: in the corners of the yard, by the telephone pole, or by the composter.

Regional Advice and Care
Use as annuals in Central and North Florida. Periwinkles in South Florida will develop yellow leaves after experiencing temperatures in the low 50s Fahrenheit.

Companion Planting and Design
Periwinkles often arrange themselves in disturbed areas or abandoned lots. They may be planted with pentas, but they offer no nectar, just personality. They make good container plants.

Try These
White periwinkles are my preference for the same reason I like other white flowers—they can be readily seen at night.

Poinsettia

Euphorbia pulcherrima

Botanical Pronunciation
you-FOR-bee-ah pull-CHAIR-eh-mah

Bloom Period and Seasonal Color
Colorful bracts for winter in red, pink, and white

Mature Height x Spread
8 feet x 8 feet

Zones 9B–11

L et's face it—it's hard to toss out a holiday poinsettia. We want to keep it for another year, either in the container or as a landscape addition. Everyone surely knows the poinsettia, but did you know they can grow quite well as an accent feature among other shrubs or as a stand-alone planting? Throughout the year they are just greenery with some unique foliage, but it's during the Christmas holidays they become spectacular landscape displays. Most gardeners probably know the really colorful portions are not the flowers but are the leaves, called bracts, which become colored. The real flowers are among the bracts and are yellowish green. Keeping a poinsettia in a container for another year takes a little work, but they are easy to care for in the ground. (TM)

When, Where, and How to Plant
Poinsettias are often saved from Christmas to continue in containers or add to the landscape. Around March add the plants to the landscape or give them a larger sized container. When added to the landscape open holes wider, but no deeper, than the rootballs. Set the plants in the ground so the tops of the rootballs are even with or slightly above the soil line. Poinsettias grow in most soils, but plants in enriched sandy soils are easier to maintain. Add a light mulch, and water frequently to keep the soil moist.

Growing Tips
After planting give poinsettias in containers and those in the landscape a heavy pruning to within 12 to 18 inches of the soil. This starts to develop a more compact plant with multiple bracts for the holidays. After the plants produce a foot of growth, remove 4 to 6 inches from the end of each shoot. Continue the prunings after each flush of new growth through the end of August. Keep the plantings moist, and provide feedings every six to eight weeks during the warm months with a general landscape fertilizer, or use a slow-release product as instructed on the label.

Regional Advice and Care
Poinsettias are light-sensitive and need short days to flower during the fall. In all areas of the state they must be shielded from nighttime light starting in early October. This is continued until the colorful bracts can be detected. In colder locations plantings must be in containers to move to a warm location when frost or freezes are expected or covered during the cold.

Companion Planting and Design
Add to the landscape where the plants can be enjoyed for the holidays. Poinsettias mix well with other shrubs, including hollies, camellias, pittosporum, and loropetalum. They can also be used as a backdrop for perennial gardens.

Try These
Many varieties are available during the holiday season. Most seem to do well, so pick a favorite color to grow for another year. Some garden centers have an older landscape variety called 'Fire Ball'. The bracts are numerous and give a colorful display.

Quailberry

Crossopetalum ilicifolium

Botanical Pronunciation
cross-o-PET-a-lum ill-liss-suh-FO-lee-um

Other Name Christmasberry

Bloom Period and Seasonal Color
Throughout the year; pink flowers and red berries

Mature Height x Spread
12 inches x 18 inches

Zones 10b–11

A charming little plant, quailberry is native to South Florida's pine rockland. It has holly-like leaves, and it branches repeatedly to spread as wide or wider than it grows tall. Its use, therefore, is primarily as a groundcover in a sunny area, as a mass planting for a rock garden, or as a component of a native garden. The quailberry produces small pink flowers throughout the year and brilliant red berries, which are eaten by quail in the wild. The plant is drought-tolerant. It also is remarkably tough, and aside from being torn from the ground, only deep shade or salt water can kill it. Quailberry is not a scene stealer, but the more you utilize this attractive plant, the better you will like it. (GBT)

When, Where, and How to Plant

Plant quailberry in a sunny location in soil that has excellent drainage. Because the *Crossopetalum* genus is from our endangered pine rockland, it is fully adapted to our alkaline soils. Rocky limestone soils hold more moisture than sandy soils, but don't just plant and walk away. Keep the soil moist until you see new growth. Once established it can be left to its own devices.

Growing Tips

I've found that a little fertilizer and occasional hit from the hose can help even native plants throughout the first two years. The chances are that the area where you are attempting to establish them is not really native soil as they knew it, but a coarser substrate that has been altered by development. So give the natives a chance. In learning to reestablish native plants, such as pines, we have discovered that most are associated with mycrorrhizal fungi that help the roots absorb minerals. Mycrorrhizae, which have a symbiotic relationship with root hairs, are sold commercially.

Regional Advice and Care

Protect this plant from cold in Central and North Florida. This plant ranges from South Florida and the Florida Keys through the Bahamas, Cuba, and Hispaniola, according to the Institute for Regional Conservation.

Companion Planting and Design

The pine rockland community has a wonderfully full cast of characters that can go with this plant. Slash pines, saw palmettos, 'Elliott' lovegrass, pineland lantana, snowberry...the list is long. If you have some limestone boulders, try using quailberry in niches at varying levels, and add man-in-the-ground, which is a dainty red-flowering morning glory endemic to the same ecosystem.

Try These

Plant the species.

Shrimp Plant

Justicia brandegeana

Botanical Pronunciation
just-TISH-see-ah bran-dee-GEE-ay-nah

Bloom Period and Seasonal Color
Year-round during warmer weather with reddish brown and white or yellow blooms

Mature Height x Spread
4 feet x 4 feet

Sometimes plants are forgotten by gardeners and need to be rediscovered. Perhaps this is what happened with the shrimp plant, a long-time favorite in perennial plantings that seemed to disappear for a while. Well, it is one you just have to grow, as it is very durable and bears persistent flowers for the landscape. It is in bloom year-round except in the coldest regions. Consider it for flower beds and to mix with shrub planting. The flower spikes do look like enlarged shrimp, which makes them good conversation starters when planted near walkways and patios. Plants can be grown in containers to keep on decks and balconies. Plants tolerate a wide range of soil conditions and are ideal for minimal-maintenance landscapes. (TM)

When, Where, and How to Plant
Plantings are best added to the landscape at the end of winter and throughout the warmer months to avoid cold damage. Select a site in full sun to filtered sun. Shrimp plants tolerate most soils but do best if sandy soils are enriched with organic matter before planting. Open holes wider but no deeper than the rootballs. Set the plants in the ground so the tops of the rootballs are even with or slightly above the soil line. Add a light mulch, and water frequently to keep the soil moist.

Growing Tips
Shrimp plants have some drought-tolerance but need frequent watering until the roots grow out into the surrounding soils. During the hot, dry times they are best watered at least weekly to keep the plants growing and flowering. Feed every six

to eight weeks during the warmer weather with a general landscape fertilizer, or use a slow-release product following label instructions. Maintain a light mulch to stretch the time between watering and control weeds.

Regional Advice and Care
Surprisingly shrimp plants are cold-resistant and tolerate frosts and light freezes with minimal damage. In colder locations plantings' flowers, foliage, and stems are severely damaged by freezes. Give these plantings a renewal pruning in mid- to late winter or whenever you cannot stand the brown. All plantings grow lanky and out of bounds during the growing season and may need periodic grooming. These too need a late-winter pruning to reshape and encourage additional growth. Few pests affect these plants. Like all perennials, plantings do decline after a few years and must be replaced.

Companion Planting and Design
One shrimp plant or a cluster can create interest in a perennial garden or along walkways. Combine with bush daisy, daylilies, caladiums, coneflower, crinums, or yellow alder for good displays of continual color.

Try These
Plants are often available as the species but a number of good varieties are found at garden centers. Some to look for include 'Jambalaya', a red; 'Fruit Cocktail', pink and yellow; 'Pink Surprise', pinkish; and 'Yellow Queen', a yellow.

Society Garlic

Tulbaghia violacea

Botanical Pronunciation
tul-BAG-eh-uh vi-o-LAY-see-ah

Bloom Period and Seasonal Color
Year-round blooms in lilac, pink, and white

Mature Height x Spread
1 to 2 feet x 1 to 2 feet

Zones 9–11

Society garlic is an enduring plant that provides delicate flowers throughout the summer. It is an herb in the onion family along with leek, garlic, and chive. Round balls of lilac, pink, or white flowers (umbels) top the slender flower stalks that are pleasing to the eye. This South African native does smell of garlic or onion and yet was thought by someone to be less offensive than true garlic, hence the common name. (*Tulbaghia* is named for Rijk Tulbagh, an eighteenth-century Dutch governor of the Cape Colony of South Africa. There also is a town named for him.) The plant forms clumps, and tubers can be separated in winter. Flowers have six tepals and a corona. On some species and hybrids, the corona is more visible, colorful, and interesting. (GBT)

When, Where, and How to Plant
Plant any time in a bed that has good drainage and some organic matter, such as compost or peat moss. These plants can take full sun or partial shade. As you would plant other rhizomes and bulbs, place society garlic tubers not too far below the surface, with a little bonemeal in the bottom of the planting hole; space about 18 inches apart. Flowers are produced from spring to fall.

Growing Tips
Keep the planting bed moist to get society garlic started, and use a slow-release fertilizer in spring, summer, and fall. Water less in winter, when it wants to rest.

Regional Advice and Care
Plants can be put into containers for winter and brought inside when freezing weather occurs. Place containers in a sunny location. These plants do not do well in shade, whether inside or out. If kept in shade or overwatered, society garlic can succumb to a fungus called southern blight, which begins at the ground level. Society garlic also attracts aphids and whiteflies.

Companion Planting and Design
Mauve, pinks, and blues remind one to think of Gertrude Jekyll's mixed herbaceous borders, yet translating that look to Florida is difficult, given our bright light and the tendency of pale flowers to wash out. Used by itself, society garlic is a pretty flower. The plants can serve as a medium-level backdrop to smaller-growing plants in a bed. For instance, they make a good foil for moss rose or miniature roses. If you have a vegetable garden, try society garlic among culinary herbs. Plant them several deep in front of pittosporum shrubs, pink hibiscus, ligustrum, or snowbush. When used in groups, rather than in long lines, these bulbs are quite spectacular.

Try These
A variegated form of *Tulbaghia violacea* is called 'Silver Lace'.

Whirling Butterflies

Gaura lindheimeri

Botanical Pronunciation
GAR-uh lind-HAY-mere-eye

Other Name Gaura

Bloom Period and Seasonal Color
Spring through fall with pink and white blooms

Mature Height x Spread
1 to 3 feet x 3 feet

Zones 8–9

Opening flowers at the ends of long stems, as if they were small butterflies, this perennial adds lots of interest to gardens. Plants are in bloom throughout most of the warmer months with variations of white to pink blossoms. Use clusters of whirling butterflies to fill large spaces in the perennial garden or just set a plant or two as accents. They can also be used in container gardens as a featured plant for decks, patios, and balconies. One unique feature of this plant is a long taproot that helps provide drought-tolerance but makes the plants hard to transplant. Plantings decline during the winter but grow back in early spring. This is a good addition to low-maintenance gardens and is relatively pest free. (TM)

When, Where, and How to Plant
Add to the landscape during the warmer months when the flowers are starting to open. The plants bloom best in full sun locations. Whirling butterfly tolerates most soils, but care is easier if sandy sites are enriched with organic matter to help extend the time between watering. Dig holes wider but no deeper than the rootballs. Set the plants in the ground so the tops of the rootballs are even with or slightly above the soil line. Add a light mulch, and water frequently to keep the soil moist.

Growing Tips
Whirling butterfly plantings are drought-tolerant but need frequent watering until the roots grow out into the surrounding soils. During the hot, dry times they are best watered at least weekly to keep the plants growing and flowering. Water container-grown plants when the surface soil begins to feel dry to the touch. Feed in-ground plantings every six to eight weeks during the warmer weather with a general landscape fertilizer, or use a slow-release product following label instructions. Feed container plantings with a slow-release fertilizer. Maintain a light mulch to stretch the time between watering and control weeds.

Regional Advice and Care
Plantings decline during the winter months in all sections of North and Central Florida. Plant portions can be removed as needed with a final cleanup around the middle of February. Leaf spot fungus and powdery mildew may be noted on the foliage, and a fungicide can be applied for these diseases if needed. Follow label instructions.

Companion Planting and Design
Cluster a number of plants in a section of the perennial or flower garden to get the best color and airy blossoms in flight displays. They can be planted with seasonal annuals and other perennials, including bush daisy, Stoke's aster, shrimp plant, perennial salvias, and Mexican heather.

Try These
Plants are often offered as the species, but a number of selections are also available. Some to try are the pinks and whites in the 'Stratosphere' and 'Ballerina' series, plus varieties 'Karalee Petite Pink' and 'Rosey Jane'.

Wild Petunia

Ruellia caroliniensis

Botanical Pronunciation
roo-EL-e-uh kare-o-lyn-ee-EN-sus

Other Name Ruellia

Bloom Period and Seasonal Color
Summer blooms in blue-lavender

Mature Height x Spread
20 inches x various

Zones 10–11

Once, before the 1992 hurricane took out the pinelands, wild petunias could be found in Larry and Penny Thompson Park in South Dade County. I know, because old notes from a taxonomy field trip tell me so. (Memorable because the field trip was in August—absolutely the hottest time to be in the pinelands.) Wild petunias grow on slender stems with hairy opposite leaves and blue-lavender sessile flowers; the flowers have no stalk, but the ends of the tubes attach directly to the plant. Wild petunias can reseed themselves, given the right opportunity. Several non-native ruellias, which like damp conditions, are found in nurseries. (GBT)

When, Where, and How to Plant
Plant during the warm season. Choose a sunny, dry location among pines and palmettos. Use a trowel to dig a hole slightly larger than the rootball of the containerized plant. Gently slip the plant from the container, holding it toward the base of the stem, not by the top. Position the plant in the planting hole, and fill with original soil. Water daily for a week to help the plant become established, and then gradually taper off watering. Ruellias are drought-tolerant, having evolved to withstand life in the pinelands. Skipper butterflies love these plants.

Growing Tips
Little care is needed after the plant has become established and is growing well. Water twice weekly. If kept too wet, you may lose this wildflower, which often is recommended for Xeriscape landscaping. Ruellias tend to clump. They are cosmopolitan (Carolina wild petunia ranges from the eastern seaboard states across west Texas), and their ease of care suggests why: they are not fussy about soil, and they self-seed. Although these characteristics are gardener-friendly, they can be ecosystem-unfriendly should plants escape into the wild. Such are the considerations that might well go into selecting plants for your garden.

Regional Advice and Care
It has few pests or diseases but won't provide much color in winter. This native is damaged by cold in Central and North Florida.

Companion Planting and Design
The popularity of butterfly gardens and native plants coupled with the increasing need to conserve water in landscapes has contributed to a recent popularity of ruellia. Planted with a yellow-flowering necklace pod (*Sophora tomentosa*) or butterfly bush, this native wildflower will help attract butterflies while making few demands on you as a gardener. Ruellias are being used in highway medians and parking lots, and they are thriving.

Try These
There are several choices: Mexican bluebell, *Ruellia amoena*, and *R. brittoniana*. Several cultivars include 'Compacta', 'Chi Chi', 'Purple Showers', and 'Snow Queen'. Still others are *R. graecizans* and *R. squarrosa*, a groundcover.

Yellow Alder

Turnera ulmifolia

Botanical Pronunciation
turn-ER-ah ulm-EH-fol-ee-ah

Other Name Buttercup

Bloom Period and Seasonal Color
Year-round in warm locations with yellow flowers

Mature Height x Spread
4 feet x 3 feet

Zones 9–11

Gardeners looking for a tough, durable plant should give the yellow alder a try. It seems to tolerate the poorer soils and still continues to flower year-round. This is a plant for the minimal-maintenance landscape that opens yellow blooms for a day and then they decline. But don't worry; there are normally plenty of buds to open the next day. Plant in clusters with a 3- to 4-foot spacing to obtain a real burst of color. Also use the plant mixed with shrubs, and add to containers to display on decks and patios. Plantings make good understory perennials for use below pines and palms with the filtered sun. Yellow alder is usually pest free but susceptible to frost and freezes in the colder locations. (TM)

When, Where, and How to Plant
Plantings are best added to the landscape at the end of winter and throughout the warmer months to avoid cold damage. Select a site in full sun to filtered sun. Yellow alder tolerates most soils but does best if sandy soils are enriched with organic matter before planting. Open holes wider but no deeper than the rootballs. Set the plants in the ground so the tops of the rootballs are even with or slightly above the soil line. Add a light mulch, and water frequently to keep the soil moist.

Growing Tips
Yellow alder is drought-tolerant but needs frequent watering until the roots grow out into the surrounding soils. During the hot, dry times they are best watered at least weekly to keep the plants growing and flowering. Feed every six to eight weeks during the warmer weather with a general landscape fertilizer, or use a slow-release product following label instructions. Maintain a light mulch to stretch the time between watering and control weeds. Few pests affect these plants. Like all perennials plantings do decline after a few years and must be replaced.

Regional Advice and Care
In colder locations plantings are damaged by freezes. Give these plantings a renewal pruning in mid- to late winter or whenever you cannot stand the brown. All plantings can grow out of bounds during the growing season and may need periodic grooming. Some gardeners shear the plants, which seem to rebound quickly with fresh flowers. All that survive the cold need a late-winter pruning to reshape and encourage additional growth.

Companion Planting and Design
Yellow alder can be a standalone perennial growing much like a shrub to use in foundation planting or to add color with other greenery of dwarf yaupon holly, pittosporum, viburnums, and loropetalum. It can be used as a backdrop for perennial gardens with other plantings of bush daisy, shrimp plants, salvias, and roses.

Try These
Only the species with yellow flowers is normally found at garden centers. A white variety, 'Alba', is also available.

SHRUBS FOR FLORIDA

For many years, I have been told by horticulturists to think of shrubs as the walls of the garden. They are the space shapers of the garden, the room dividers, and the plants that we see at eye level. Shrubs most often set off property lines, and they are also used as entryway accents. These are among the most common reasons for growing them.

For small spaces, shrubs are often more convenient than trees. A large shrub (which also may be a small tree) won't have to be brutally pruned should it outgrow its spot; it won't lift the pavers with massive roots; it won't shade out the other plants in the garden.

Shrubs will bring color, and, often, alluring fragrance, to an area, be it townhouse garden or suburban yard. Some bring fruit with them, which can be appealing to you or to birds. Some attract butterflies and moths. Carefully selected shrubs will bring fall color (crape myrtles) or winter flowers (*Clerodendron quadriculare*). Others, such as azaleas and rhododendrons, are the very essence of early spring.

Bush and climbing roses

Attracting Birds and Butterflies

Using native shrubs can go a long way toward helping not only resident birds, such as the cardinals that nest in shrubs, but also migrants in need of a stopover shelter and food. Provisioning the landscape for wildlife is a vital part of contemporary gardening, because so much of the natural area of this country has been covered over by cities and farms.

Shrubs also play a key role in butterfly gardening; many of the nectar-bearing flowers that attract butterflies are shrub-borne. One South Florida shrub that comes to mind is *Cordia globosa*. It produces round heads of tiny white flowers and all kinds of skippers and little butterflies can be found there throughout the day. In Central and North Florida, *Buddleia* is the butterfly bush par excellence.

Shrub Considerations

Although we may give special deference to roses, they are in fact shrubs (as well as climbing plants).

Ixora

The returning popularity of old roses is welcome in Florida, where finicky hybrid teas have a hard time with the fungus called blackspot, requiring too many applications of chemicals. Old roses are hardier, less disease prone, and some, such as chinas, teas, and noisettes, flower off and on all year. And many of them can be mixed right in with other shrubs in a border planting.

As our lives have become more hectic and time more precious, there is a greater need to reduce household chores, including those in the garden. One way to do so is to landscape informally, so that shrubs are not clipped and pruned but are allowed to billow and assume their natural shapes. That is not to say pruning is never required, but it will be needed less often if plants can assume hazy or flowing shapes rather than rigid and boxed ones. For such shrubs as gardenia and ixoras, hibiscus, and orange jasmine, the flowers are produced on new growth, so regular pruning means fewer flowers.

In recent years, new shrubs have entered our gardening and landscaping vocabulary. *Tibouchina*, for instance, is now widely available. It is popularly called glory bush for its purple flowers. *Mussaenda* is another tropical shrub finding wide use in protected southern areas. Croton is making a comeback. Crotons may be included in mixed borders and groupings rather than sun-bleached, leggy hedges or foundation plants.

Shrubs are the workhorses of the garden. We can assign them many roles, and they can take them on. But like workhorses, they need a good diet. Fertilize shrubs in spring, summer, and fall (February/March, June/July, October). Most shrubs will need supplemental irrigation in the dry season.

Prune flowering shrubs after they flower and fast-growing large shrubs in the spring. Watch for aphids, which love new and succulent growth, and use insecticidal soap, or 2 tablespoons of nonperfumed dish detergent and 2 tablespoons vegetable oil in a gallon of water. Shrubs will perform well in return.

Azalea

Rhododendron spp.

Botanical Pronunciation
ROW-doh-den-dron

Bloom Period and Seasonal Color
Spring blooms in pink, red, white, and purple

Mature Height x Spread
2 to 6 feet x 2 to 6 feet

Zones 8–9

Nothing heralds spring's arrival better than azaleas. Most gardeners have heard of old-time favorites such as 'Duc de Rohan', 'Formosa', 'George Lindley Taber', and 'Southern Charm'. Azaleas have been a Florida favorite for almost a hundred years. The more common types include the Southern Indian, Satsuki, Rutherford, and Pericat. Most plantings bloom for three to four weeks and then fade into the background as a space divider or transition plant. Low-growing azaleas are also used as ground covers and small hedges along walkways. Florida is home to four native azaleas. The species *Rhododendron austrinum*, *R. calendulaceum*, and *R. canescens* are deciduous, and *R. chapmannii* is an evergreen type. These are medium to large shrubs found mainly in the northern portion of the state. (TM)

When, Where, and How to Plant

Azaleas are best transplanted from one area of the landscape to another between December and February. Plants in containers can be added at any time. Filtered sun is okay, but azaleas grow best in partial shade and acidic soil conditions. They grow good foliage in the shade but give poor flower displays. A well-drained soil is best. Make sure the plantings have an acidic soil. Improving the planting site with compost, peat moss, or manure helps with care, as azaleas also like a moist soil. Dig a hole that's much wider than the rootball but not deeper. Position the azalea plant at the same depth as it was growing in the container or original planting site. The top of the rootball may be set a little higher above the soil level, especially in a poorly drained location. After planting, form a berm and add a 1- to 2-inch mulch layer.

Growing Tips

Once established, most shrubs grow well with minimal care. It may be two years before azaleas grow a substantial root system. The best plantings receive regular feedings and enough water. Feed azaleas once in March, May, and September. Use an azalea-camellia or slow-release fertilizer. Azaleas need frequent watering, especially during periods of drought, because of their fine root systems.

Regional Advice and Care

Native azaleas are limited to the colder areas of the state. They are recommended for North Florida, but some have been planted in the central regions. Most hybrids are also limited to North and Central Florida. Azaleas need rejuvenation pruning every three to five years. Prune to keep the plants in-bounds yearly. Some pests that affect azaleas are caterpillars, lace bugs, and mites.

Companion Planting and Design

Plant in clusters for the best color in partially shady spots. Use as a backdrop or edging with cast iron plants, cocculus, gardenia, ferns, liriope, philodendron, crossandra, impatiens, and begonias.

Try These

Only a few azaleas have really become popular and are grown in most landscapes. One group, the Southern Indian hybrids, are known to survive some of the poorer, drier soils found in Florida.

Beautyberry

Callicarpa americana

Botanical Pronunciation
KAL-leh-car-pa AH-mere-E-cane-AH

Other Name American beautyberry

Bloom Period and Seasonal Color
Spring blooms in pink; magenta berries in the fall

Mature Height x Spread
6 feet x 6 feet

American beautyberry is a native plant of the southeastern United States. It grows where other shrubs do poorly, often in sandy, dry soils, and it requires little care. The real beauty of this shrub is evident during the fall and winter months when the fruits turn a magenta color in large clusters along the stems. This great accent shrub is possibly best used in naturalistic areas and along walkways. It makes a good space divider and view barrier. It remains semievergreen during the winter months. Consider this plant for minimal-maintenance landscapes and areas receiving mainly natural rainfall. It's frequently planted in clusters of three or more to create a display of fall color. Plants of beautyberry that produce white berries are available. (TM)

When, Where, and How to Plant
Transplanting from one area of the landscape to another is best performed between December and February to take advantage of the cooler weather. Plants in containers can be added at any time of the year. Beautyberry grows well in moist to dry soils. A well-drained soil is best. Many gardeners like to enrich sandy soils with compost, peat moss, and manure. Dig a hole that's much wider than the rootball but not deeper. Position beautyberry at the same depth it was growing in the container or original planting site. It may be set a little higher above the soil level, especially in a poorly drained location. After planting, form a berm and add a 1- to 2-inch mulch layer.

Growing Tips
Once established, most shrubs grow well with minimal care. Beautyberry is drought-tolerant and, after the roots of new plants have grown into the soil, seldom needs special watering. It can also survive with nutrients from mulches and what's provided other trees and shrubs in the area. If additional growth is desired, water more frequently. Feed once in March, May, and August. Use a general landscape or slow-release fertilizer.

Regional Advice and Care
Beautyberry grows well throughout the state with similar care. In South Florida it may bloom year-round. No pruning is needed at planting time. It grows lanky and should be pruned during late winter before new growth begins. Remove older stems, and cut back to a few feet below the desired height. Pests include caterpillars and grasshoppers. They are seldom a problem. Many can be handpicked from the plantings.

Companion Planting and Design
Use in a natural low-maintenance setting with other low-moisture-requiring plants. Beautyberry forms a nice backdrop for coreopsis, asters, or daisies or with contrasting greenery of saw palmetto, hollies, and ornamental grasses.

Try These
This native plant has a white-berried form often called variety 'Lactea' or 'Alba', but the common magenta-berried forms are most popular. Some like to plant one of each for a contrast.

Bush Rose

Rosa hybrids

Botanical Pronunciation
ROW-sah

Bloom Period and Seasonal Color
Year-round in all colors

Mature Height x Spread
5 to 6 feet x 5 feet

Modern roses began in 1867 with the introduction of the first hybrid tea named 'La France'. All roses prior to this date are considered old varieties, and those produced after this date, the new roses. Those old and new consist of a large group of nonclimbing plants separated into floribunda, grandiflora, hybrid tea, miniature, and old garden or heirloom roses. The main differences are in the size of the plants and the number and sizes of the blooms. All are admired for their beautiful blooms that open year-round but are their best during the warmer months. Roses are often planted in beds devoted to their culture and are focal points in the landscape. Sometimes they are mixed with shrubs or perennials and many are grown in containers. (TM)

When, Where, and How to Plant
The best time for planting is during spring or fall. Add compost, peat moss, and manure; then till the soil deeply. If planting in a container, use potting soil. Position each new rose so that the top of the rootball is even with the soil. If planting bare-root plants, use the color change along the trunk as an indication of how deep to plant. In poorly drained gardens, plant the bushes in mounds or raised beds. Add a 2- to 3-inch mulch layer over the surface.

Growing Tips
Feed monthly during warm weather with a general landscape or rose fertilizer and every six weeks during cooler weather. Keep the soil moist. Most established plants need a watering every three or four days.

Regional Advice and Care
During January or February, prune bush roses to reduce their height by one-third to one-half. This is also the time to remove weak stems and limit the bushes to no more than seven strong stems. Throughout the growing season, gardeners should be constantly giving the plants a light grooming to remove weak stems and direct the plant's growth. North Florida growers may also have to remove cold damage, and South Florida growers may add an extra pruning in August. South Florida growers may not need to reduce the feedings during the winter. Blackspot attacks mainly during hot, rainy weather. When it's severe, spray weekly with a fungicide. Mites are a major problem during dry weather. Wash light infestations off the foliage, or apply a miticide. Other pests are thrips, powdery mildew, aphids, caterpillars, and stem cankers.

Companion Planting and Design
Plant a bed or a few clusters of bush roses. Make sure they have adequate spacing, and then leave room for annuals and perennials, including ageratum, alyssum, periwinkle, and lantana, around the edges.

Try These
So many great roses are available for planting that it is hard to pick a few. Some favorites include 'Double Delight', 'Mr. Lincoln', 'Sun Flare', 'Europeana', 'Louis Philippe', 'Old Blush', and 'Gold Medal'. Ask a rosarian or your extension agent for a more complete list.

Climbing Rose

Rosa hybrids

Botanical Pronunciation
ROW-sah

Bloom Period and Seasonal Color
Year-round in a wide array of colors

Mature Height x Spread
6 to 8 feet x 6 to 8 feet

Almost every gardener would like to add a climbing rose to the landscape. It's a quick way to disguise a wall, fence, or trellis. Many gardeners like to have a climbing rose near the side of the home or at the entrance to form an accent feature. Climbing roses have lots of limbs, which means there should be bouquets to cut at any time. Some older types are quite colorful but flower only once a year. It is best to give climbing roses their own trellis or arbor rather have them climb a wall or side of the home. This practice provides good air movement to reduce disease. Create a display that's easy to see at the end of a focal point or along a walkway. (TM)

When, Where, and How to Plant
The best time to plant is fall through early spring. Choose a site where each plant has plenty of room to grow. Climbers can be grown in containers, but the size of the plant is often restricted by the available space. Sandy soils benefit from lots of organic matter, including compost, peat moss, and manure. Provide good drainage. If the soil is naturally wet, plant the rose bush in a mound of soil or a raised bed. When planting, dig the hole wider but no deeper than the rootball. Position the bush so that it is at the same depth it was in the pot. Finish the planting by adding a berm and 2 to 3 inches of mulch.

Growing Tips
Apply a general landscape or rose fertilizer once a month through the warmer months. During the cooler times, reduce feedings to every six to eight weeks. Roses need lots of water to maintain good growth. Established rose plantings need watering every three to four days.

Regional Advice and Care
Rose care is similar throughout the state. Climbing roses get limited pruning. Allow the long canes to develop with many laterals to bear the roses. After two to three years of growth, thin out the weak shoots, and prune laterals back to the main stems, leaving just two to three buds. Residents of North Florida may find more winter injury and need additional pruning after periods of cold. Residents of South Florida may not need to reduce winter feeding but stay on the once-a-month schedule. Two pests that can kill a rose bush are blackspot, which is a disease, and mites.

Companion Planting and Design
Send plants up a trellis or train to a fence as accents and space dividers. Use them as backdrops for bush daisies, pentas, gaura, salvias, and shrimp plants.

Try These
Perhaps the best climber for the Florida landscape is 'Don Juan', a hybrid with large, red, fragrant blossoms. Others favorites include 'Prosperity', a white; 'Altissimo', a medium red; 'Fourth of July', a red-and-white striped rose; and 'Cecile Brunner', a light pink.

Cocculus

Cocculus laurifolius

Botanical Pronunciation
KOK-you-lus laur-eh-FOI-ee-us

Other Name Snail seed

Bloom Period and Seasonal Color
Spring and summer blooms in yellow

Mature Height x Spread
12 feet x 12 feet

Zones 9–11

Every now and then you have to give a new plant a try. Cocculus might be that plant, with bright green leaves that have prominent veins and a very shiny appearance. The stems are arching and fairly open in habit, which can be thickened with timely pruning. The plant may be grown just because it's a curiosity, with seeds that resemble a coiled snail shell. It's the most interesting end of the flowering process, as the yellow blooms are insignificant. Cocculus make great hedges, shrubby borders, or specimens. They are tolerant of most soil conditions and need little care, which makes it ideal for minimal-maintenance or water-wise landscapes. The foliage can be added to arrangements and used to make wreaths, but take care—the leaves are poisonous. (TM)

When, Where, and How to Plant
Transplant cocculus from one area to another between December and February. Container plants can be added to the landscape at any time of the year. The plants grow in some of Florida's poorer soils. A well-drained soil is best. Many gardeners like to improve the site with compost or peat moss and manure before planting, but it is not necessary. Dig a hole that's much wider than the rootball but not deeper. Position the cocculus plant at the same depth it was growing in the container or original planting site. The top of the rootball may be set a little higher above the soil level, especially in a poorly drained location. After planting, form a berm at the edge of the rootball and add a 1- to 2-inch mulch layer.

Growing Tips
Once established most shrubs grow well with minimal care. Feed cocculus once in March, May, and September. Use a general landscape or slow-release fertilizer at label rates. Cocculus plantings are relatively drought-tolerant. Most plantings receive adequate moisture from rainfall. Water weekly to encourage growth, especially during a drought.

Regional Advice and Care
Cocculus suffers cold damage in North Florida in most years and in Central Florida during severe winters. Affected plantings need a late-winter pruning to remove the damaged portions and reshape the plants. Pruning is not usually needed at planting time. All shrubs need periodic pruning to keep the plantings in bounds, compact, and full of foliage. One pest that may affect cocculus is scale. Where needed, apply a pesticide recommended by the University of Florida, following label instructions.

Companion Planting and Design
Here is a great evergreen for minimal-maintenance landscapes to use as a hedge for sun or shade. It can also be used as a contrasting backdrop with perennials of bird-of-paradise, heliconias, gingers, and ornamental bananas.

Try These
Only the species of this snail seed is available in Florida. The Carolina snail seed, *Cocculus carolinus*, is native to North Florida. It has a vining growth habit with oval leaves with red fruits.

Cocoplum

Chrysobalanus icaco

Botanical Pronunciation
kry-so-ba-LAN-us eye-KAY-ko

Bloom Period and Seasonal Color
Year-round foliage

Mature Height x Spread
3 to 20 feet x 15 feet

Zones 9–11

A medium to large evergreen shrub, cocoplum has an upright or spreading shape. Two forms occur: red-tipped and green-tipped. The round leaves march alternately along the twigs and point skyward. The shrub has a more or less symmetrical shape, and it can become quite full and large inland. The sprawling, low, coastal form is *C. icaco* 'Horizontalis'. Cocoplum fruit is eaten by birds and wildlife—and humans too. When creating a native garden or wildlife habitat, cocoplum is a good addition. The genus name *Chrysobalanus* comes from the words *chryso*, meaning "gold," and *balanos*, or "acorn." Some species have golden fruit. Those in Florida have pink, white, or dark red-purple fruit. But as landscape plants, they are worth their weight in gold. (GBT)

When, Where, and How to Plant
Plant at the beginning of the rainy season, late May to early June, or from March to midsummer if consistent irrigation is practical early on. Dig a hole twice as wide but just as deep as the rootball. If roots in the container are circling, then make several ¼-inch cuts in the rootball with a sharp knife to promote new, outward root growth. Add compost or peat moss to make up one-third of the backfill to enrich the planting hole. Water as you shovel in the backfill to eliminate air pockets. Mulch to a depth of 3 or 4 inches, making sure the mulch is several inches away from the trunk of the shrub to prevent fungus.

Growing Tips
Cocoplum benefits from 6-6-6 or 7-3-7 fertilizer twice a year to keep growing vigorously. If using cocoplum in a hammock setting or a native garden and you don't want to add synthetic chemical fertilizers, you can add well-aged compost or cow manure to the root zone along with mulch. The compost is really a soil conditioner with a few nutrients in it. When adding mulch to planted shrubs, work it into the top couple of inches of the soil in the bed or around the trunk or trunks, out as far as you care to take it. Microorganisms are available that can be added to the soil to stimulate other microorganisms to breakdown compost into usable form. You'll find these at garden centers or where organic gardening products are sold.

Regional Advice and Care
This shrub grows through Central Florida but not into North Florida.

Companion Planting and Design
Use these plants in any number of situations, from background shrubs and screening to clipped hedges. Cocoplum brings a feeling of the Everglades to a native Florida planting that also might include cabbage palms, Fakahatchee grass, and willows or wax myrtle. It can be pinched to remain a particular size.

Try These
The red-tipped version of this Florida native plant is especially pretty and can be used to pick up the red of nearby plants or grown simply for itself.

Crape Myrtle

Laegerstroemia indica

Botanical Pronunciation
lay-ger-STOM-ee-ah IN-de-ka

Bloom Period and Seasonal Color
Summer and fall blooms lavender, white, coral, pink, and red

Mature Height x Spread
20 feet x 20 feet

Zones 7–10B

Reliable bloomers that put on a nice show, crape myrtles are from Japan, Korea, and China. Breeding efforts in this country have produced many colors and disease-resistant varieties. The flowers are outstanding in late summer and fall, but come winter, the leaves drop. If bare twigs are not something you can ignore, then plan ahead and mix with other shrubs in the background. The leaves on the crape myrtle turn yellow and then orange-red before falling in midwinter, and the dried seeds stay on the twig ends, gradually splitting open and falling. After a few years, the bark peels and becomes quite attractive. Three cultivars are mildew-resistant: 'Muskegee', a lavender flowering shrub; 'Natchez', with white flowers; and 'Tuscarora', with coral flowers. (GBT)

When, Where, and How to Plant

Plant at the beginning of the rainy season, late May to early June, or from March to midsummer if consistent irrigation is practical early on. Crape myrtles are drought-tolerant and do well in many kinds of soils as long as they don't stand in water. Dig a hole just as deep but 1 foot wider than the rootball (two to three times as wide in rocky ground). If roots in the container are circling, then make several ¼-inch cuts in the rootball with a sharp knife to promote new, outward root growth. Water as you shovel in the backfill to eliminate air pockets. Build a saucerlike basin of soil around the edge of the planting area to retain water.

Growing Tips

Fertilize in March, July, and November (make this a low-nitrogen fertilizer, such as 4-6-8). Mulch to a depth of 3 or 4 inches, making sure the mulch is several inches away from the trunk of the shrub to prevent fungus.

Regional Advice and Care

Older varieties get powdery mildew. Prune in late winter before the new growth begins, as flowering occurs on new branch ends. If too many twigs grow out, thin to shape. The plants can sucker at the base and become multistemmed in spite of your best efforts. Do not remove stems larger than pencil size in diameter. The "dignity" of the plant's shape will remain and the plant will bloom more profusely in a habit more appealing to the eye if these stems are left in place. Crape myrtles grow throughout Florida with similar care.

Companion Planting and Design

Use in a mixed, informal planting or as a specimen plant. White-colored crape myrtles tend to get lost in the din unless used as specimens; reds, pinks, and lavenders are more noticeable. Let this big shrub grow tall and, during the summer flowering period, shine above landscape begonias.

Try These

Crape myrtle 'Seminole' is a medium pink-flowered plant with a compact habit (many crape myrtles can become quite large) and keeps its panicles of flowers close enough together to make an impact.

Croton

Codiaeum variegatum

Botanical Pronunciation
co-DIE-ee-um vare-E-gate-um

Bloom Period and Seasonal Color
Year-round foliage in green, pink, yellow, and red

Mature Height x Spread
3 to 8 feet x 3 feet

Zones 9B–11

One croton fancier used to collect crotons on trips throughout Florida and ended up with more than 60 different-looking plants—and that was probably just the beginning. Gardeners love the variety of leaf colors, greens, pinks, yellows, and reds, in addition to the leaf shapes available in the croton genus. Crotons have to be kept consistently warm. In cooler portions of the state, protection is needed to survive any dip below 32 degrees Fahrenheit. These relatively narrow plants are ideal for cramped gardens and the small spots between the home and the sidewalk. In the cooler regions of Florida, the plants are often set in containers. Some have been used as foliage plants indoors. You can create croton hedges and use the plants as screens. (TM)

When, Where, and How to Plant
Transplant crotons from one area to another between December and February. Add container plants to the landscape at any time. Most selections tolerate the lower light levels under a large tree, but the colors are somewhat subdued. A well-drained soil is best. The plants take well to sandy soils. Many like to improve the sandy sites with compost or peat moss and manure, but it is not necessary. Dig a hole that's much wider than the rootball but not deeper. Position the croton plant at the same depth it was growing in the container or original planting site. The top of the rootball may be set a little higher above the soil level, especially in a poorly drained location. After planting, form a berm and add a 2- to 3-inch mulch layer.

Growing Tips
Crotons can exist with feedings given nearby plants but make the best growth when fertilized once in March, May, and September. Use a general landscape or slow-release fertilizer at label rates. Crotons are relatively drought-tolerant; normal rainfalls are often sufficient for them. During an extended drought, water the plantings weekly.

Regional Advice and Care
Growing crotons in North Florida and parts of Central Florida is restricted to containers due to winter cold. Plant in a loose potting soil, and feed with a slow-release container fertilizer during periods of active growth. Protect these plants from frosts and freezing. No pruning is needed at planting time. They need periodic pruning to produce compact plants with plenty of colorful new shoots. Some pests that may affect crotons include scale, thrips, and mites. Where needed, apply a pesticide recommended by the University of Florida.

Companion Planting and Design
Producing lots of color, crotons make great accent plants for container or in-ground culture in sun or shade. Plants are best used with surroundings of greenery, including ferns, philodendron, cast iron plant, viburnum, and similar shrubs.

Try These
Many selections have been marketed. All are enjoyable with virtually a rainbow of color combinations, including varieties 'Banana', 'Dreadlocks', 'Fiesta', 'Gold Dust', 'Lucia', and 'Petra'.

Firebush

Hamelia patens

Botanical Pronunciation
ha-MEEL-yah PAY-tens

Other Name Scarlet bush

Bloom Period and Seasonal Color
Year-round blooms in scarlet

Mature Height x Spread
15 feet or more x 6 feet

Zones 10–11

Firebush is a fast-growing shrub with whorls of textured leaves that take on a reddish color in full sun. Though it may grow to 15 feet or more, it can be kept much shorter by pruning. A South Florida native, firebush is a valuable plant for its nectar-rich flowers that attract hummingbirds and butterflies. The slender, tubular flowers are in clusters toward the ends of the branches. Firebush takes heat and drought like a champ. Mix it with wild coffee, necklace pod, spicewood, beautyberry, and other native shrubs in a mixed border. Use it along with native trees to create a wildlife habitat or as a part of the yard you do not irrigate (once the plants are established) in a water-conserving landscape design. (GBT)

When, Where, and How to Plant
Planting just before the rainy season is ideal. Or plant in March, if you are willing to irrigate until the rainy season begins. Avoid transplanting anything in the high heat of August and September, as high heat adds an extra burden of stress to plants trying to develop new roots. Plant firebush in an area that drains well. Dig a hole twice as wide but just as deep as the rootball. If roots in the container are circling, then make several ¼-inch cuts in the rootball with a sharp knife to promote new, outward root growth. As you work, water the backfill to eliminate air pockets. Mulch to a depth of 3 or 4 inches, making sure the mulch is several inches away from the trunk of the shrub to prevent fungus.

Growing Tips
Keep the roots moist until the shrub is established. Water daily for the first week and then every other day for two weeks; reduce to every three or four days for two weeks. During the first growing season, water weekly if rain is irregular or if the shrub wilts.

Regional Advice and Care
In Central Florida, this shrub will be damaged by cold. Each spring, prune out the affected area once new growth has begun to indicate what must be pruned away. You may want to prune this back hard to keep it small or under control. The caterpillars that are larvae of a sphinx moth, *Xylophanes tersa*, often prune it back naturally. Cold wind can burn the leaves. This *Hamelia* species is good at recovering from such plunder, however—and not just from caterpillars, but also from aphids, which find it delectable.

Companion Planting and Design
Incorporate this plant into a butterfly garden or use several near your patio where you can watch the butterflies flock to the pretty orange-red flowers. Hummingbirds also like the flowers. Mix with wax myrtle, West Indian lilac, and cocoplum. As a butterfly-attracting shrub, firebush is excellent and serves well in a South Florida butterfly garden to buffer wind.

Try These
Non-native forms of *Hamelia* include *Hamelia cuprea*, with larger, orange flowers.

Gardenia

Gardenia jasminoides

Botanical Pronunciation
gar-DEEN-ya jazz-min-OY-dees

Other Name Cape jasmine

Bloom Period and Seasonal Color
Spring blooms in white

Mature Height x Spread
8 feet x 3 to 4 feet

The gardenia is a slow-growing evergreen shrub with textured dark green leaves and fragrant white flowers in the spring. She sends her intoxicating perfume across the heavy air, and at night even moths that would be drawn to the moon return for the gardenia. For who, once captivated by her powers, can resist this siren? We grant you that some people cannot bear to be in the same room with her. For our part, we think she is the queen of tropical scents. She has virginal white flowers that are large, most often double, and roselike in appearance. 'Miami Supreme' is the biggest-selling cultivar in Florida. It has large flowers, is extremely fragrant, and also grows in partial shade. *Gardenia jasminoides* 'Radicans' is a dwarf species. (GBT)

When, Where, and How to Plant
Gardenias prefer an acidic soil and will grow in full sun to light shade. Plant from March through summer, although late May or early June is the best. The soil should be kept moist. Fluctuation in soil moisture leads to yellowing leaves on this shrub. Dig a hole twice as wide but just as deep as the rootball. If roots in the container are circling, then make several ¼-inch cuts in the rootball with a sharp knife to promote new, outward root growth. Add peat moss or compost to the planting hole so that about one-third of the soil is enriched. If you mix too much organic material in the hole in rocky soils, the roots will be disinclined to move out into the rocky substrate. Add mulch to a depth of 3 or 4 inches, making sure the mulch is several inches away from the trunk of the shrub to prevent fungus.

Growing Tips
Gardenias are heavy feeders, and in alkaline soils they thrive on high-nitrogen, acid-forming fertilizer. A 12-6-8 or 12-6-10 fertilizer formula is appropriate. Use small amounts every two or three months. A lack of micronutrients also causes yellow leaves; use a foliar micronutrient spray. For iron deficiency, use an iron drench once a year.

Regional Advice and Care
Prune lightly after the major flowering period to keep the shrub compact. Cold winters can damage gardenias in Central and North Florida. Prune out affected portions after new growth appears in the spring. Thrips are attracted to the buds, which are spirally twisted before opening. Predatory insects such as lacewings can attack thrips. Use a paraffin-based horticultural insecticide or a systemic insecticide. Don't plant near the orchid house.

Companion Planting and Design
When in full flower, gardenia wants to be admired by itself, and using it as a specimen plant allows that. Or blend it with snowbush, crotons, or green and white acalypha for nonblooming months.

Try These
Gardenia taitensis, Tahitian gardenia, is less fussy in South Florida, presenting single, pure white flowers against glossy green leaves. It takes pruning well.

Hibiscus

Hibiscus rosa-sinensis

Botanical Pronunciation
hi-BIS-kus row-sa sa-NEN-sis

Other Name Chinese or Hawaiian hibiscus

Bloom Period and Seasonal Color
Summer blooms in all colors

Mature Height x Spread
20 feet or more x 15 feet

Zones 10–11

Hibiscus flowers, like palms, say tropical. Big, flashy, and strong bloomers, hibiscus flowers begin with white and go to mauve, gray, brown, orange, red, yellow, blue, brown with yellow edges, yellow with orange centers...combinations that are reminiscent of tie-dyed T-shirts of those hippie days so long ago. Yet some people love the single white, the bright red, the bell-like clarity of the single yellow, and the plain pink. Most blossoms last only a day, so they don't make great cut flowers, but they perform well in the garden. *Hibiscus schizopetalus*, sometimes called the fringed hibiscus, has upside-down red flowers that hang from long stems. *Hibiscus syriacus* is the rose-of-Sharon that produces blue single flowers and is deciduous. It does well in alkaline soils. (GBT)

When, Where, and How to Plant
Plant in March through midsummer, with late May and early June as the best times. Find an area where plants won't sit in water. Dig a hole twice as wide but just as deep as the rootball. Add peat moss or compost to the planting hole so that about one-third of the backfill is enriched. As you work with the shovel, water the backfill to eliminate air pockets. Mulch to a depth of 3 or 4 inches, making sure the mulch is several inches away from the trunk of the shrub to prevent fungus.

Growing Tips
Once established shrubs are drought-tolerant. You may have to water in the dry season if there is not any rain. Watch for wilt. Use a slow-release fertilizer with a 3-1-3 ratio. Hibiscus in alkaline soils can show minor element deficiencies, so a micronutrient foliar spray three times a year is advisable. Growers warn not to mix water-soluble 20-20-20 with a micronutrient spray because the phosphorus in the 20-20-20 will tie up micronutrients.

Regional Advice and Care
Hibiscus can be grown in Central Florida in protected areas—such as a sunny southeast side of a house. In North Florida, use in containers or as an annual. Prune any cold damage off in spring. In South Florida, hibiscus are best grown on 'Anderson's Crepe' rootstock, which withstands nematodes and heat stress. Control whitefly and aphids with insecticidal soap or 2 tablespoons of liquid Ivory in 1 gallon of water. If armored scale attack hibiscus prune off the affected area. Never use Malathion; it can kill hibiscus. Gall midges cause bud drop, and pink hibiscus mealybugs cause deformed terminal growth. Hibiscus need good gardening, and many gardeners have chosen less-challenging plants.

Companion Planting and Design
A coconut palm or areca palm can be bordered or interplanted with hibiscus for a true tropical picture. Use along a fence line. Don't mix lots of colors. Pure white hibiscus flowers are appealingly unaffected and look cool in summer's heat.

Try These
Turk's cap, *Malvaviscus arboreus* var. *drummondii*, sometimes is called the sleeping hibiscus because the flower resembles an unopened hibiscus flower.

Hydrangea

Hydrangea macrophylla

Botanical Pronunciation
HI-drain-GEE-ah MAC-row-phil-ah

Other Name Mophead hydrangeas

Bloom Period and Seasonal Color
Spring through summer blooms in pink, blue, purple, and white

Mature Height x Spread
5 feet x 5 feet

Zones 8–9

When you think of Easter plants, one shrub that always comes to mind is the hydrangea. The ball-shaped inflorescences are prominent from mid-spring through early summer. Hydrangeas on display at Easter have been forced to bloom and are a little earlier than the landscape plantings. You may be able to convince any hydrangea to be either pink or blue by regulating the soil acidity where it's growing. But many varieties have been selected for the better blue or pink color. Hydrangeas are best used in mass displays of three or more plants. They can be planted as background shrubs, hedges, or accents. Central and North Florida gardeners can also plant the oakleaf hydrangea, *Hydrangea quercifolia*. It grows to about 6 feet tall and produces a white inflorescence for spring. (TM)

When, Where, and How to Plant
Transplant hydrangeas from October through February. Container plants can be added to the landscape at any time. Hydrangeas need protection from the hot, drying sun. They are best planted where they get filtered or morning sun and afternoon shade. Select a well-drained soil, but it should be able to hold some moisture. Improve the planting site with compost or peat moss and manure. Dig a hole that's much wider than the rootball but not deeper. Position the hydrangea at the same depth it was growing in the container or original planting site. The top of the rootball may be set a little above the soil level, especially in a poorly drained location. After planting, form a berm and add up to a 2-inch mulch layer.

Growing Tips
Hydrangeas need extra care to grow in most landscapes. Feed plantings once in March, May, and September. Use general landscape or slow-release fertilizer. Hydrangeas need *lots* of water; the plants frequently wilt with just a little moisture stress. Check the plantings several times each week during periods of drought. Plants need watering at least every three to four days during hot weather.

Regional Advice and Care
Hydrangeas grow well only in Central and North Florida where they have some cold weather during winter. Some years they suffer freeze damage that needs to be groomed during the early spring season. Hydrangeas are usually pruned after flowering is complete in early to midsummer. Remove older flower heads, and do any reshaping of the plants. Handpick caterpillars from plants, or treat them with a natural pesticide.

Companion Planting and Design
Plants grow well in a container for the porch, for the patio, or along a walkway. Display in ground with other filtered sun lovers, such as allamanda, ardisia, jacobinia, Indian hawthorn, nandina, viburnum, azaleas, and camellias.

Try These
New free-flowering hydrangeas that repeat blooms for 15 or more weeks are arriving at garden centers. A good selection is the 'Endless Summer' series. Others to try include long blooming 'Oak Hill', 'David Ramsey', 'Decatur Blue', and 'Penny Mac'.

Ixora

Ixora coccinea

Botanical Pronunciation
ig-SORE-a cock-SIN-ee-ah

Other Name Flame of the woods

Bloom Period and Seasonal Color
Spring through summer blooms in red, orange, pink, and yellow

Mature Height x Spread
2½ to 8 feet x 6 feet

Zones 10B–11

Ixoras are evergreen shrubs that produce many small but bright flowers in large heads throughout the warm season. Once the darling of South Florida builders, the plants experienced a period of disuse and then came back to the landscapes. The reasons for this swing had to do with the way the shrubs were originally maintained and the development of new cultivars to make maintenance easier. With the development of *Ixora* 'Nora Grant', which is resistant to nematodes, tolerant of rocky soil, and shapely enough that hard pruning isn't needed, the picture changed. *Ixora duffii* 'Super King' has large heads of deep red flowers and is susceptible to nematodes; but it looks healthier and is bigger (to 10 feet) than *I. coccinea*. *Ixora javanica* produces orange flowers. (GBT)

When, Where, and How to Plant
Plant at the beginning of the rainy season, late May to early June. Good drainage is important. Dig a hole twice as wide but just as deep as the rootball. If roots in the container are circling, then make several ¼-inch cuts in the rootball with a sharp knife to promote new, outward root growth. Add peat moss or compost to enrich the planting hole so that about one-third of the backfill is organic.

Growing Tips
Ixoras like fertilizer to keep producing those big balls of flowers called umbels. They prefer acidic soil, so they benefit from mulch and high-nitrogen fertilizer. Micronutrient deficiencies are often seen in alkaline soils, particularly magnesium deficiency, which causes yellowing of older leaves. Manganese deficiency causes yellowing in new leaves. Iron deficiency creates yellow areas between green veins. One or two handfuls of Epsom salts (magnesium sulfate) around the root zone when you fertilize will help with the magnesium problem. An iron drench once a year is beneficial. Manganese sulfate combats yellowing of new leaves, and the sulfate helps make soil acid as well. Use a micronutrient foliar spray. Do not overwater in winter.

Regional Advice and Care
Very cold weather, in the upper 30s, will cause leaves to develop brown spots. If freezing occurs, wait until spring before pruning so you can allow the emergence of new leaves to indicate how far back twigs and branches were damaged. Lightly prune to shape; ixoras perform best when they're not sheared.

Companion Planting and Design
Resist hedging, except informally, and instead combine them with crotons, palms, and copper leaf for easy-care plantings that are colorful but not confusing.

Try These
The medium pink, rather dwarf cultivar 'Nora Grant' is a good performer. 'Maui' has yellow-orange or reddish orange flowers that are just as striking. 'Maui Yellow' bears light yellow flowers.

Jamaica Caper

Capparis cynophallophora

Botanical Pronunciation
CAP-er-is SIGH-no-fal-a-for-a

Bloom Period and Seasonal Color
Spring, with pinkish white flowers; fall, red fruits

Mature Height x Spread
10 to 20 feet x 10 feet

Zones 10–11

One of the most beautiful native shrubs in South Florida, Jamaica caper also grows in Mexico and Central America. Oh, that we could be the sole claimant! The leaves are notched at the tip, with a covering of rusty hairs on the undersides. Spring flowers resemble miniature fireworks, with the stamens and a pistil seeming to explode from the sepals and calyx. The flowers open white and turn pink. They are fragrant at night to attract a moth pollinator. It is the larval host for the Florida White butterfly, and a few nibbled leaves will tell you when the larvae are in residence. Seedpods are long and skinny, opening to red seeds and pulpy interior. Jamaica caper should be a native plant ambassador. (GBT)

When, Where, and How to Plant

Select a prime location for this shrub so you can admire the flowers on an up-close and personal basis. Also, you'll need a planting area that has some shade. I grow several that have an eastern exposure, allowing them full sun in the morning and shade in the afternoon.

Growing Tips

Jamaica caper may take one or two years to settle in and two or three more to gear up for lots of flowers. But the wait is worth it. Fertilize two or three times a year to encourage it along, keep mulch around the base (but keep mulch from touching the trunk), and after three or so years,

prune away lower branches if you want a more treelike shape. You also can pinch the tops for more density.

Regional Advice and Care

This is a plant for the warmer parts of the state, up to the coastal areas of Pinellas County on the west coast and to Brevard County on the east coast, according to the Institute for Regional Conservation.

Companion Planting and Design

You can allow this shrub to become a small tree or use several together as a screen, planting them about 4 to 5 feet apart and keeping them pruned to 8 or 10 feet tall. Jamaica caper may be used as an understory tree in a native garden or as part of a butterfly garden.

Try These

Limber caper, *Capparis flexuosa*, is a more sprawling cousin to Jamaica caper. Because of its long, flexible branches, it remains a shrub. It also is a larval host for the Florida White and Great Southern White butterflies. Its flowers are more exuberant, which is to say showier, than those of the Jamaica caper, and its seeds are white.

Juniper

Juniperus spp.

Botanical Pronunciation
joo-NE-per-us

Bloom Period and Seasonal Color
Spring, some with dark blue fruits for winter

Mature Height x Spread
30 feet x 20 feet, depending on variety

Zones 8–10

Needle-leaf evergreens are a favorite of many new residents relocating to Florida. Yet they are much fewer in number than you find in the cooler states. One favorite gardeners can bring with them is the junipers to grow in most of Florida. Perhaps the most popular is the native red cedar that grows upright to use individually, in hedges, or maybe even as a Christmas tree. But junipers of other species also make good groundcovers, space dividers, and foundation plantings. They are fairly prickly, so some say they might be planted to keep intruders out of the home. The main thought is to pick the right juniper for your landscape, which can be done by consulting a nursery expert or your extension agent. (TM)

When, Where, and How to Plant
Container-grown plants can be added to the landscape at any time of the year. Balled-and-burlapped plants are best added during the cooler months. Select a sunny site with good drainage. Be sure to give the taller and wider growing selections adequate room to grow. Dig a hole wider but not deeper than the rootball. You can improve the fill soil, but it is not necessary. Position the rootball so the top is even with the soil line or slightly above, and backfill with soil. Water well and build a 4- to 6-inch berm of soil at the edge of the rootball to hold and direct water down through the root system. Add a light layer of mulch over the root system. Water frequently until the new junipers are established.

Growing Tips
Keep the soil moist until the plants grow roots out into the surrounding soil. Junipers are drought-tolerant but do best with watering once a week during the very hot, dry times. Encourage growth with a slow-release fertilizer applied once in March, June, and August. Mites and scale insects are occasional pests and are best controlled with a natural insecticide when needed.

Regional Advice and Care
Find the best juniper for your location to plant in the landscape. Most grow best only in Northern and Central Florida. Plantings can grow very rapidly when given good care. Prune shoots to keep them in-bounds. Many gardeners like to use some of the longer shoots from shrub types for holiday decorations, but pruning can be done as needed. Junipers are best not sheared or pruned back past where there are green needles along the stems.

Companion Planting and Design
Use with most shrubs and groundcover plantings. They are especially useful in minimal-maintenance landscapes with yaupon holly, camellias, pineapple guavas, Asiatic jasmine, and anise.

Try These
The shore juniper makes a most durable groundcover, with 'Blue Pacific' being a favorite for growing throughout the state. Some good shrub types include 'Blue Vase', 'Hetzi', and 'Mint Julep'. Upright types include 'Brodie', 'Sylvestris', and 'Spartan'.

Lady-of-the-Night

Brunfelsia nitida

Botanical Pronunciation
brune-FELL-zee-ah NIT-a-da

Bloom Period and Seasonal Color
Summer blooms in white

Mature Height x Spread
8 to 10 feet x 5 to 10 feet

Zones 10B–11

On the softest summer nights, when the moon is hazy through the humidity and the screech owls call in little whinnies from the avocado tree, the sweet scent of cloves may drift or linger. Unlike jasmine, with its cloying ways, *Brunfelsia nitida*'s clove perfume seems never to be in excess, never overripe. It lasts two, maybe three nights and then is gone until the next wave of flowers washes over the twigs. This shrub is incredibly showy when flowering; it blooms profusely all at once. Yesterday-today-and-tomorrow is a winter-flowering cousin, *Brunfelsia pauciflora*. The 3-inch flowers open blue-purple and fade to white, hence the name. *Brunfelsia grandiflora* blooms in the warm season, also with purple flowers and white centers. *Brunfelsia australis* is another purple-to-white bloomer. (GBT)

When, Where, and How to Plant
Plant lady-of-the-night where she gets five or six hours of sun in the summer. If roots in the container are circling, then make several ¼-inch cuts in the rootball to promote new, outward root growth. Add compost or peat moss to make up one-third of the backfill to enrich the planting hole. Water while shoveling in backfill to eliminate air pockets. Add mulch to a depth of 3 or 4 inches. Do not use cypress mulch, but look for melaleuca mulch, a more environmentally friendly choice.

Growing Tips
Water every few days in the dry season. Fertilize three times a year with an 8-4-12 with 4 percent magnesium and micronutrients in the spring and summer and a 4-6-8 right before winter to avoid pushing out new leaves. Apply new mulch twice a year, because it wears thin every six months or so. When spraying liquid fertilizer on orchids, spray this shrub at the same time. *Brunfelsia nitida* thrives on this regimen. Cut back after the flowering has ceased or in late winter. This shrub tends to have lots of dead twigs beneath its leaves. It also will occasionally self-seed.

Regional Advice and Care
Brunfelsia grows throughout Central Florida but may be damaged by cold. Prune off damage in early spring after new growth appears as an indication of where live wood begins. Prune to shape, but bear in mind that this *Brunfelsia* likes to sprawl naturally. To sow seeds, remove the skin and pulp, push seeds just beneath the surface of a 50-50 mix of peat moss and perlite, and keep moist.

Companion Planting and Design
Lady-of-the-night laces summer nights with rich perfume, so place this shrub where you can take delight in it. It wants to sprawl, so allow it to spill like milk from a grouping of shrubs. Placed on the southeast corner of the house, this shrub will float its clovelike perfume on the prevailing evening breeze and show off its flowers in the moonlight.

Try These
Brufelsia pauciflora from Brazil has purple flowers but needs acid-forming fertilizer.

Ligustrum

Ligustrum japonicum

Botanical Pronunciation
LEH-guss-trum JAH-pon-eh-come

Other Name Japanese privet

Bloom Period and Seasonal Color
Spring blooms in white; blue berries in fall

Mature Height x Spread
12 feet x 8 feet

Zones 8–10

Talk about a plant that is a backbone of the landscape industry, and you must be discussing the ligustrum. It's planted as a hedge, view barrier, accent plant, and tree. Ligustrums have large, very shiny leaves and open white blossoms in the spring. A blue berry follows in fall for extra color. They survive in all but the wettest soil and can live with minimal care. Ligustrums can be pruned to almost any shape or permitted to grow naturally for a slightly upright to spreading form. It has rapid growth to fill in voids and give the landscape a quick, recognizable form. Gardeners also plant the glossy privet, *Ligustrum lucidum*, which grows to 20 feet tall as a tree in the landscape. (TM)

When, Where, and How to Plant
Transplant ligustrums from one area of the landscape to another between December and February. Add container plants to the landscape at any time. Ligustrum will tolerate filtered sun where they develop a more open growth habit. A well-drained soil is best. They are very tolerant of Florida sands. If you wish to improve the planting site with compost or peat moss and manure, but it is not necessary. Dig a hole that's much wider than the rootball but not deeper. Position the ligustrum plant at the same depth it was growing in the container or original planting site. The top of the rootball may be set a little higher above the soil level, especially in a poorly drained location. After planting, form a berm, and add a 2- to 3-inch mulch layer.

Growing Tips
Ligustrums make the best growth if fed once in March, May, and September. Use a general landscape or slow-release fertilizer. Ligustrums are fairly drought-tolerant—able to exist with natural rainfall for all but the drier times. The best growth is made with weekly watering, especially during periods of drought.

Regional Advice and Care
Ligustrums grow well in all but the most southern regions of the state. Care is similar in all areas. Pruning is normally not needed at planting time. Formal hedges may need pruning several times during the growing season. The tree forms need periodic pruning to keep an open habit of growth and remove lower sprouts along the trunks. Ligustrum may get caterpillars, grasshoppers, and scales. Handpick pests from the plantings, or treat them with a pesticide recommended by the University of Florida. Good care will overcome fungal leaf spots.

Companion Planting and Design
Ligustrum is often used as a hedge or backdrop for gardens or a border for the home site. It also makes a great tree to use in small designs and near patios.

Try These
Gardeners typically purchase a green leaf shrub or tree form of ligustrum. Some selections with varying leaf forms and colors to try include 'Gold Tip', 'Howardii', and 'Recurvifolium'.

Locustberry

Byrsonima lucida

Botanical Pronunciation
bur-so-NIM-ah LEW-sah-da

Bloom Period and Seasonal Color
Spring flowers in pink and white

Mature Height x Spread
10 to 15 feet x 10 to 15 feet

Zones 10B–11

ocustberry produces amazing flowers. It is a member of the family Malpighiaceae. Most members of this family bear pink and white flowers with clawed petals and sepals that produce oil for particular oil-collecting bees. It is thought that *Oncidium* orchids mimic these flowers in shape, and bees are fooled into visiting them as they hunt for oil, pollinating the orchid flowers accidentally. Clusters of showy flowers may appear all year but are most numerous in the spring and summer. Leaves are simple and entire and occur in pairs. Locustberry is the larval host for the Florida Duskywing, a skipper butterfly. Mockingbirds and the little Key deer on Big Pine Key eat the fruits. (GBT)

When, Where and How to Plant

Planting is best at the start of the rainy season to reduce irrigation needs. Locustberry is not hard to cultivate if it's given a good start in life. A good start includes daily watering for the first week after planting, gradually reducing irrigation to no more than twice weekly. Like most natives, locustberry likes some fertilizer to help it become established, and then both water and fertilizer may be greatly reduced.

Growing Tips

When planting, remember that winter's sun is quite low, and shadows may overtake areas that in the summer are sunny. If this happens, locustberry will be less floriferous, and its branches will stretch and thin, making it a less attractive plant. Pruning can help shape this shrub, making it more compact.

Regional Advice and Care

As the climate becomes warmer, the USDA hardiness zones are moving northward. This means that plants previously thought too cold-sensitive for Central Florida may be able to be grown with protection—such as being planted in a south-facing area of the garden, sheltered by walls or windbreaks. This plant grows into Palm Beach County without a problem. It has virtually no pests.

Companion Planting and Design

Locustberry is a great candidate for a native garden, a butterfly garden, or a bird-attracting garden. Locustberry mixes well with other natives, such as pearl berry, pineland strongbark, firebush, snowberry, and beautyberry.

Try These

Thryallis, *Galphimia glauca*, is another member of the Malpighiaceae family that does well in South Florida, with its claw-shaped yellow petals in clusters in summer and fall. This plant from Mexico and Central America is drought-tolerant.

Nandina

Nandina domestica

Botanical Pronunciation
nan-DEE-nah doh-MES-tea-kah

Other Name Heavenly bamboo

Bloom Period and Seasonal Color
Spring blooms in yellow, red fruit in fall and winter

Mature Height x Spread
5 to 6 feet x 3 to 4 feet

Zones 8–10

According to folklore, planting nandina at the entrance to your home brings good luck. Its colorful berries and unique foliage add to the list of reasons to plant it. As the name suggests, it resembles bamboo, producing upward growth from canelike stems plus bamboolike foliage. The plants produce clusters of yellowish flowers for spring, but they may be hidden within the branches. Depending on how much cold weather the plants endure and on the variety, they may be evergreen to semievergreen. Nandina are often planted in clusters as accents or groundcover. They can be grown in containers for patio and entrance displays. Older varieties seeded freely and should be avoided to prevent them from invading native habitats. Berries are considered toxic if eaten. (TM)

When, Where, and How to Plant
Transplant nandina from one area of the landscape to another between December and February. Container plants can be added to the landscape at any time. A well-drained soil is best. The plants grow well in Florida's sandy soils. Many like to improve the planting site with compost or peat moss and manure. Dig a hole that's much wider than the rootball but not deeper. Position the nandina plant at the same depth it was growing in the container or original planting site. It may be set a little higher above the soil level, especially in a poorly drained location. After planting, form a berm, and add a 2- to 3-inch mulch layer.

Growing Tips
Nandina exist with care given nearby shrubs and trees. They make the best growth when fed once in March, May, and September. Use general landscape or slow-release fertilizer at label rates. Nandina can tolerate short periods of drought but grow best with weekly watering.

Regional Advice and Care
Plantings in the cooler parts of the state are likely to show the best leaf color and exhibit deciduous growth habit during the winter months. Protect plantings in the southern and hotter areas of the state from midday sun. Many of the older canes lose their leaves and grow too tall for the garden site. An annual rejuvenation pruning in late winter takes out the older canes to allow new growths to fill in from the base. One pest that may affect the nandina is the scale insect. If needed, apply a pesticide recommended by the University of Florida.

Companion Planting and Design
Fill beds as a groundcover, or cluster a few together as an accent. Use the contrasting foliage with deeper green shrubs of Indian hawthorn, dwarf hollies, hibiscus, viburnums, and ligustrum.

Try These
Breeders have been improving the quality of the nandina for local landscapes. A few for Florida are 'Alba', with white fruits; 'Nana', growing to 2 feet tall; 'Compacta', with a low-growing, dense habit; 'Firepower', a dwarf with red and yellow foliage; and 'Harbor Dwarf', a low-growing type.

Oleander

Nerium oleander

Botanical Pronunciation
near-EE-um oh-LEE-and-der

Bloom Period and Seasonal Color
Spring through late fall blooms in white, pink, red, and salmon

Mature Height x Spread
12 feet x 12 feet

Give your yard a tropical look with an oleander. It is one of the showiest shrubs you can add to your landscape, in bloom from spring through fall. It can be planted as a hedge or space divider. Many gardeners plant larger oleanders to the rear of the yard to enjoy the distant color. You can plant just one shrub as an accent, but three or more provide a cluster of color. Large varieties can be trained as single-trunked trees, and dwarf types can be used in foundation plantings. Plantings do not mind the poorer soils and tolerate dry conditions. For all its beauty, all portions of the oleander are *extremely poisonous*. Teach family members not even to taste this plant. (TM)

When, Where, and How to Plant
Transplant from one area of the landscape to another between December and February. Add container plants at any time. A well-drained soil is best, but they also thrive in Florida sands. Gardeners often improve sands with compost or peat moss and manure, but it is not necessary. Dig a hole that's much wider than the rootball but not deeper. Position the oleander at the same depth it was growing in the container or original site. The top of the rootball may be set a little higher above the soil level, especially in poorly drained locations. After planting, form a berm, and add a 2- to 3-inch mulch layer.

Growing Tips
Oleanders can exist with the nutrients obtained from feeding nearby trees, shrubs, and lawns. Where extra growth is needed, they can be fed once in March, May, and September. Use a general landscape or slow-release fertilizer at label rates. This is a very drought-tolerant plant that needs watering only to encourage growth or withstand periods of severe drought. Normal rainfall is often sufficient.

Regional Advice and Care
Northern plantings and some in Central Florida are sure to suffer cold damage. Plants in cold locations may be frozen back to the ground but usually grow back from the base. Plants in warmer locations get tall and out of bounds. Provide a renewal pruning every few years. Prune in late winter to take out the dead and allow spring growth from the base. Pests include caterpillars, aphids, and scale insects. Handpick them or treat with a natural pesticide.

Companion Planting and Design
Probably it is best to keep oleanders away from walkways and play areas where children would be present. Use them to the rear of flower gardens and landscape designs. They can be used as backdrops for lower-growing plumbago, crinums, canna, pentas, and roses.

Try These
Gardeners can pick a dwarf form such as 'Petite Salmon' or 'Petite Pink'. Also available are colorful selections, including 'Hardy Red', 'Calypso', and 'Cardinal Red'.

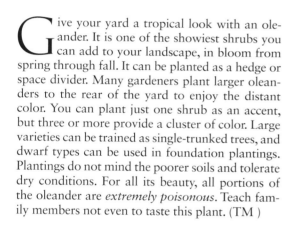

Pineland Strongbark

Bourreria cassinifolia

Botanical Pronunciation
boo-RARE-ee-ah ka-SIN-ah-pho-lee-ah

Other Name Little strongbark

Bloom Period and Seasonal Color
Warm season white flowers and orange fruit

Mature Height x Spread
6 feet x 6 to 10 feet

Little two- and three-flower clusters of white flowers, followed by orange fruit, keep this native shrub attractive all year, although flowers are most numerous in the warm months. The alternate leaves are small, with the tiniest little soft barb at the tips. Although it likes to billow, pineland strongbark is amenable to shaping. Best of all, the flowers often glisten with nectar, and bees and butterflies, even the occasional hummingbird, love it. As its common name tells us, it hails from South Florida's pine rockland, but also is found in the Caribbean. However, in Florida, the plant is listed by the state as endangered. (GBT)

When, Where, and How to Plant
Plant at the onset of the rainy season or any time throughout the warm months until August, when heat makes it difficult for plants to establish roots and transpire at the same time. Keep the soil moist for the first growing season. Plant with the root crown at the same level as it was in the container. Do not amend the soil, as this tough shrub is used to the rocky soils of South Florida. Initially, water and fertilize to help the shrub become established, and then stand back.

Growing Tips
Mulch will help regulate soil moisture and add some nutrients to the soil over time. It has no known pests, and with sufficient air circulation, this plant also will be disease free.

Regional Advice and Care
This is not a plant for North and Central Florida. It prefers Zones 10B–11.

Companion Planting and Design
Little strongbark is a wonderful addition to any South Florida native garden that features pine rockland plants. It also is an outstanding specimen plant in its own right. The Connect-to-Protect program at Fairchild Tropical Botanic Garden encourages homeowners to use pine rockland plants as a way to establish corridors for insects, germplasm, and critters of the ecosystem. Very little is left of this once-plentiful habitat. Because it is so widely used by butterflies, this can be a star of any butterfly garden and will feel at home with wild sage, locustberry, beautyberry, salvia, Bahama coffee, and milkweed.

Try These
Bourrera succulent, Bahama strongbark, is the bigger brother to pineland strongbark. It is found in the Florida Keys and throughout the Caribbean and northern South America. It grows to about 15 feet by 15 feet. It is a great nectar plant for Bahamian and Giant Swallowtail butterflies and many others. This shrub also is known as Bahama strongback.

Plumbago

Plumbago auriculata

Botanical Pronunciation
plum-BAY-go or-ick-you-LAY-tuh

Other Name Cape leadwort

Bloom Period and Seasonal Color
Spring through summer blooms in blue

Mature Height x Spread
3 to 4 feet x 8 feet

Cobalt blue flowers have taken the unexciting out of plumbago, a plant originally from South Africa. The blue of the 'Royal Cape' cultivar is worthy of Monet's pond. It is a jubilant color and jumps out of the cloud of green behind it. Although it straggles and sprawls unless pruned regularly, it also mounds and mushrooms, and it may be just what you need at an entry gate. Flowers are terminal, but growth is rapid and flowers return quickly after pruning. This is a host plant for the Cassius Blue butterfly. It is somewhat salt-tolerant, though you should not use it where it can catch spray. *Plumbago indica* is red flowering with many of the same characteristics of the blue *P. auriculata*. It commonly is called scarlet leadwort. (GBT)

When, Where, and How to Plant
Plant plumbago at the beginning of the rainy season, from late May to early June, or plant the shrub from March to midsummer if consistent irrigation is practical early on. Dig a hole twice as wide but just as deep as the rootball. If roots in the container are circling, then make several ¼-inch cuts in the rootball with a sharp knife to promote new, outward root growth. Because plumbago likes fertilizer, add compost or peat moss to make up one-third of the backfill to enrich the planting hole. Water in backfill to eliminate air pockets. Mulch to a depth of 3 or 4 inches, making sure the mulch is several inches away from the trunk of the shrub to prevent fungus.

Growing Tips
Use slow-release fertilizer in late February or early March, in July or August, and again at the end of October or early November. Although the plant is moderately drought-tolerant, water in the dry season. Long twigs of plumbago tend to fall over and root as well as sucker, so don't be afraid to use a firm hand with this beauty. Or, tie it to a support such as an arbor or a gate for a dramatic effect.

Regional Advice and Care
Plumbago prefers Zones 10–11. It may be grown in Central Florida, but it will be affected by freezing weather. Prune away damage after new growth appears in early spring. Prune back hard at the end of winter (late February in South Florida) to encourage pretty new growth. Flowers are terminal.

Companion Planting and Design
It can serve as a short shrub or even a giant groundcover and would complement magenta bougainvillea, yellow *Turnera*, or buttercup. Because it's low and sprawling, plumbago can serve as an underplanting to disguise the legginess of taller shrubs.

Try These
The deep sky-blue cultivar 'Imperial Blue' makes the most impact. Pair it with yellow shrimp plant.

Thryallis

Galphimia glauca

Botanical Pronunciation
GAL-fim-ee-ah GLAU-kah

Bloom Period and Seasonal Color
Spring through fall in yellow

Mature Height x Spread
8 feet x 6 feet

Zones 9–11

When the summer flowers start to fade, you can pop up the color with thryallis. Its bright yellow blossoms open along a terminal spike to put the color above the foliage. The blossoms start to open from late spring through fall, but some color may occur at any time of the year in the warmer areas of the state. Thryallis makes a good natural hedge or barrier. Establish thryallis as a cluster of several shrubs for a burst of color. Plants can also be set in the landscape as individual accents. Keep it back from walkways; the wood is brittle and may be damaged by traffic or maintenance. This evergreen shrub tolerates a frost and light freeze and, if damaged, grows back in spring. (TM)

When, Where, and How to Plant
Transplant thryallis from one area of the landscape to another between December and February. Container plants can be added to the landscape at any time. Be careful during transporting and planting to avoid breaking the limbs. Thryallis plants can survive light shade but at the lower light levels they develop a more open growth habit and limited flowering. A well-drained soil is best. The plants grow well in sandy soils. Many gardeners like to improve these planting sites with compost or peat moss and manure, but it is not necessary. Dig a hole that's much wider than the rootball but not deeper. Position the thryallis at the same depth as it was growing in the container or original planting site. The top of the rootball may be set a little higher above the soil level, especially in a poorly drained location. After planting, form a berm, and add a 2- to 3-inch mulch layer.

Growing Tips
Thryallis can exist with feedings given nearby lawns and flower beds. For best growth, feed once in March, May, and September. Use a general landscape or slow-release fertilizer. Thryallis can tolerate short periods of drought but grow best with weekly watering.

Regional Advice and Care
Because of its cold-sensitivity, thryallis is limited to Central and South Florida. In the colder regions, give the plants a protected location, and be ready to prune in late winter. All plantings grow lanky with time; give them an early spring rejuvenation pruning. Some pests include caterpillars and grasshoppers. Handpick pests from the plantings, or treat them with a pesticide recommended by the University of Florida, following instructions.

Companion Planting and Design
Plant thryallis as a backdrop for summer color with cannas, periwinkle, begonias, coleus, caladiums, pentas, and plumbago. It can also be used as a free-form hedge to enclose the landscape, but keep it out of the way of traffic and maintenance equipment to prevent limb breakage.

Try These
Only the species is marketed in Florida. The species *Galphimia gracillis* may be marketed, but it's likely the same plant.

Viburnum

Viburnum spp.

Botanical Pronunciation
vi-BURN-num

Bloom Period and Seasonal Color
Winter through spring blooms mainly in white

Mature Height x Spread
6 to 15 feet x 6 to 15 feet

Zones 8–10B

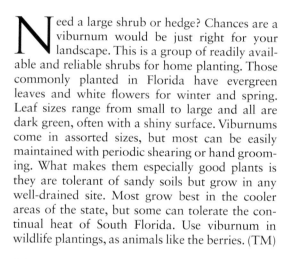

Need a large shrub or hedge? Chances are a viburnum would be just right for your landscape. This is a group of readily available and reliable shrubs for home planting. Those commonly planted in Florida have evergreen leaves and white flowers for winter and spring. Leaf sizes range from small to large and all are dark green, often with a shiny surface. Viburnums come in assorted sizes, but most can be easily maintained with periodic shearing or hand grooming. What makes them especially good plants is they are tolerant of sandy soils but grow in any well-drained site. Most grow best in the cooler areas of the state, but some can tolerate the continual heat of South Florida. Use viburnum in wildlife plantings, as animals like the berries. (TM)

When, Where, and How to Plant

Transplant viburnums from one area to another between December and February. Add container plants at any time. Viburnum plants prefer a full sun location but can tolerate some filtered shade. A well-drained soil is best. These plants grow well in sandy soils, but when possible, improve the planting site with compost or peat moss and manure before planting. It's best to dig a hole that's much wider than the rootball but not deeper. Position the rootball at the same depth it was growing in the container or with the top of it a little higher, especially in a poorly drained location. Form a berm at the edge of the rootball, and add a light mulch layer. Keep new plantings moist until established.

Growing Tips

Viburnums should be fed once in March, June, and September, to encourage growth. Use a landscape or slow-release fertilizer. Most viburnums are drought-tolerant but should be watered at least once a week during periods of drought.

Regional Advice and Care

Viburnums grow best where they receive some cool winter weather. During extremely cold winters, some species suffer limb damage that can be pruned away before spring growth begins. Many viburnums are sheared to form a hedge. This pruning is performed as needed. It's best if you pick a viburnum that needs minimal pruning so as to reduce landscape work. Some pests that affect viburnum are thrips, scales, white fly, mites, and downy mildew. Control with a natural pesticide, if possible.

Companion Planting and Design

Some viburnums grow tall and wide; select only the lower growing types for foundation plantings. Most make great hedges, space dividers, or backdrops for lower growing shrubs and flowers. Combine with other common landscape plants.

Try These

Viburnums for Florida include the sweet viburnum, *Viburnum odoratissimum*, that grows to 15-plus feet tall; the native Walter viburnum, *V. obovatum*, to 12 feet tall; Sandankwa viburnum, *V. suspensum*, to 6 feet tall; and Laurustinus viburnum, *V. tinus*, to 6 feet. Many have varieties you can select to fit your location.

Wax Myrtle

Myrica cerifera

Botanical Pronunciation
mah-REE-Kah sir-IF-er-ah

Bloom Period and Seasonal Color
Winter blooms in green to greenish yellow

Mature Height x Spread
15 to 25 feet x 15 to 25 feet

Native to the entire state, wax myrtle wanders among the cocoplum, the pond apples, and the sweet bay magnolia in the estuaries and strands of the Everglades, then heads into the hammocks and meanders through the open pinelands. It is twiggy and dense, but can be more open growing in light shade. Flowers are tiny and grow on catkins, which usually appear as early as December. The female flowers are green; male flowers are greenish yellow. Wax myrtles can grow into screens or be shaped into hedges. The plant sends up root suckers, but the aroma is so pleasant and uplifting that it outweighs the troublesome suckering. *Myrica heterophylla* is green bayberry, and *M. inodora* is an odorless bayberry. (GBT)

When, Where, and How to Plant
Plant at the beginning of the rainy season, late May to early June, or from March to midsummer if consistent irrigation is practical early on. Plant it wherever your heart desires. This is a supremely versatile plant. Dig a hole twice as wide but just as deep as the rootball. If roots in the container are circling, then make several ¼-inch cuts in the rootball with a sharp knife to promote new, outward root growth. Wax myrtle can flourish under moist as well as dry conditions; however, to allow the shrub to become established, keep the root zone moist (not soggy) during the first growing season.

Growing Tips
Sharp pruning shears for an occasional pruning and 8-4-12 fertilizer with micronutrients in spring and fall are about the only things needed for this hardy shrub after it is established. It will sucker from the roots, so you may have to keep it under control. But it will form screening clumps by virtue of this same habit.

Regional Advice and Care
Care is similar throughout Florida. Once established, the plants require very little care other than shaping or removal of root suckers.

Companion Planting and Design
It's an excellent plant for low-maintenance and native landscapes. Use wax myrtle for a screen or background plant or with other native shrubs. It grows too large for use next to your home. The male and female flowers are on separate plants, and the female's fruits occur in winter and are much appreciated by wildlife and birds. The vireos, catbirds, bluebirds, warblers, as well as many other birds, utilize the waxy fruit.

Try These
For a bird-attracting garden, this is a must. Soldierwood, *Colubrina elliptica*, a seldom-used and endangered Florida native large shrub/small tree, is another excellent choice, as it is a bird magnet during fall migration when tiny flowers line its branches, attracting insects that attract warblers. Wild coffee's red fruit in fall serves the same purpose.

Wild Coffee

Psychotria spp.

Botanical Pronunciation
sigh-CO-tree-ah

Bloom Period and Seasonal Color
Spring and summer, white flowers; red berries follow in late summer and fall and may stay into winter

Mature Height x Spread
6 to 15 feet x 5 to 6 feet

Zones 10B–11

When finely grown, wild coffees are among South Florida's loveliest shrubs. *Psychotria nervosa*, shiny-leaf wild coffee, has beautifully quilted leaves, tiny white flowers over the summer, and red fruit in fall and winter. The shrub stretches out and becomes lanky in the shade, but stays compact in partial to full sun. For shady conditions, *Psychotria ligustrifolia*, or Bahama wild coffee, is unbeatable. It also produces white flowers and red fruit, but has less shine to its smaller leaves. *Psychotria sulzneri* is soft-leaved wild coffee. The leaves have a slightly velvety texture and are gray-green. (GBT)

When, Where, and How to Plant

Plant wild coffee plants at the beginning of the rainy season, from late May to early June, or from March to midsummer if consistent irrigation is practical early on. Plant these coffees in partial shade to full sun. Filtered sunlight or sun in the morning or late afternoon will produce beautiful plants. The coffees like more moisture than many other natives because they are hammock plants. Mulch, to a depth of 3 or 4 inches, helps retain the moisture that coffees like.

Growing Tips

Keep the root zone moist until the shrub is established, then water during periods of drought. Coffee plants wilt when thirsty. Use a slow-release 8-4-12, two or three times a year for these plants to look their best. Or replenish compost in spring and fall, working it into the soil. Wild coffee will reseed itself in mulched areas of the garden. Without the proper air circulation, wild coffees will get scale. Prune away affected areas and look for ways to increase air flow around the plants.

Regional Advice and Care

Wild coffee takes well to pruning, but not shearing. Pruning in spring will make a fuller shrub; pruning done in summer, after renewal growth has flushed, serves to shape a shrub. This plant is recommended for use in South Florida. Wild coffee is not a landscape plant for Central or North Florida.

Companion Planting and Design

Wild coffee and Bahama coffee (*P. ligustrifolia*, whch is less often available) make beautiful hedges in semishade. Plant these shrubs beneath a lysiloma or wild tamarind, or cabbage palms that will provide shade and sun. White flowers are so small as to be insignificant, although butterflies and bees like them. The deep red berries in the summer are quite beautiful and beneficial for birds.

Try These

Grow the species. Shiny-leafed wild coffee, when growing on the edge of a hammock, is a familiar and reassuring sight as natural areas disappear. In the garden, the shrub's textured leaves and red berries are first rate.

TREES FOR FLORIDA

A Southern live oak may live for three hundred or more years. Its massive branches can stretch horizontally, if allowed, so that the canopy is wider than the tree is tall. Its furrowed bark and leathery leaves support millions of living creatures, smaller than we can see, and a good many large enough for us to discern: lichens, mosses, liverworts, a couple of squirrel nests, gnats, aphids, hairstreak butterfly larvae, germinating seeds of bromeliads, mats of resurrection fern and whisk fern, an ant highway, and a well-worn path of raccoons that teeter from topmost branches and watch the goings-on below. A whole world lives in this one organism, and on, around, and under it, while it, too, thickens, stretches, and lengthens through complex metabolic activities.

It pulls water from the ground at the rate of hundreds of gallons a day, and it takes in carbon dioxide from the air and releases oxygen. The mycorrhizae attached to its roots are probably connected to other trees around it, like the invisible strings of matter in the universe, linking and interacting with other trees. Dissolved minerals flow into the vascular tissue, up and out to the limbs and leaves. The cellulose of the cells is thicker on the tops of branches to act like muscles, allowing the tree to bear the great weight.

Slash Pine

Trees Are a Living Canvas

Florida has an enormous number of native trees that have adapted and evolved to suit the conditions in which they find themselves, from mangroves that grow in salt water to scrub oaks that make do in arid and infertile sands. Some of these natives are North Florida residents only and don't venture into the warmer parts of the state, and vice versa. Dogwood, sweet gum, black gum, sycamore, and linden stay away from the likes of gumbo limbo, fiddlewood, and sea grape. A handful of temperate trees venture south, including red maple, persimmon, and live oak. In the southern tip

Live Oak

of the peninsula and the Florida Keys, tropical trees of the West Indies such as West Indies mahogany, lignum vitae, and wild tamarind are found in sun-dappled forests and hammocks.

Be sure you know the mature size of trees you select for your home so that you can locate them properly in the right soils and drainage conditions, in ways that will cool and shade the house but won't threaten it in storms or invade the water pipes or the drain field. If a breathtaking flowering tree will be too large for your yard when it is mature, then you may want to find a shrub with the same color that will serve you better.

Think before You Dig

Look up when selecting a planting site. Are there power lines that will result in years of hard pruning for the tree you have in mind? If so, select a smaller tree. Before you begin digging, call your local utilities company to come out and check the site for underground pipes or cables. If you are planning to plant on a swale, remember it is public property. Contact your local building and codes department for restrictions.

If planting your own trees, you most likely will buy them in containers. Professional arborists who have the equipment that can more easily move the enormous rootballs should transplant large, field-grown trees.

When buying a containerized tree, slip the container off the rootball, and look at the root system. Roots should be white and healthy, not soggy or brownish black. They should fill the container but not poke out the bottom drain holes or circle the inside of the pot.

Avocado

Persea americana

Botanical Pronunciation
per-SEE-ah ah-MERH-ee-can-ah

Other Name Alligator pear

Bloom Period and Seasonal Color
February through March, greenish, green to
purple fruits mid-summer through early winter

Mature Height x Spread
30 feet x 30 feet

Zones 9B–11

Avocados are pretty trees with large green leaves that offer tasty fruits eaten fresh with a little salad dressing or used in salads and other dishes. There are many varieties to choose from, each with different characteristics. Even if you don't want the fruit of an avocado, it is a good tree for providing shade and visual framing for a home. The trees grow quite fast and the wood, therefore, is brittle. Residents in the colder areas should select a hardy variety that can withstand temperatures in the 20s Fahrenheit. Seed-started trees from saved pits are normally the least hardy. Avocados are usually picked from the tree hard and left to ripen indoors. They are also a favorite food of squirrels, so expect to share a few. (TM)

When, Where, and How to Plant
Avocados are best planted from a container during the warmer months starting in March. Position the tree at least 15 to 20 feet from buildings, sidewalks, and streets. Provide a site without overhead wires and away from drain fields. Avocado trees grow best in a well-drained soil; wet soils may lead to root rot. Prepare a hole that's two times wider than the rootball but no deeper. Plant the avocado so the top of the rootball is even with the soil line or a little above. After planting, create a berm at the edge of the rootball, and add a light mulch layer.

Growing Tips
Water every day for the first few weeks, and then gradually taper off to watering on an as-needed basis. Fertilize four to six weeks after planting. Continue feeding new trees every other month,

March through September. Fertilize established trees in March, June, and September with an avocado-type fertilizer. Established avocado trees require watering only during periods of severe drought—but for best production, water weekly.

Regional Advice and Care
Avocado trees needs pruning to keep a straight trunk and develop even branching. Major pruning is performed after harvest. Most gardeners like to limit the height of their trees to ensure an easy harvest. They can be kept around 20 feet tall by topping as needed. Choose cold-resistant varieties for Central Florida. When cold does affect the trees, late-winter pruning is needed. Pests include lace bugs, scales, caterpillars, and grasshoppers. Apply a control recommended by the University of Florida.

Companion Planting and Design
Start the tropical fruit collection with tall and wide-growing avocados. Some additional fruit trees for the planting might include citrus, mangos, lychee, and carambola. Avocados can also be added to large containers for patio culture.

Try These
Many avocado varieties have been developed for Florida planting. Some with the most cold resistance are 'Brogdon', 'Gainesville', 'Lula', 'Mexicola', 'Taylor', 'Tonnage', and 'Winter Mexican'. Other good varieties for warmer locations are 'Booth 7', 'Choquette', 'Hall', 'Monroe', 'Pollock', 'Ruehle', 'Simmonds', and 'Waldin'.

Bald Cypress

Taxodium distichum

Botanical Pronunciation
tax-Odd-ee-um DISS-tea-come

Bloom Period and Seasonal Color
Spring flowers are inconspicuous, fall yellow to bronze foliage color

Mature Height x Spread
100 feet x 30 feet

The native bald cypress are large deciduous evergreen trees that can grow in the water and are often seen at the edge of neighborhood lakes in Florida. Cypress roots develop short protrusions called "knees" that help stabilize the tree in mucky soils—or perhaps they help with gas exchange for the plant. The bald cypress is just as happy growing in sandy soils with limited amounts of water as it is growing in water. The needlelike leaves have a feathery appearance, giving a light airy feeling to the landscape. Throughout the summer the leaves are bright green. During the fall they turn a coppery color and drop from the trees. These are large trees best located as a shade tree away from the home and near the water. (TM)

When, Where, and How to Plant

Transplant bare-root trees during the dormant time of the year, normally between December and February. Container-grown bald cypress can be added to the landscape at any time. Position at least 20 to 25 feet from buildings, sidewalks, and streets. Provide a site without overhead wires and away from drain fields. Bald cypress is one of the few Florida trees that can grow in wet or dry soils. Dig a hole that is wider but no deeper than the rootball. Plant the tree so the top of the rootball is even with the soil line or a little above. If planted in a dry area, create a berm to catch and direct water though the rootball and add a light mulch layer. When planted in wet areas, trees establish quicker if the rootballs are not completely submerged.

Growing Tips

Keep bald cypress trees moist if planted in the drier areas. Some growers like to water every day for the first few weeks, and then gradually taper off to watering as needed. Trees planted out of the water are ready for their first feeding four to six weeks after planting with a general product. Continue the feedings in March and June for the first two to three years. Trees along the lakes and in water do not need special feedings. Established bald cypress trees growing out of the wet areas need watering only during severe drought.

Regional Advice and Care

Bald cypress grows throughout the state of Florida. It needs similar care in all areas. Prune during the winter months to keep a straight trunk and to develop even branching around the trunk. Caterpillars are sometimes a pest; if needed, the natural insecticide *Bacillus thuringiensis* can be applied.

Companion Planting and Design

Can be planted in the dry sites but best used lakeside. Add one or two trees with plantings of loblolly bay, wax myrtle, pickerel plant, horse-tail, bulrush, and arrowhead.

Try These

Only the species is available in Florida. The pond cypress, *Taxodium ascendens*, is often found growing near lakes and has a similar appearance.

Black Ironwood

Krugiodendron ferreum

Botanical Pronunciation
krug-ee-o-DEN-dron FAIR-um

Bloom Period and Seasonal Color
Flowers from spring to late fall

Mature Spread x Height
25 feet x 10 feet

Zones 9–11

A handsome tree that may reach 25 feet, black ironwood has the densest wood of any tree in North America. It will not float. A slow-growing tree, black ironwood comes from coastal hammocks and ranges from Cape Canaveral south through the Florida Keys, Mexico, and throughout the West Indies. The leaves have undulating margins, they form in opposite pairs, and the apex has a small notch. Flowers appear in spring and summer, and they are greenish yellow and quite tiny but have sufficient nectar to attract bees and butterflies. The fruits are black drupes and are eaten by birds and wildlife. The small trunk of an older tree is furrowed and craggy. (GBT)

When, Where, and How to Plant
Because it is a hammock tree, it prefers a more organic soil than plants of the pine rockland. And it loves full sun but will be fine in part shade. Plant in spring to early summer; mulch around the root zone, but keep mulch 2 inches away from the trunk. This is a slow grower, so don't hold your breath for it to shoot up in the first or second years. A slow-growing tree can be a plus in South Florida: usually this means it has wood strong enough to endure hurricanes. And with this tree, you can rest assured it will endure.

Growing Tips
Use aged compost with or as mulch to gradually enrich rocky or sandy soils. Use a low-phosphorus fertilizer two or three times a year to help push

growth. Once it is established, black ironwood should only require mulch/compost replacement. It will be quite happy with the water nature gives it, although in times of drought it should be watered.

Regional Advice and Care
Black ironwood can be used along Florida's east coast as far north as Cape Canaveral.

Companion Planting and Design
Because it is a bird-attracting plant, *Krugiodendron ferreum* is a good component of native or habitat gardens, featuring wax myrtle, soldierwood, satinleaf, and Jamaica caper. Black ironwood with Bahama coffee and firebush (if kept as a shrub) make a nice birdy threesome. Black ironwood's black fruits are borne between September and November, just in time for bird migration to South America.

Try These
Krugiodendron ferrum is a monotypic genus, meaning there is only one species in the genus. Leopold Krug was a German diplomat who did extensive botanical work in Puerto Rico.

Black Olive

Bucida buceras

Botanical Pronunciation
boo-SEE-da boo-SEAR-us

Bloom Period and Seasonal Color
April blooms in white

Mature Height x Spread
40 to 50 feet x 30 feet

Zones 10–11

Black olive is a tree for large yards or for use as a street tree. A moderately fast-growing tree, it has dark gray bark, simple leaves, and zigzagged branches. If you look carefully at the crown, you can see that it grows in tiers, like its relative the tropical almond. When selected for the right place and maintained properly, the black olive is a fine tree, resistant to wind and tolerant of salt breezes. It grows well on rocky soil. Black olives drop leaves and replace them throughout the year, so the tree is evergreen except after a cold spell. The flowers are tiny, appearing in April. *Bucida spinosa*, a native of the Bahamas, is a small tree that is often used as a bonsai subject. (GBT)

When, Where, and How to Plant

Plant a black olive from spring through midsummer. Plant in a large area so that the crown can develop without being cut back severely. Dig a hole as deep as the rootball and two to three times as wide. If you enrich the soil, use not more than one-third peat, compost, or aged manure to two-thirds of the backfill.

Growing Tips

Keep the rootball moist until the tree is established—which means until the growth rate of the new tree is that of a mature tree. Water daily for one month to three weeks, gradually taper off to every other day, and then every third day. Fertilize young trees three times a year, in late February to early March, June to July, and late October to early November, until established. Once mature, the black olive needs little attention, except for pruning. Its leaves will stain concrete.

Regional Advice and Care

Plant in a protected area or southern exposure outside southern Florida because the black olive can be cold-sensitive. Many black olives are hat-racked (limbs cut back to stubs). This practice causes massive resprouting and results in an extra-dense canopy that is vulnerable to wind toss. Some black olives develop long spiraling fruits as a result of galls from mites. Black olive can have whiteflies and mealybugs, but they do not seem to harm this robust tree.

Companion Planting and Design

This is a large shade tree that too often is used where a smaller tree would be a better solution. It requires a big space. When mature, it can be underplanted with bird's-nest anthuriums, big-leafed philodendrons, and bromeliads. Staghorn ferns and hoyas are plants that find black olive a generous companion.

Try These

The cultivar 'Shady Lady' has a compact growth habit and smaller leaves than the *Bucida buceras* regular or 'Oxhorn' bucida with leathery leaves at the ends of branches.

Bottlebrush

Callistemon rigidus

Botanical Pronunciation
KAL-LISS-ta-mon reh-GEA-dos

Bloom Period and Seasonal Color
Year-round blooms in red, pink, purple, and green

Mature Height x Spread
15 feet x 15 feet

Zones 9–11

Bottlebrush trees add a tropical look to the landscape. The flowers cluster along the ends of the stems, resembling red bottlebrushes for cleaning jars. This is a good accent plant for an area near the entrance, off the patio, or at the end of a view. The plants sporadically produce flowers throughout most of the year. They can be grown as an unclipped hedge and used as a view barrier. One species, *Callistemon citrinus*, resembles the species *Callistemon rigidus*. The main difference is a shorter, broader leaf that has a citrus aroma when crushed. *Callistemon viminalis* has a weeping growth habit. Some varieties of bottlebrush have flowers that are a deeper red than the standards. There are also bottlebrush trees that have green and violet flowers. (TM)

When, Where, and How to Plant
Transplant and plant container-grown trees during the dormant time, between December and February. Position this tree at least 10 to 15 feet from buildings, sidewalks, and streets. Plant bottlebrush away from drain fields. These trees grow best in a well-drained soil and grow well in sandy Florida soils. Dig a hole that is wider but no deeper than the rootball. Plant the bottlebrush so the top of the rootball is even with the soil line or a little above. After planting, create a berm at the edge of the rootball, and add a light mulch layer.

Growing Tips
Bottlebrush thrive with regular care throughout the state. Keep the bottlebrush tree moist after planting. Water every day for the first few weeks,

and then gradually taper off to watering as needed. This tree is ready for a first feeding four to six weeks after planting, with a general landscape or slow-release fertilizer. Continue the feedings, once in March and once in June, for the first two to three years. Established bottlebrush trees need watering only during periods of severe drought.

Regional Advice and Care
Bottlebrush trees are usually grown with several trunks that branch out from the base, starting a few feet from the ground. They may need pruning to help them develop an even branching habit. Prune during late spring after the major bloom. Pruning usually consists of removing limbs that interfere with traffic or plant care. Bottlebrush grows well throughout the central and southern parts of Florida. In Central Florida, give the plantings a warm location. Prune cold damage before spring growth begins.

Companion Planting and Design
Use as focal point accent trees or cluster several together as a view barrier. Plantings can be made near a patio or walkway to get a good view of the unique flowers. Use with shrubs that flower at other times of the year, including thryallis, plumbago, hydrangeas, and jasmine.

Try These
Most bottlebrush trees are sold by color, but a few varieties to look for include 'Little John', 'Red Cluster', and 'Captain Cook'.

Chinese Elm

Ulmus parvifolia

Botanical Pronunciation
UHL-moss par-VEH-fol-ee-ah

Other Name Lacebark elm

Bloom Period and Seasonal Color
Late summer, greenish yellow flowers; yellow leaves in fall

Mature Height x Spread
35 feet to 40 feet x 35 feet to 40 feet

Zones 8–9

Gardeners in need of a small tree will be quite happy with the Chinese elm. Seldom do you plant the pure species but usually add one of the selections for patio, street, or general landscape use. The trees are semievergreen, which means they lose their leaves during late fall to allow the sun in for a warm spot during winter. Gardeners also like the smaller leaves with a bright green look and the peeling bark that adds extra interest. As the trees grow older they develop an open habit that make them ideal for an under planting with shrubs and perennials that like just a little shade. Another relative for the landscape is the native winged elm *Ulmus alata*, which is also a small tree with interesting bark. (TM)

When, Where, and How to Plant

Chinese elms are full sun plants that can be grown as a single specimen tree or in a cluster of three or more spaced 25 or more feet apart. Because most selections are spreading in habit they are best planted 20 or more feet away from buildings. Open a hole that is wider but no deeper than the rootball. Plant so the top of the rootball is even with the soil line or a little above. After planting, create a berm at the edge of the rootball, and add a light mulch layer. The trees do need staking for a year, as they are often affected by winds when young.

Growing Tips

Keep the soil moist during the first year or two to help the trees establish a root system out into the surrounding soil. Thereafter they are quite drought-tolerant and can usually exist with moisture from seasonal rains. Feed lightly with a general landscape or slow-release fertilizer once in March and June during the first three years. Thereafter the trees can obtain needed nutrients from nearby lawn and shrub feedings.

Regional Advice and Care

Maintain a central leader until the trees are 6 to 8 feet tall, and then allow branching to establish a rounded to weeping look as appropriate for the variety. Most need periodic pruning to keep limbs above sidewalks and patio areas. The elms are usually pest-free but are a favorite feeding site during fall for squirrels that chew off the ends of limbs noticed on the ground. Leaf spots may be found on trees where air movement is not adequate for good tree growth.

Companion Planting and Design

Plant with other drought-tolerant selections in minimum-maintenance landscapes to reduce waterings after establishment. Use shade tolerant plants under the branches, including bromeliads, ivy, and Asiatic jasmine.

Try These

Often selected is the variety 'Drake Elm', with a weeping and wide spreading habit. Other more recent selections include a rounded 'Athena' and very upright 'Allee'. All grow into good small shade trees.

Desert Senna

Senna polyphylla

Botanical Pronunciation
SEN-uh polly-FILL-ah

Other Name Desert cassia

Bloom Period and Seasonal Color
Fall to spring in yellow

Mature Height x Spread
12 to 15 feet x 8-10 feet

Zones 9–11

A small tree with butter yellow flowers, desert senna is a good candidate for a townhouse and zero-lot-line yards. The canopy is open, the slender branches are weeping, leaves are tiny and pinnate. Its bark is dark to black. The West Indies native is said to flower there after a rain (it hails from dry habitats). In South Florida it blooms profusely in winter, but five-petaled flowers appear off and on throughout the year. The petals are uneven, with the bottom petal larger than the rest. Like other sennas, this is a larval host for the Orange, Cloudless, and other Sulphur butterflies. And although I frequently see Sulphurs on the canopy, I have never found caterpillars or chrysalids on either of my trees. (GBT)

When, Where, and How to Plant
Plant in spring or early summer so the tree can establish roots and bloom in the fall. Select a site where the tree can receive full sun and there is good air circulation. Water initially as you would other newly planted trees, then once new growth has begun, lightly fertilize. Reduce watering over the first growing season.

Growing Tips
This is a legume, which means it fixes nitrogen in the soil. And because it comes from arid conditions, I find it needs less water and fertilizer than many other tropical or subtropical trees. A low-nitrogen fertilizer is appropriate for the desert senna and only once or twice a year.

Regional Advice and Care
With a warming climate, some have reported that desert cassia is growing in the lower part of Zone 8. However, it still is a good idea to give this a southern exposure if living in Central and North Florida. Because of its size, desert cassia is a good candidate for container growing so it can be protected from cold fronts. A small spider likes to weave together leaflets on the ends of the branches. They don't harm the tree, but I sometimes cut them off because they can be unsightly. One nursery in Homestead has found the sap-sucking pink hibiscus mealybug on this tree. Mealybug destroyer and parasitic wasps are predators.

Companion Planting and Design
Use desert senna as a standalone specimen. Plant it where you can watch butterflies from a window. Add it to a butterfly garden, making sure it is not in shade. Yellow flowers are attractive to butterflies, and other yellow companions might include silkgrass (an aster), and pineland lantana.

Try These
Senna mexicana var. *chapmanii*, once called Bahama cassia, is native to Florida, Cuba, and the Bahamas. *Senna alata*, or candlestick cassia, produces upright racemes of brilliant yellow flowers.

Dogwood

Cornus florida

Botanical Pronunciation
CORE-nuss FLOR-ah-da

Bloom Period and Seasonal Color
Late winter white blooms, red fruits in fall

Mature Height x Spread
20 feet x 20 feet

Zones 8–9

One of the trees reminiscent of northern living is the flowering dogwood. Gardeners love the white to almost red flowerlike portions opening in spring. Gardeners in Central and North Florida won't have to leave the dogwoods behind but only the white forms are going to be good performers. Dogwoods need winter cold to be good flowering trees. They make great accents growing beside and in the light shade of larger trees. Some good specimens can be found in the full sun, but the light shade seems to remove some of the stress encountered in Florida. They make great fillers for woodland settings and can be used as a backdrop for other smaller shrubs and perennials. Select a Florida-grown tree already adapted to our environment. (TM)

When, Where, and How to Plant
Dogwoods do grow in the full sun, but they seem to be better adjusted to the filtered sun under taller trees in this state. Try to improve the sandy soils with lots of organic matter. Dogwoods prefer the moist but not wet soils and the organic matter with microbes that many feel can help the roots become established. Open a hole that is wider but no deeper than the rootball. Plant so the top of the rootball is even with the soil line or a little above. After planting, create a berm at the edge of the rootball, and add a light mulch layer.

Growing Tips
You do not own a dogwood for two years. That is how long it takes them to become established. Keep the plantings moist and maintain a 2- to 3-inch mulch layer over the root system but back a little from the trunk. Water to keep the soil moist but not wet, usually when the surface inch begins to dry, especially during the hot dry months. Provide light feedings in March and June using a slow-release landscape fertilizer for the first two years. Thereafter the trees can normally obtain needed nutrients from decomposing mulches and the feeding of nearby plants.

Regional Advice and Care
Only North and Central Florida gardeners can grow dogwoods. The trees need good care the first few years. Keep each trained to a single trunk, and maintain as many limbs as possible. Twig beetles often cause the ends of the limbs to decline. Limbs are best cut back into healthy wood as needed. Powdery mildew may be a leaf disease, but it is usually ignored.

Companion Planting and Design
Dogwoods grow well under tall oaks, sweet gum, and similar trees. They look especially good blooming in the spring with redbuds, native plums, and tabebuias. Combine them with camellias and azaleas, also late winter and spring bloomers.

Try These
Red and pink are normally not good choices for Florida landscapes. Try one of the white varieties, 'Cherokee Princess', 'Cloud 9', 'Weaver's White', and 'White Cloud'.

Geiger Tree

Cordia sebestana

Botanical Pronunciation
KORD-ee-uh seb-a-STAY-na

Other Name Orange Geiger tree

Bloom Period and Seasonal Color
Year-round blooms in orange

Mature Height x Spread
20 feet x 15 feet

Zones 10–11

The Geiger tree is one of the few flowering trees native to South Florida and the Florida Keys. Two Geiger trees at what is now the Audubon House in Key West are said to be more than 100 years old. The Audubon House originally belonged to Capt. John Geiger, a harbor pilot. John James Audubon stayed with the Geigers in 1832, when he painted many of the area's birds. The tree is named for Captain Geiger. The Geiger's leaves have the texture of sandpaper, and the crepe-textured flowers are bold orange, appearing throughout the year. Hummingbirds are attracted to the bright flowers. It's a tough little tree that is salt- and drought-tolerant, but not cold tolerant. (GBT)

When, Where, and How to Plant

Plant a Geiger tree any time from early spring through midsummer. Plant in full sun in a well-draining or dry area, perhaps with other native trees on the perimeter of the yard where irrigation doesn't reach. When transplanting from a pot, dig a hole three times as wide as the rootball and as deep. Situate the tree in the planting hole so that the top of the rootball is even with the soil surface. Fill in with soil from the planting hole. Use a hose to water in the soil as you fill the hole to remove any air pockets. Mulch to a depth of 3 to 4 inches. To avoid disease, be careful to keep mulch from getting next to the tree's trunk.

Growing Tips

Fertilize in the spring when the tree is young. Once established, this hardy tree needs little more than occasional irrigation in the dry season. It will drop leaves in cold weather and die back to the roots in a freeze but will resprout.

Regional Advice and Care

Used away from the coast in South Florida, the Geiger will need some winter protection, such as a windbreak of trees or a cozy southeast corner. This tree is not appropriate for Central or North Florida. The Geiger beetle can be a nuisance. A metallic green and blue beetle that menaces the trees in the spring, it can cause defoliation. Adults eat the leaves, and larvae damage roots. Use an insecticide containing carbaryl on the larvae. A single Geiger tree is less likely to attract beetles than several in close proximity.

Companion Planting and Design

Geiger trees may be planted with seven-year-apple and sea grape for a natural-looking setting along the coasts or simply honored by a place of its own. Use as background for a butterfly garden. The orange flowers are hard to pair with other flowering trees and yet will become part of a scheme with multiple colors of bright flowers.

Try These

Whereas the orange Geiger brings an unusual color to the landscape, the white-flowering *Cordia boissieri*, called Texas wild olive, is more pleasingly shaped and flowers profusely year-round.

Gumbo Limbo

Bursera simaruba

Botanical Pronunciation
BURR-sir-ah sim-ah-RUE-bah

Other Name Tourist tree

Bloom Period and Seasonal Color
Spring blooms are insignificant

Mature Height x Spread
30 to 40-plus feet x 20-plus feet

Zones 10B–11

From the coastal hammocks of South Florida and the West Indies, the gumbo limbo is instantly recognizable by its red to silver-red and peeling bark. Mockingbirds, vireos, and naturalized parrots noisily appreciate fruit, which develop over summer. When working with the gumbo limbo to plant or prune, you may notice a sticky sap that smells a little like turpentine. The sap once was boiled into a gum and used to make varnish or glue for canoes. Use mineral spirits to remove sap from your hands. Trees grown from seed have better root systems than those planted from limb cuttings. The leaves are compound, with three to seven opposite leaflets. Small, greenish flowers occur in winter to spring, and fruit follow but may take a year to ripen. (GBT)

When, Where, and How to Plant
Plant in sun or light shade in a spot with good drainage. The trees can be started from branch cuttings, but they often grow with unattractive, twisted, polelike trunks, whereas those from seed develop great character. That said, should you decide to plant a gumbo limbo branch, do this: make the planting hole 12 to 18 inches deep, and water the cutting faithfully until leaves begin to emerge, which can take several weeks. It pays to water the entire branch as well as the root zone.

Growing Tips
Once established, the gumbo limbo needs little care. Water in periods of drought; keep mulched. The tree is cold-sensitive and will drop leaves after cold snaps.

Regional Advice and Care
This is not a tree for use in Central and North Florida. The rugose white fly is a current pest problem for these trees. Often the white flies are so numerous that you can see them in the air when you are walking down a street. Their excretions also lead to a black covering on leaves, streets, or even cars below the trees. This "sooty mold" will reduce photosynthesis of the plants on which it occurs. There are natural predators for the white fly, but it takes a long time for them to appear, and currently the problem is widespread.

Companion Planting and Design
For light, high shade, a mature gumbo limbo is a great native. Because the bark is frequently shed, it is not a tree for epiphytes, such as orchids. The trunks can become almost sculptural, and should be seen, so the tuber sword fern or medium-sized bromeliads make good plants for the base. An older tree can develop remarkable girth, with heavy branches and a spare canopy. Its shade is more or less mottled and shifting. In late winter, the gumbo begins to lose leaves, and new growth can begin in late February or March. It makes a beautiful specimen tree. The tree is briefly deciduous.

Try These
When buying a young tree, look for the reddest bark you can find; silvery bark is not as attractive. Also, ask for a seed-grown tree.

Holly

Ilex spp.

Botanical Pronunciation
EYE-lex

Bloom Period and Seasonal Color
March to April; white to greenish, many with red berries for winter

Mature Height x Spread
20 to 40 x 15 to 25 feet

Zones 8–10

Hollies compose a large group of trees that provide shade and also serve as view barriers, hedges, and accents in the landscape. Perhaps the most popular is the American holly, *Ilex opaca*, with dark green spiny leaves and deep red berries, but it's the one that is used the least in most of Florida. Gardeners are more likely to plant the attenuate holly, *Ilex attenuata*, or the yaupon holly, *Ilex vomitoria*. For damp locations gardeners can also plant the dahoon holly, *Ilex cassine*. They are all exciting trees that offer numerous varieties to make them very adaptable landscape plantings. For the best color, gardeners should select the female varieties, which are usually the named selections that produce berries. (TM)

When, Where, and How to Plant

Container-grown hollies are an easy way to add new plantings to the landscape. Gardeners may also find balled-and-burlapped plants at garden centers. Most hollies like well-drained, acid soils. A few, including the dahoon species, grow in damp sites. Give them a full sun location. Hollies have a more upright growth habit than most other trees and can be planted at closer spacings of within 10 to 20 feet of other trees and buildings. Position the rootball in the ground so the top is at or slightly above the soil line. Add a 4- to 6-inch berm at the edge of the rootball to hold water during the establishment period, and a light mulch layer.

Growing Tips

Most hollies are drought-tolerant once established. They grow best with watering when other plantings are irrigated during drought. Feed once in March and June with a general landscape fertilizer for the first three years after planting. Thereafter the trees normally receive adequate nutrients from decomposing mulch and feedings of nearby shrubs and lawns. Most hollies change out their leaves during late winter, which is often of concern to gardeners. The leaf drop is in conjunction with lots of new growth that quickly renews the green.

Regional Advice and Care

Give the trees minimal trimming to allow the limbs to develop berries with fall and winter color. Lower limbs can be trimmed as needed to allow movement and maintenance under the trees. Where pruning is needed, sterilize the pruners between trees to prevent a gall-forming fungal disease from affecting the attenuate and American hollies. Otherwise the trees are relatively pest free and seldom need pesticide applications.

Companion Planting and Design

Hollies are best planted with other small trees and large shrubs. They are especially attractive with dogwoods, red buds, azaleas, hydrangeas, camellias, and gardenias that prefer acidic soils.

Try These

Yaupon holly trees have to be the most durable, withstanding poor soils. A weeping form is an attractive accent. Many holly hybrids are commonly planted, including 'East Palatka', 'Foster's', 'Savannah', 'Mary Nell', and 'Nellie R. Stevens'.

Lignum Vitae

Guaiacum sanctum

Botanical Pronunciation
GWHY-ah-cum SANC-tum

Other Name Holy wood

Bloom Period and Seasonal Color
Spring blooms off and on through summer;
blue-violet

Mature Height x Spread
15 to 20 feet x 10 to 15 feet

Zones 10B–11

Slow growing, with extremely hard wood and black heartwood, the lignum vitae is a tree much loved in Florida. The tree has a rich history, not only because of medicinal uses of the sap for arthritis, rheumatism, and skin diseases, but also because the wood itself is so heavy it will not float and has been employed in boat and even submarine construction. The United States Navy harvested trees from the Florida Keys during the 1940s, where the tree naturally occurs in Florida, and so few are left today that they are endangered. Lignum Vitae Key is a state botanical preserve and a protected site. The blue flowers are lovely, with contrasting yellow stamens, followed by fruit pods that split to reveal red drupes. (GBT)

When, Where, and How to Plant
Plant lignum vitae at the beginning of the rainy season or throughout early and midsummer. Plant this where guests entering the house, near a patio, can see the small flowers or grow it in a large container, where it may stay for years. Though extremely slow growing, lignum vitae can produce a considerable canopy when grown in the ground. Plant in full sun in a spot with excellent drainage. Follow normal planting procedure—keeping the root crown at the same level in the soil as it was in the container—without amending the planting hole.

Growing Tips
Make sure you keep the rootball moist after planting. Fertilize with 20-20-20 at half strength weekly for seedlings; use slow-release fertilizer every three to four months for larger trees. Transplanting is tricky. Root prune at least a month ahead in the rainy season; take the taproot with the rootball if possible; water daily, not only root zone but wood and canopy as well. Leaves will drop with transplant shock, but new ones will emerge.

Regional Advice and Care
This tree is recommended for use in South Florida only, where it is pest-free.

Companion Planting and Design
The blue of the flowers is unusual in a tree, so you would want to use this as a specimen, in your parking court, or at the front door. Or keep it in a mega-container of terracotta to show its character. The trunk can be pruned to display this character so the tree may resemble a rather over-large bonsai.

Try These
The national tree of Jamaica is *Guaiacum officinale*, which is more plentiful than *G. sanctum*, with lighter blue flowers. It sometimes is called roughbark lignum vitae. The specific name *officinale* means the tree once was used in medicinal compounds in the West Indies.

Live Oak

Quercus virginiana

Botanial Pronunciation
kwer-kus VIR-jin-ee-an-ee-ah

Bloom Period and Seasonal Color
February through March, brown

Mature Height x Spread
50 or more feet x 80 feet

Strong, long-lived, and beautiful, the live oak is a native plant highly prized as a shade or street tree. A single, mature live oak in a front yard may be ornament enough. Once the trees were thought to be slow growing, but fertilizer, water, and mulch when the trees are young can bring much faster results than benign neglect. Leathery, simple leaves are toothed when young and gray-green on the undersides. Young trees can be twiggy. As the crown grows, lower limbs die and drop. Oaks drop their leaves over a couple of weeks in February to March before new leaves flush. *Quercus laurifolia*, the laurel oak, is a taller (to 100 feet), shorter-lived tree. It can drop limbs because of weak wood. (GBT)

When, Where, and How to Plant

In more northern parts of the state, live oaks are planted in the dormant season. In the 1930s, the Florida legislature declared the state's Arbor Day to be in January because that was the best time to plant oaks. In South Florida, plant any time. Select a spot in sun and with ample room for the horizontally inclined limbs. Oaks can take a wide range of soils. Be sure to allow for canopy development. Builders often plant oaks too close together in an attempt to "tree" the property.

Growing Tips

Some oaks send up multitudes of root suckers if the soil around the root zone is disturbed. Mulch around the root zone or plant the area with a ground cover, such as ferns, which have shallow surface roots. Once the tree is established, little care is necessary. An oak in front of my house root suckers so profusely that the lawn service trims the seedlings as if they were a ground cover.

Regional Advice and Care

The large crown may require fine pruning to remove deadwood, but live oaks usually don't need hard pruning. Limbs grow naturally low and horizontally. Some of the most beautiful have been allowed to touch the ground around the city of Orlando's Lake Eola, and elsewhere. Live oaks thrive all over the South, many reaching their most beautiful character in North Florida, especially when they are draped with Spanish moss.

Companion Planting and Design

Whether in a hammock setting with other trees or as a singular shade tree, the live oak creates the perfect shade for nursing back to health any houseplants that are declining.

Try These

There are many other oaks in Florida, including the scrub oak that is found in an ecosystem called the scrub, a desertlike area that survived the last interglacial period. The scrub, which runs down the center of the state and has remnants in South Florida, has a flora and fauna distinct to itself, including the gopher tortoise and the scrub jay, both endangered species.

Mahogany

Swietenia mahagoni

Botanical Pronunciation
swee-TEA-knee-ah mah-HAG-uh-knee

Bloom Period and Seasonal Color
February through March, greenish, large fruits of interest follow

Mature Height x Spread
40 to 60 feet x 40 to 60 feet

Zones 10–11

Once a major lumber tree, the native Florida mahogany is now used mainly as a good landscape tree for the warmer climates. It's an upright-growing tree with a rounded crown that gardeners like to use for shade, to plant streetside, or to frame the home. It's a tree with good salt-tolerance, so it's suitable for planting in coastal landscapes. The shape of the tree makes it wind resistant, and the wood is tough. The leaves are persistent into the fall and winter months; in the spring, they quickly drop from the tree and new growth begins. Because the foliage casts a light shade it is possible to grow grass below it. This is a tree for a minimal-maintenance landscape. (TM)

When, Where, and How to Plant
Transplant between December and February. Add containers to the landscape at any time, though the cooler and more dormant times are best. Mahogany trees can tolerate some light shade. Position this tree at least 15 to 20 feet from buildings, sidewalks, and streets. Give street trees a 25- to 30-feet spacing. Provide a site without overhead wires and away from drain fields. Mahogany trees grow well in well-drained acid, alkaline, and sandy Florida soils. Open a hole that is wider but no deeper than the rootball. Plant so the top of the rootball is even with the soil line or a little above. After planting, create a berm at the edge of the rootball, and add a light mulch layer.

Growing Tips
Water every day for the first few weeks, and then gradually taper off to watering as needed. Feed four to six weeks after planting with a general landscape or slow-release fertilizer following label instructions. Continue the feedings, once in March and once in June, for the first two to three years. Established mahogany trees are drought-tolerant and need watering only during periods of severe drought. They do not need additional feedings after the first few years.

Regional Advice and Care
In South Florida, the mahogany is considered semi-deciduous. Planting is done when leaves are beginning to drop. Mahogany is cold-sensitive and restricted to use in frost- and freeze-free locations. Mahogany trees need winter pruning to keep a straight trunk and to develop even branching around the trunk. Pests include caterpillars and borers. Use a *Bacillus thuringiensis* caterpillar control, a borer spray, or other University of Florida-recommended controls.

Companion Planting and Design
Mahogany is a great tree to combine with other small to medium trees and greenery. Add the tropical look with bamboo, hibiscus, oleander, bird-of-paradise, and bananas. Use where light shade is needed.

Try These
The native mahogany is the only species used in the Florida landscape. Another Central and South American relative, *S. macrophylla*, is used for timber, growing too tall for ornamental landscape use.

Mango

Mangifera indica

Botanical Pronunciation
man-JIF-er-ah IN-duh-cah

Bloom Period and Seasonal Color
Winter blooms in yellow

Mature Height x Spread
30 to 50 feet x 30 feet

Zones 10B–11

One of South Florida's most treasured and delicious fruits, mangos are neighborhood friendly, making great shade and climbing trees as well as fruit trees, and can be long-lived. Mangos are big trees, having broad to round crowns, depending on the cultivar, although some dwarf types are available. Trees among the Indian types should be grafted to come true to seed. Fruit, depending on type and cultivar, mature from May to September. Plant cultivars that are resistant to anthracnose, such as 'Earlygold', 'Florigon', 'Van Dyke', 'Saigon', 'Edward', 'Glenn', 'Carrie', 'Tommy Atkins', and 'Keitt', 'Fairchild', 'Jean Ellen', and a host of newer cultivars have been developed at Fairchild Tropical Botanic Garden, which has an annual International Mango Festival in July. (GBT)

When, Where, and How to Plant
Plant your mango at the beginning of the rainy season (end of May or early June), throughout early and midsummer. Plant in a sunny location at least 30 feet from the house, where dropping fruit are not a problem. Plant where the tree does not receive irrigation. The fruit is best when the tree experiences a long dry season. Add organic amendments such as peat moss, compost, or aged manure, but do not allow them to exceed one-third of the backfill. Use a hose to water in the soil as you fill the hole to remove air pockets.

Growing Tips
Newly planted trees need faithful irrigation so that the root zone stays moist but not wet. Fertilizers such as 6-6-6 or 10-10-10 with additional 3 or

4 percent magnesium are good for juvenile trees. A fertilizer with high potassium is best for mature trees. Those grown at Fairchild Tropical Botanic Garden's farm are given only potassium. Use 1 pound for each inch of trunk diameter, measured 1 foot above the ground. Apply micronutrient sprays about three times a year in rocky soil, and use an iron drench once a year.

Regional Advice and Care
Smaller varieties, such as 'Carrie' and 'Cogshall' can be grown in protected areas in Central Florida. Many mangos are susceptible to anthracnose, a fungus that attacks leaves, twigs, and fruit. Often no harm is done to the fruit, although the skin may have tearstains running from the stem down the sides. Commercial growers spray frequently; homeowners don't have to unless the fungus is severe.

Companion Planting and Design
In South Florida, more than four hundred cultivars are now growing at Fairchild Tropical Botanic Garden's farm. Keep the root zone mulched, but avoid planting expensive or rare plants beneath it, because fruits can damage what they hit.

Try These
The 'Edward' cultivar is my favorite mango, tastewise, but 'Nam Doc Mai' is not far behind. 'Irwin' is a less robust tree, easier to manage and delicious, though prone to anthracnose. 'Keitt' has a great flavor. It's really hard to decide, but every South Floridian has a different favorite.

Pigeon Plum

Coccoloba diversifolia

Botanical Pronunciation
ko-ko-LOW-bah di-verse-a-FO-lee-ah

Bloom Period and Seasonal Color
Spring blooms in white; fruit dark red to purple

Mature Height x Spread
30 to 50 feet x 15 to 20 feet

Zones 9–11

Pigeon plum is plentiful in the coastal hammocks, from the center of the state to the Keys. And increasingly, it is being used in landscaping. Its dense, columnar crown and pretty bark make it useful for street planting as well as for framing a house, even in a formal design. The simple, bright green leaves are generally large when the tree is young and reduced in size when it is older. With the appearance of flowers, in March or thereabouts, comes the first flush of new leaves. A second follows later in spring. Fallen leaves turn distinctively golden on the forest floor or in your backyard lawn or mulch. The fruit of this tree is eaten by the white crowned pigeon, hence its name. (GBT)

When, Where, and How to Plant
Plant this tree in sun or shade, with natives or even in formal settings. The pigeon plum is able to thrive in harsh conditions; it takes wind and drought well. There are male and female trees. Dig a hole as deep as the rootball and two to three times as wide. Remove the container from the rootball, and position the tree in the planting hole. Water in the soil as you fill the planting hole to eliminate air pockets that kill roots. Mulch, keeping mulch 2 or 3 inches away from the trunk to avoid disease. The female trees often have raccoon scratches on the trunks when seen in the wild. And trunks are recognizable by their splotchy bark.

Growing Tips
Water and fertilize consistently when the tree is young to help it get a good start in life. When your pigeon plum is a few years old, you can let go of the reins. If growing in a shady group of natives, a pigeon plum will grow tall and narrow; in sun, it will be shorter and fatter.

Regional Advice and Care
Use this tree in coastal areas of Central Florida. Care is similar. It is not for use in North Florida. Pigeon plum grows throughout the Bahamas and the Antilles, and in Florida from Monroe and Miami-Dade Counties into Broward and Lee. It is a mainstay of the forests on North Key Largo.

Companion Planting and Design
Use as a formal planting along a wall, or an informal grouping in a native habitat. This versatile tree can blend with stoppers, wild coffee, Florida privet, beautyberry, and other plants of coastal woodland areas. This is a versatile tree, upright and handsome in any setting, but when in the company of stoppers, soldierwood, wild tamarind, and other bird-attracting trees, it will serve birds well.

Try These
Coccoloba uvifera, the sea grape, is a close relative. There are male and female trees, with females producing hanging clusters of grapes.

Redbud

Cercis canadensis

Botanical Pronunciation
SER-sis KA-nah-den-sis

Other Name Judas tree

Bloom Period and Seasonal Color
Spring pink flowers, fall leaf color yellow
to bronze

Mature Height x Spread
25 feet x 25 feet

Zones 8–9

Redbud trees help announce spring's arrival with a unique display of pinkish blooms along the stems. This is a special flowering habit as the buds are held flush against the stems. The tree is also interesting for its heart-shaped leaves, which in some selections open a magenta color before turning green. Here is a tree that is ideal for the small landscape. It is an accent and shade tree all in one. The trees can also grow in the full sun or light shade. Set them as a backdrop for gardens, along walkways, and near entrances. This is a deciduous tree dropping golden yellow leaves during the fall. It needs little care, which makes it nice for the minimal-maintenance landscape. (TM)

When, Where, and How to Plant

Redbuds grow in any well-drained soil in full sun to light shade. They prefer enriched sites, so consider adding organic matter to sandy soils if you can improve a large area. Plant bare-root trees during the winter months and container trees any time of the year. The trees grow small in size but are best planted 15 feet or more from sidewalks, drives, and buildings. Open a hole that is wider but no deeper than the rootball. Plant so the top of the rootball is even with the soil line or a little above. After planting, create a berm at the edge of the rootball, and add a light mulch layer.

Growing Tips

Keep the plantings moist and maintain a 2- to 3-inch mulch layer over the root system but back a little from the trunk. Water to keep the soil moist but not wet, usually when the surface inch begins to dry, especially during the hot dry months. Provide light feedings in March and June using a slow-release landscape fertilizer for the first two years. Thereafter the trees can normally obtain needed nutrients from decomposing mulches and the feeding of nearby plants.

Regional Advice and Care

Plant redbuds in North and Central Florida, as they need cold to mature their leaves and flower buds for spring. Grow with a short trunk and allow branching to begin at 4 to 5 feet. Train to a rounded shape. Give a light trimming in February to remove crisscrossing limbs and declining tree portions. This is also a good time to remove any remaining seedpods from summer. Trees grow best when kept moist, but they can tolerate drier sites.

Companion Planting and Design

Plant alone or with other spring flowering trees, including dogwoods, native plums, and tabebuias. Plants that grow well under the trees include jacobinia, azaleas, impatiens, Asiatic jasmine, and liriope.

Try These

A number of varieties have been selected, including 'Alba', with white blossoms; 'Forest Pansy', with purplish new foliage; and 'Oklahoma', with purple blooms. A similar species, *C. chinensis*, can also be grown in cooler landscapes.

Red Maple

Acer rubrum

Botanical Pronunciation
A-sir ROO-brum

Other Name Scarlet maple

Bloom Period and Seasonal Color
Red foliage in the fall

Mature Height x Spread
40 to 50-plus feet x 30 feet

Zones 8–10B

The red maples of the Everglades do not grow with their feet in deep water, but they can be found nearby and in slightly drier areas or periodically wet hammocks with acid soils. Red maples, you may have guessed, have a low tolerance for drought. At the southern end of its range, the red maple is variety 'Trilobum', with three pointy leaf lobes edged in teeth to distinguish it. It does not venture into the tropical Florida Keys. In addition to its red fall color, the leaves have leaf stems or petioles that are red, as are its flowers that appear in December and January. Silver maple, *Acer saccharinum*, occurs in North Florida. (GBT)

When, Where, and How to Plant
Plant in late winter. In South Florida's natural areas, the seeds germinate in the dry season and shoot up before rains return and flood the swamps. Shallow-rooted, red maples have brittle wood and can break in storms. Look for trees with a single leader to prevent splitting. Plant in full sun in a low-lying, wet area. When transplanting from a pot, dig a hole two to three times as wide as the rootball and just as deep. Remove the container from the rootball; situate the tree in the planting hole so that the top of the rootball is even with the soil surface. Add at least one-third as much organic material to the planting soil from the planting hole, as red maples like rich soil. Use a hose to water in the soil as you fill the hole to remove any air pockets. Mulch.

Growing Tips
Little care is required if the tree is properly located. Some South Florida cities have elected to plant red maples in swales—those low-lying drainage areas found in front of suburban homes—so they can take advantage of the water that runs off roads.

Regional Advice and Care
Use other maple species or varieties in Central and North Florida. Flowers tend to be male or female on the same tree, but sometimes they occur on different trees. Fruits develop quickly after December flowering and may be ripe by January or February before new leaves appear.

Companion Planting and Design
This is a big, handsome tree adapted to wet areas. If you have a lakefront or low-lying wet area, use red maple with cabbage (sabal) palms, leather fern, and dahoon holly. As a general rule, wetland plants may be planted upland, but upland plants do not grow in wetlands.

Try These
There are many good varieties; ask your favorite nursery to recommend one for your area.

Satinleaf

Chrysophyllum oliviforme

Botanical Pronunciation
kry-so-FILL-um awl-liv-ih-FOR-me

Bloom Period and Seasonal Color
Year-round blooms in white; purple fruit

Mature Height x Spread
30 feet x 15 feet

Zones 10–11

Few other trees have leaves as beautiful as those of the satinleaf. When they dance in the wind and show the backs of their hunter green leaves covered with bronze or copper hairs, they become the Fred Astaire of trees, all dazzle and grace in movement and light. The crown is erect and, in shade, the tree will squeeze through small spaces to reach light. The long, loppy branches tend to come out on one plane when the tree is young. When you plant it, notice that direction so you don't end up replanting the tree later. The little flowers occur in the leaf axils; purple fruit is not edible by humans, but is good for wildlife. (GBT)

When, Where, and How to Plant

Plant a satinleaf tree in a grouping of native trees or in a perimeter planting. The tree is drought-tolerant and once established doesn't require irrigation. The branches are long and often without many twigs. Planting instructions, as for any tree, are digging a hole two to three times as wide and just as deep as the rootball. Although satinleaf deserves a special spot, it may be damaged by hurricanes, and protection by other trees is a good idea.

Growing Tips

Keep roots moist throughout the first growing season. Fertilize with an acid-forming fertilizer according to package directions as the tree prefers slightly acid soils. Once the tree becomes a large specimen, mulching consistently should be ample care.

Regional Advice and Care

Plant along the coasts up to the center of Florida; inland, it will freeze back when unprotected. Seedlings may proliferate around the base and can be dug at any time.

Companion Planting and Design

The sweetly scented flowers, according to P. B. Tomlinson in *The Biology of Trees Native to Tropical Florida* (Harvard University), can persist a long time before they open and may be stimulated to open after rain. Fruits are dark purple berries, which make this a good tree for attracting birds to your yard. If landscaping for wildlife, use this tree with wild coffee, pigeon plum, sea grape, cocoplum, and other fruit-bearing natives that offer birds and small animals food and shelter. Used as a specimen tree, the copper undersides of satinleaf are clearly visible when the wind blows or when you're beneath it looking up.

Try These

Equally pretty is a relative with larger leaves and edible fruit. This is the caimito, *Chrysophyllum cainito*. In the West Indies, it is a "dooryard" fruit, with sweet, granular flesh.

Sea Grape

Coccoloba uvifera

Botanical Pronunciation
coco-LOW-bah you-VIFF-er-ah

Bloom Period and Seasonal Color
Year-round white flowers followed by
purple fruits

Mature Height x Spread
20 to 25 feet x 20 feet

Zones 9B–11

Gardeners in warmer locations should plant the sea grape, if for no other reason than its exotic look. Even in the cooler spots, a protected site can be chosen. The leaves are circular in shape and grow to 8 inches in diameter. Each leaf has red veins, and the entire leaf turns red before dropping. This is a small, broad, spreading tree with a very open branching habit. The sea grape is quite salt-tolerant. Clusters of edible purple fruits are produced by female trees throughout the year in the warmer locations. Use sea grapes as view barriers, accent trees, and space dividers. When planted near a patio they are bound to be conversation starters. They are ideal for the minimum-maintenance landscape. (TM)

When, Where, and How to Plant
Add containers of sea grape to the landscape at any time, though the cooler and more dormant times are best for planting. Position this tree at least 5 to 10 feet from buildings, sidewalks, and streets. The sea grape can usually be used in sites with overhead wires. Sea grapes grow best in a well-drained soil and are very tolerant of salt exposures. Sea grape grows well in sandy Florida soils. Enriching planting sites with compost or peat moss and manure makes care easier. Open a hole that's about two times wider than the rootball but no deeper. Plant at the same depth it was growing in the field or container. Create a berm, and add a 2- to 3-inch mulch layer.

Growing Tips
Water every day for the first few weeks, and then gradually taper off to watering as needed. The tree is ready for a first feeding with a slow-release fertilizer four to six weeks after planting. Continue the feedings, once in March and once in June, for the first two to three years. Established trees are drought-tolerant and need watering only during periods of severe drought. They do not need additional feedings after the first few years.

Regional Advice and Care
All sea grapes are cold-sensitive, limiting most to South Florida and the coastal areas of Central Florida. Inland plantings of Central Florida need winter protection. In South Florida, plant in spring (if you plan to water consistently) or at the start of the rainy season. Sea grape trees need winter pruning to keep a straight trunk and to develop even branching around the trunk.

Companion Planting and Design
Use in view barriers as a standalone planting. Or use as an accent in foundation plantings or near patios with Indian hawthorn, lantana, coontie, beautybush, firebush, and fetterbush.

Try These
Only the species is available in Florida. Consider planting some relatives like the pigeon plum, *Coccoloba diversifolia*, a medium native tree that grows to 40 feet tall. The big-leaf sea grape, *C. pubescens*, is sometimes planted in the landscape or a container for its 3-foot-diameter foliage.

Southern Magnolia

Magnolia grandiflora

Botanical Pronunciation
mag-NOL-lee-ah gran-DAH-floor-ah

Other Name Bull bay magnolia

Bloom Period and Seasonal Color
May through July; sporadically the rest of summer, white flowers; brown pods; red seeds in summer

Mature Height x Spread
40 to 90 feet x 30 to 40 feet

Zones 8–10B

No tree represents the South more than the Southern magnolia, with its large green leaves and fragrant white flowers. Many are planted not too far from the home or patio to take advantage of the late-spring blooms. Selections grow from medium to large trees—ideal to frame a home site or serve as a backdrop for landscape plantings. This is an evergreen tree that can provide shade for the hotter months and then make a good windbreak during the winter. Most gardeners just ask for a magnolia, but you should request this tree by variety. A number have been selected that can provide early flowering and leaf interest. Many have a brown lower surface that's obvious when moved by the wind. (TM)

When, Where, and How to Plant

Gardeners can add a new container-grown or balled-and-burlapped magnolia to the landscape at any time of the year. It's best to pick a time when you can provide adequate water, as the trees appear to be very moisture-sensitive during the establishment period. Give the trees a full sun location and position 25 or more feet from a building or outer limbs of other trees. Be sure the top of the rootball is positioned at or slightly above the level of the soil. Create a berm of soil around the edge of the rootball to catch and hold water during the establishment period. Add a light mulch layer. Keep the soil moist with frequent waterings until established.

Growing Tips

Magnolias grow in moist soils and are drought-tolerant when established. Best growth is made when they are watered with lawns and other shrub plantings. Feed the trees in March and June with a general landscape or slow-release fertilizer for the first three years to encourage growth. Thereafter, feedings are normally not needed. Keep the soil mulched within 4 to 5 feet out from the trunk.

Regional Advice and Care

Allow the limbs of magnolias to grow near the ground or trim them off as needed to allow walking or traffic flow under the trees. The trees do shed most of their leaves during the late winter and spring months, which often makes gardeners think they are declining. This is normal and new growth soon follows. Scale and black sooty mold can be ignored or controlled with an oil or systemic insecticide as needed.

Companion Planting and Design

It's often difficult to find plants to grow under magnolia trees, but bromeliads don't seem to mind. Also plant Asiatic jasmine, begonias, ivy, and impatiens.

Try These

Some selections available at garden centers include 'Bracken's Brown Beauty', 'Little Gem', and 'Saint Mary'. 'Little Gem' flowers at an early age and over an extended period of time. Gardeners should also consider the sweet bay magnolia, *M. virginiana*, a native especially good for moist sites.

Stoppers

Eugenia spp.

Botanical Pronunciation
yew-JEAN-ee-ah

Bloom Period and Seasonal Color
White flowers off and on throughout the year, most in spring; black fruit

Mature Height x Spread
20 feet x 10 feet

Zones 10B–11

A long "drip-tip" on shiny leaves is your key to identifying redberry stopper, the rarest of the so-called "stoppers" that are small understory hammock trees. A drip-tip is an elongated, pointy apex of the leaf that allows raindrops to drip from the surface—a characteristic of many tropical trees found in areas of high rainfall. The strong musky smell of the white stopper, *Eugenia axillaris*, perfumes the air in our hammocks. Many of the old stoppers in Miami have fallen to housing developments, especially along the bay front, but many more should be planted because of their beauty and small size, including Spanish stopper, *Eugenia foetida*, and Simpson stopper, *Myrcianthes fragrans*, with beautiful red and peeling bark. All like a moist soil and produce nectar-filled flowers and fruit for birds. (GBT)

When, Where, and How to Plant
Understory trees tolerate the shade of the hammock. A useful screen is a mix of stoppers, which will grow together, up to 12 to 20 feet. To use as a screen, plant on 5-foot centers in a zigzag pattern. Plant as you would other trees, making sure you water in the backfill to remove air pockets. Be sure to mulch around the root zones, and keep mulch away from the trunk. Stoppers generally are slow growers with hard wood, but they are worth cultivating, particularly because of their use by bees and migratory birds.

Growing Tips
Keep the planting area moist for the first growing season. In severe drought, you may have to water if you detect wilt. Stoppers like fertilizer in moderate amounts—the leaves will complain when the tree is hungry, turning a little yellow. Because they are well adapted to South Florida, reading the leaves for signs of fertilizer needs is better than just applying fertilizer routinely.

Regional Advice and Care
Stoppers are recommended for use in South Florida.

Companion Planting and Design
Adapted to rocky soil, these are wonderful trees for small gardens and patios or with a group of natives. Wild coffee, either *Psychotria nervosa* or *Psychotria bahamensis*, works exceptionallywell with stoppers. Plant several stoppers along a fence or in a group, and you will learn to identify these hard-to-tell-apart plants. I have a hedge of wild coffee planted in front of my stoppers so the coffee will provide low screening as the trees get taller.

Try These
Spanish stopper has rounded leaves that curl under slightly at the edges; white stopper has light bark and pink new growth; Simpson's stopper tends to be multitrunked and has peeling red bark; red stopper, *Eugenia rhombia*, also has a distinctive drip tip.

Sweet Gum

Liquidambar styraciflua

Botanical Pronunciation
lick-wah-DAM-bar sty-RAH-siff-lou-ah

Bloom Period and Seasonal Color
Yellowish small flowers cluster late winter; fall foliage is yellow, red, and purple

Mature Height x Spread
50 feet x 20 feet

Zones 8–9

The sweet gum is one of the truly reliable native trees that has a good shape and won't get too tall for the average landscape. It's ideal for smaller properties. The trees are upright and pyramidal in habit. The shape of the leaf, with its five to seven lobes, gives it a starlike appearance. It is often confused with the red maple. As the limbs grow older, they often produce a corky ridge. Don't get alarmed—this is not a scale insect, and the growths are normal. Mature sweet gums produce a seed ball with prickles that can hurt bare feet so do keep it away from walkways. Use the sweet gum as a street tree, a backdrop for other shrubs, and a shade tree with good fall color. (TM)

When, Where, and How to Plant

Add container specimens to the landscape any time, though the cooler and more dormant times are best for planting. Give sweet gums a full sun to slightly shady location. Position at least 15 to 20 feet from buildings, sidewalks, and streets. Provide a site without overhead wires and away from drain fields. Sweet gums grow best in a well-drained soil and in Florida sands. Some like to enrich planting sites with compost or peat moss and manure, but it is not necessary. Open a hole wider but not deeper than the rootball. Be sure the top of the rootball is positioned at or slightly above the level of the soil. Create a berm of soil around the edge of the rootball to catch and hold water during the establishment period. Add a light mulch layer starting six inches from the trunk.

Growing Tips

Keep the sweet gum tree moist. Water every day for the first few weeks, and then gradually taper off to watering as needed. Feed four to six weeks after planting with a general landscape or slow-release fertilizer. Continue the feedings, once in March and once in June, for the first two to three years. Established sweet gum trees are very drought-tolerant and need watering only during periods of severe drought. They do not need additional feedings.

Regional Advice and Care

All sweet gums grow through North Florida down to the uppermost portions of South Florida. Sweet gum trees need a late winter pruning to keep a straight trunk and to develop even branching around the trunk. Pests that commonly affect sweet gums include caterpillars and thrips. Use *Bacillus thuringiensis* caterpillar control, an oil spray, or other University of Florida-recommended control, following label instructions.

Companion Planting and Design

This is a great tree for smaller yards with upright growth. Plant with maple, pine, and river birch.

Try These

A number of native sweet gum varieties have been selected for landscape plantings, including 'Festival', a columnar form; 'Moraine', with reddish fall foliage; 'Purple Majesty', with good fall color; and 'Variegata', with green-and-cream-colored foliage.

Tabebuia

Tabebuia spp.

Botanical Pronunciation
tah-BAH-boo-ee-ah

Other Name Trumpet tree

Bloom Period and Seasonal Color
Late winter to spring blooms in yellow or pink

Mature Height x Spread
15 to 40 feet x 40 feet

Zones 9B –11

At least two tabebuias with yellow flowers are commonly grown in home landscapes. *Tabebuia caraiba*, or silver tabebuia, grows mainly in South Florida, and *Tabebuia chrysotricha*, or golden trumpet tree, grows from Central Florida southward. Both are showstoppers with bright yellow flowers produced during the late winter to early spring months. The flowering period lasts for up to a month, and the fading blossoms drop to the ground to produce a yellow carpet. They hold their leaves through the winter and drop them just before the flowers appear. Some additional yellow-flowering tabebuias found in Central and South Florida are *Tabebuia chrysantha* and *Tabebuia umbellata*. A very popular pink flowering tabebuia is *Tabebuia impetiginosa*, which has similar growth habits and is often called 'Ipe'; it also flowers during the winter. (TM)

When, Where, and How to Plant
Add container plants to the landscape at any time of the year. Position at least 10 to 15 feet from buildings, sidewalks, and streets. Tabebuias grow best in well-drained soils, including the Florida sands. Many like to enrich sandy planting sites with compost or peat moss and manure, but it is not necessary. Dig a hole that's about two times wider than the rootball but no deeper. Be sure the top of the rootball is positioned at or slightly above the level of the soil. Create a berm of soil around the edge of the rootball to catch and hold water during the establishment period. Add a light mulch layer starting six inches from the trunk.

Growing Tips
Keep the tabebuia tree moist. Water every day for the first few weeks, and then gradually taper off to watering as needed. Feed four to six weeks after planting with a general landscape or slow-release fertilizer. Continue the feedings, once in March and once in June, for the first two to three years. Established tabebuia trees are drought-tolerant and need watering only during periods of severe drought. They do not need special feedings after the first few years.

Regional Advice and Care
The northern limit for tabebuias is mid-Central Florida. In this upper region, the trees need the warmest location in the landscape. Areas near a lake are best, as they remain a few degrees above the coldest winter temperatures. If they become frozen, the trees do grow back, but they need training to keep one central trunk. Trees should be pruned to remove crossed or dead limbs after flowering has finished.

Companion Planting and Design
So spectacular is the bloom that you will want to use the tabebuia as a specimen tree, perhaps near the walk to the front door, where you can accent it with sun-loving roses, plumbago, and coreopsis.

Try These
Pick a tabebuia with your section of the state in mind. *Tabebuia chrysotricha* has the most intense gold color, and *Tabebuia* 'Ipe' has the new year pink blooms all enjoy.

Texas Wild Olive

Cordia boissieri

Botanical Pronunciation
KOR-dee-ah BWA-see-air-ee

Other Name White Geiger

Bloom Period and Seasonal Color
Year-round blooms in white

Mature Height and Spread
About 20 feet x 10 to 15 feet

Zones 8B–11

A small tree that blooms with funnel-shaped white flowers year-round and has no major diseases, the Texas wild olive is a wonderful landscape component. In addition to its practicality, it's a handsome tree with a round canopy and dark green, sandpapery leaves. A member of the Boraginaceae family, this tree's flowers, with golden throats, are sprinkled over the canopy in small, neat, terminal clusters. Like all white flowers, they stand out in the moonlight. Texas wild olive makes a beautiful front yard tree, where it can charm passersby. It is not sensitive to cold, as is its cousin, the orange-flowered Geiger tree (*Cordia sebestena*), and the large shrub to small tree, the yellow-flowered *Cordia lutea*. This appears to be a superb tree for landscape use in South Florida. (GBT)

When, Where, and How to Plant
Plant Texas wild olive any time except November through January. Use a hose to water in as you shovel in backfill. Mulch heavily around the root zone so mulch is about 4 inches deep but not touching the trunk. Keeping mulch a couple of inches from the trunk will avoid disease. It can take a wide range of soils, including South Florida's alkaline soil.

Growing Tips
Keep the root zone moist for the first growing season, and gradually allow nature to take over. Texas wild olives don't like to be in areas that flood or to be near sprinklers. Otherwise these hardy little trees have no special problems. Fertilize with appropriate amounts of fertilizer formulated for palms, 8-4-12 with micronutrients, slow-release nitrogen and potassium. The fall application of fertilizer for flowering and fruit trees is sometimes a low-nitrogen one to dissuade them from producing too many young leaves over winter, but this tree seems oblivious to seasonal changes and not only handles cold but blooms throughout.

Regional Advice and Care
They may flower at quite an early age, perhaps even at a foot high. No major pruning is necessary. Eliminate dead wood, rubbing, or diseased branches in the late winter or early spring.

Companion Planting and Design
Because of its size, this flowering tree could be used near an entryway, in a swale, or set off by itself as a specimen tree. Its good behavior and blooming habit make it a candidate for wider planting as a street tree, able to produce flowers for tourists all year. Choose other drought-tolerant plants, such as trailing lantana (*Lantana montevidensis*), liriope, kalanchoe, or plumbago. Used as a small specimen tree to give it maximum visibility, this one is excellent.

Try These
Cordia bahamensis, found in the Bahamas and once found in South Florida, is a shrub.

Wild Tamarind

Lysiloma latisiliquum

Botanical Pronunciation
lie-suh-LOW-mah lah-ta-suh-LEE-qum

Other Name False tamarind

Bloom Period and Seasonal Color
Warm months with white puffball flowers; flat, black seedpods

Mature Height x Spread
50 feet x 50 feet

Zones 10b–11

Wild tamarind is a wonderful tree for attracting birds; this big native is the perfect candidate for using as a shade or specimen tree—providing you give it sufficient room, because it can reach nearly 50 feet tall with a spread just about as wide. Its white, dandelion-like puffball flowers occur from spring through summer, rising above compound leaves with tiny individual leaflets. The seedpods are distinctive and a field characteristic: black, white and flattened. If winter stays warm, the tree will gradually shed leaves; if cold, they will all drop. This readily distinguishes it from the non-native tamarind, *Tamarind indicus*, which have long, brown leguminous seedpods. Wild tamarind is where you are likely to find endangered tree snails, which eat lichens off the bark. (GBT)

When, Where, and How to Plant

This is a great specimen tree, and when planted on the south side of your home, it will allow winter's sun to shine through its sometimes-bare branches to warm you. Because of its mature spread, make sure you plant it far enough away from your house. Plant in the warm season, March (if you can use a hose to water heavily for the first few weeks) through early summer, in full sun.

Growing Tips

Give any native tree or shrub fertilizer for the first year or two to help it become well established in your landscape. Keep the soil moist during the first growing season, and then once established allow wild tamarind to thrive without supplemental irrigation.

Regional Advice and Care

This is a tree for South Florida only.

Companion Planting and Design

This is a tree that grows in rocky hammocks, and its shade is not dense. *Tetrazygia bicolor*, or West Indian lilac, pearl-berry, and locustberry might make good companions. Just one wild tamarind will a shady spot make. This is the larval host for the Cassius Blue, the Large Orange Sulphur, and Mimosa Yellow butterflies.

Try These

Lysiloma sabicu, the weeping or shaggy-bark lysiloma, grows to about 30 feet by 25 feet. New growth is pinkish. Its flowers are small white fuzzballs, rather like mimosa flowers, and the fruits are thin, flat pods. The bark splits and peels, giving it one of its common names. This is a drought-resistant tree that will take full sun to part shade with good drainage. It also is salt-tolerant. Often used in South Florida parks, the tree is from Cuba and the Bahamas. It is the larval host for the Pink Spot Sulphur butterfly, recently discovered as having been misidentified as a Statira butterfly.

TROPICALS FOR FLORIDA

Most of the world's biological diversity is found in the tropics. If we look closely at tropical plants, they may serve as gateways to our understanding of larger tropical ecosystems and help us to care about their rapid destruction. The stories of tropical plants are tales of adaptation, exploitation, temptation, seduction, and unlikely triumph in a climate that promotes ceaseless competition for life itself.

Start with the story of a vine, *Monstera dubia*, that begins its life on the forest floor where it seeks not light at germination but darkness. For darkness means shadow, and shadow in all likelihood means a tree trunk. Once there, a small leaf emerges and flattens itself against the damp bark of the buttressing root, itself an architectural wonder. The next leaf is thrust over the top of the first, slightly higher on the tree, until eventually, the clamping vine has worked its way into the upper canopy. There it can quit making these tiny, clinging-for-dear-life leaves. There it detects more light and more air, and so it begins growing bigger leaves, better able to take in the sun, to bask in the rain, to reach out from the trunk and wobble in the wind, vigorous, and, yes, victorious.

Or repeat the story of the strangler fig that is deposited as a seed in the crotch of an unsuspecting tree. Tell how it germinates and sends down a single root, long and thin but for a corklike covering.

Then it produces another root, then another, and wraps them around the trunk of the tree that is its host. Its leafy shoots squirm and wedge their way through the canopy of the host until they can produce carbohydrates at a good clip in order to swell the

Walkway bordered by exotic tropicals

roots and strengthen them. And eventually, the perch becomes the victim, the fig becomes the strangler, not literally strangling its host but suffocating it, stealing its sunlight and its place in the forest.

Bromeliads open special cells when it rains to allow water into their leaves along with the nitrogen that is carried in rain.

Great Stories from the Tropics

These remarkable stories turn the tropics from abstract forests to living organisms, flirting, tempting, reproducing, and communicating in ways that

Anthurium

are stunning to behold—once you have the Rosetta stone of understanding.

Additionally these plants are enormously resourceful because of the competition with other plants for space, light, air, water, and reproductive success. They have devised all kinds of strategies for surviving: they climb, they soar, they perch, they strangle, they jump into the light at the first opportunity. You would, too, if your life depended on it. And in the process, they have become glorious garden specimens.

Plants in the aroid family (Araceae) are among the most numerous of tropical plants and bring glamor to subtropical areas by climbing trees, perching on tree limbs, adding a sophisticated velvety texture to gardens and containers. Other tropicals include the gingers, which attract their pollinators with flower spikes of brilliant color; bromeliads that store water in their vase-like rosettes; herbaceous low-lying plants that have lens-shaped leaf cells to catch the dimmest of light on the forest floor, or holes to keep from tearing in wind, or drip tips to let the rain run off...these plants are the fine details for subtropical gardens, or, in some cases, they are the bling.

Most of the plants in this section thrive best in South Florida gardens. Many will also do well outside in other areas of Florida during the summer. In pots, they can easily be moved back and forth, provided there is adequate humidity indoors.

Don't be afraid to try them. They bring wonderful foliage patterns and colors, beautiful flowers, and an intriguing way of life with them. And they tell stories that you can repeat to your friends.

Anthurium

Anthurium spp.

Botanical Pronunciation
an-THUR-ee-um

Bloom Period and Seasonal Color
Year-round foliage and blooms in red, pink, white, and occasionally green and red

Mature Height x Spread
Both varies with species

Zones 10–11

Anthuriums have some of the most prized leaves in tropical gardens, offering deep green, velvety leaves with white or silver veins, such as *Anth. warocqueanum* or the queen anthurium. They are members of the aroid family, Araceae, and cousins include philodendrons, peace lilies, and Swiss cheese plants. *Anthurium andraeanum* is the "flamingo flower" that is grown in Hawaii by the millions and sold by florists and street vendors. The spathes of these plants are protective bracts that surround the upright spadix, and hybrid colors now include maroon, orange, red, and green. The velvet-leaved anthuriums are seductively beautiful: *A. crystallinum*, *A. magnificum*, and *A. clarinervium*, each of which has white veins against dark, velvety green with slightly different veining and size. (GBT)

When, Where, and How to Plant
Think of *Anthurium plowmanni* and *Anth. faustomirandae*, with leaves up to several feet in length, and know that these need plenty of room—in the garden. The bird's-nest anthuriums, *Anthurium salvinea* and *Anth. plowmanii*, grow in rosettes on fat columns of roots. To transplant, slice off a reasonable clump with roots and relocate. Plant in shady beds with other tropicals, in pots, or as specimens throughout the garden. For aroids in clay pots, use peat moss, perlite, sand, and pine bark for drainage. An orchid mix also works well, providing you add some sphagnum moss. Drainage is the key. To attach climbing and pendant types to tree limbs, use plastic-coated or 16-gauge wire and some osmunda (dried fern roots) to wrap around their roots for moisture retention. If you can run a sprinkler extension up the tree to water the plants, do so. If not, use a hose. Gradually rely on rain, except during the dry season.

Growing Tips
If using terracotta, check moisture levels closely. Soil in clay dries faster because the pot is porous. In windy weather, water daily if you grow these in pots. In the ground, they require less watering, depending on location. When thirsty, flamingo flowers lower their leaves instead of holding them straight up. Anthuriums do well with slow-release fertilizer, supplemented with occasional foliar sprays of 20-20-20. For aroids in trees, use a nylon mesh bag filled with slow-release 14-14-14 so that when it rains the plants will be fertilized.

Regional Advice and Care
Anthuriums may be used in shade as summer flowers in Central and North Florida or grown in containers in well-draining soil. Brown leaf edges may indicate the need for higher humidity.

Companion Planting and Design
With their heart-shaped leaves, anthuriums add distinction to a tree trunk, a garden path, or a garden bed. They complement bromeliads and fussy ferns and even serve to soften rocks and boulders.

Try These
The gorgeous *Anthurium magnificum* has large leaves that almost defy belief, with a deep green suede finish and silver veins.

Aroids

Many genera

Botanical Pronunciation
Varies

Bloom Period and Seasonal Color
Warm season, colors vary

Mature Height x Spread
Depends on growth habit; height ranges from
6 inches to many feet

Zones 10–11

Philodendron species and monsteras are aroids, as are caladiums, anthuriums, alocasias, and colocasias. These plants are grown for their gorgeous, sometimes giant, foliage. All aroids have this characteristic: a flower stalk that bears a protective leaf, called a spathe, and a cylindrical spadix, which holds female flowers at the base and male flowers at the top. Many philodendrons climb palms to bring instant "jungle" to your garden; others grow upright on tall trunks. Alocasias and colocasias are the "elephant ears" of the tropics, especially *A. macrorrhiza* 'Borneo Giant' and *A. portora*, a hybrid created in South Florida. Colocasias, which Hawaiians grow as taro, are water-loving, often aquatic plants. (GBT)

When, Where, and How to Plant
If the plant likes to climb, (*Philodendron mexicanum* or *P. subincisum*) place at the base of a palm just below the soil and beneath a cover of mulch. *Alocasia* 'Nancy's Revenge' thrives in a pond. Caladiums usually are shade plants, yet there are new *Caladium* cultivars that take full sun. Most grow in containers or hanging baskets. Anthuriums vary in size from pot plants to spectacular specimens such as *Anthurium faustomiraendae*. The International Aroid Society's annual show and sale at Fairchild Tropical Botanic Garden is a good place to get advice and expert identification.

Growing Tips
Aroids generally grow well in a fast-draining mix that includes Pro Mix (a commercial blend that can be found at agricultural supply stores), peat

moss to retain some moisture, and small pine bark chips or sand to promote drainage. Warm months allow the best planting window, as some of the plants are quite cold-sensitive. Water needs depend on the genus or species. A liquid fertilizer may be applied weekly in the warm months, whereas plants in containers are helped along with slow-release pellets applied in the spring and weekly applications of liquid fertilizer. Cut back fertilizer and water in winter. A 30-10-10 or a slow-release fertilizer formulated for foliage plants also works.

Regional Advice and Care
Even in South Florida gardens, some aroids need protection from cold. Those with coriaceous leaves may not need cover. Bird's-nest anthuriums are tough. Watch for mites in dry weather; mealybugs may be a problem if you bring them inside during winter because of lack of air circulation. Use cotton soaked with rubbing alcohol to wipe away mealybugs, and employ a Q-tip to reach those in the leaf axils. Use some of the low-light species, such as aglaonemas, as houseplants in colder areas of the state, keeping them out of drafts.

Companion Planting and Design
Aglaonemas, caladiums, and sprawling philodendrons such as 'Burle Marx' make excellent groundcovers if given room to spread.

Try These
There are more and more hybrids available today. *Philodendron* 'McDowell' and *Alocasia* 'Polly' can be used with great effect.

Banana

Musa x paradisiaca

Botanical Pronunciation
MEW-sa para-DEE-sika

Other Name Plantain

Bloom Period and Seasonal Color
About 10 to 15 months after planting, bananas
will flower; fruit should mature at about 18 months

Mature Height x Spread
5 to 20 feet x various

Zones 10–11

The banana is a popular backyard fruit in South Florida. The plants are evocative of the tropics, with oblong, smooth leaves on succulent stems. We plant bananas from corms, or underground stems, which sucker after each new growth has bloomed and fruited. The fruit take from 12 to 18 months to form and develop. Male flowers form at the end of the stem, females closest to the top of the stalk. The fruit may then take two to three months to mature. When the ridges on the individual fruit round out, bananas can be picked and tied up in a garage or carport to ripen. If you allow bunches to remain on the plant, individual skins will split. 'Dwarf Cavendish' is among many bananas suitable for South Florida. (GBT)

When, Where, and How to Plant

Plant bananas at the beginning of the rainy season to allow plenty of growing time before winter. Choose an area where the plant will be protected from winds. Bananas like plenty of water, so put your stand where you easily can irrigate it, but not in a low spot where water will stand, because the underground stem will rot. Dig a hole 2 or 3 feet across by about 2 feet deep, and enrich it with aged compost or potting soil. Do not use manure or peat moss in the planting hole because such materials hold too much moisture and may breed fungi. Place the corm in the hole to a depth of 8 inches, with its white roots on the bottom, and then backfill. Mulch only after the plant has become established and is pushing out a new leaf.

Growing Tips

When new leaves begin growing, water daily. Young plants need small but frequent applications of fertilizer. Apply 1 pound every two months, increasing the amount until you apply 5 or 6 pounds by the time the plant begins to flower 10 to 15 months later. Use a 6-6-6 fertilizer initially, and then switch to 9-3-27 or another high-potassium fertilizer. Manganese and zinc can be applied as a foliar spray.

Regional Advice and Care

Bananas can tolerate cold weather but should be covered with a cloth over poles, like a tepee, when frost or freezing is expected. Freezes can take them back to the ground, but usually they will resprout. If leaves begin to flag and your cultural program is good, you may be seeing nematode infestation, sigatoka, or Panama disease. Consult the Cooperative Extension Service about control.

Companion Planting and Design

Given their need for water and fertilizer, bananas in beds by themselves are easiest to manage.

Try These

For ornamental use, the rojo, or red, banana excels at bringing a tropical feel to a garden, but for taste, a Honduran hybrid, SH 3640, produces great-tasting, sweet dessert bananas that are far better than the store-bought type. The 15-foot 'Ae-Ae' banana is a gorgeous green-and-white variegated specimen.

Bird's-Nest Fern

Asplenium nidus

Botanical Pronunciation
as-PLEE-nee-um NI-dus

Other Name Nest fern

Bloom Period and Seasonal Color
Grown for foliage

Mature Height x Spread
3 to 4 feet x 3 to 4 feet

Zones 10–11

Ferns have managed to take on myriad sizes and shapes in their ancient history, from filmy ferns that are but one cell thick to tree ferns that hold themselves aloft with great dignity in the cloud forests of the tropics. The bird's-nest fern, sporting strap-shaped leaves in a rosette, is found near the rivers and streams, where humidity is high and light often dappled. It grows as an epiphyte, occasionally balancing on a thin tree branch above a stream. The new fronds form in the center of the rosette, lengthening and unfolding gradually, and may reach 4 feet in length. As the base of roots elongates, the fern may tipple to one side, and you know it's time to repot. (GBT)

When, Where, and How to Plant
Growing ferns from spores is beyond the capabilities of all but the most dedicated gardeners, so plants usually are acquired from society sales or nurseries. Although bird's-nest ferns grow epiphytically, they also grow well in organic mulch or a mix with excellent drainage. Plant in a shaded area in the warm season, and keep the root mass moist but not wet.

Growing Tips
Biweekly liquid fertilizer or fish emulsion may be used from spring through fall. Controlled-release fertilizer applied in the spring will be useful throughout the summer. Some ferns develop a totally different "fertile" frond on which they produce spores; the bird's-nest produces stripes of brown sori that contain spores on the undersides of the leaves. Spores germinate in water and produce another plantlet called a gametophyte. Sperm and eggs develop in water from these plantlets. That's why water is such a crucial part of the fern's lifecycle. Don't allow your ferns to dry.

Regional Advice and Care
As the plants mature, the old leaves will yellow and die. Remove these to keep the plant looking neat and tidy. Be alert for snails; handpick in the early morning. Bird's-nest ferns may be grown in containers in Central and North Florida, as they need protection from cold in winter.

Companion Planting and Design
Because of their shape, bird's-nest ferns stand out in planting beds with selaginella or club moss used as a ground cover. The simplicity of the fern blades against the highly articulated club moss makes a wonderful combination.

Try These
Asplenium nidus 'Osaka' is a form with wavy edges. *Asplenium nidus* 'Fimbriatum' is a cultivar with leaf edges cut into thin sections. This is quite similar to a cultivar called 'Feather'.

Bromeliad

Many genera

Botanical Pronunciation
Varies with genus

Bloom Period and Seasonal Color
Varies with genus and species

Mature Height x Spread
Few inches to several feet

Zones 10–11

Bromeliads are all-around performers, bringing tropical color and architecturally interesting shapes to a subtropical setting. They can grow in trees or under them, on rocks or in mulch, in sun or shade, as accents or mass plantings. Their brilliant colors render many of them extroverts in a garden, whereas others produce astoundingly tall, many-branched inflorescences that last months before fading. The cup that forms inside the rosette of bromeliad leaves holds water, and in areas with distinct dry seasons, these often are the refuge for frogs and a whole universe of microscopic living things. *Aechmea blanchetiana*, when exposed to full sun, turns its leaves a glowing coppery-red; *Alcantaria odorata* is silver-blue; *Cryptanthus* species are small, ground-hugging types called earth stars, and the list goes on. (GBT)

When, Where, and How to Plant
Plant any time, particularly if putting bromeliads in trees. If you wish to remove a pup from a mother plant, wait until the pup is one-third the size of the mother, and then cut away close to the mother stem. Plant in beds of mulch beneath the canopy of a shade tree, such as a live oak; use large bromeliads as accents. Orchid mix or equal parts peat, perlite, and bark are wonderful for bromeliads grown in terracotta pots. Or, in rainy South Florida, rocks often serve as a useful medium.

Growing Tips
Keep the bromeliad cups filled with water; fertilize at one-fourth strength every two weeks. Fertilize, if at all, less often or at decreased strength for banded, spotted, or colorful leaves, or color/spotting can disappear.

Regional Advice and Care
If the water in bromeliad cups is allowed to stagnate, mosquito larvae can take up residence and make life miserable when they hatch. Use a home or garden spray, or flush the cups with the hose every couple of days. Or use horticultural oil in the cups to keep mosquitoes from laying eggs there. When the plant produces offshoots, remove with secateurs (pruners), and pot or plant. When bromeliads get old and crowded in beds, the original plants begin to rot and stink. Periodically remove them, prune away the old plants, and reposition. If working with bromeliads that have spines, use beekeeper gloves that cover your forearms to keep from being scratched. These gloves have leather hands and canvas arm coverings. Watch for scale in overcrowded conditions. Bromeliads often are grown outdoors in Central and North Florida, but they must be removed from their beds or protected with covers in freezing weather.

Companion Planting and Design
There's a bromeliad for every use, from groundcover to specimen. Use full sun types on rocks with cycads, patterned leaf species in partial shade with palms, and *Neoregelia* cultivars in beds with gingers.

Try These
Elegant bromeliads are appealing without spines. Two wonderful specimens are *Alcantarea imperialis* and *Vriesea hieroglyphica*.

Mussaenda

Mussaenda philippica

Botanical Pronunciation
mew-see-END-ah fa-LIP-a-kuh

Bloom Period and Seasonal Color
Year-round, more summer blooms in pink, white, and yellow

Mature Height x Spread
9 to 10 feet x 6 feet

Zones 10–11

When morning sunrises are pastel, with the softest peach light on the clouds gradually turning to pink, and the sky's deep blue dissipates into robin's-egg—that's when the tropical of subtropical seems most at hand. Those pink colors can be found covering the landscape when mussaendas are allowed to wander the grounds. The sepals are all enlarged and fluffy, so the pink never fails to conjure up visions of cotton candy. This is not a shrub to assign the everyday duty of running alongside a fence. Its lusciousness is best taken in smaller doses, and its cold-tenderness makes it vulnerable to damage below 45 degrees Fahrenheit. *Mussaenda philippica* 'Dona Aurora' has white sepals; other 'Dona' cultivars are pink. *Mussaenda glabra* is yellow with a single cream-colored sepal. (GBT)

When, Where, and How to Plant

Plant mussaendas any time from the beginning of the rainy season through midsummer. Locate in full sun for best color, or in high, light shade. Dig a hole as deep and twice as wide as the rootball of the plant in a container. Add organic material, such as compost, peat moss, or aged manure. Carefully remove the container from the plant, and slip the shrub into the planting hole. Water in the soil to eliminate air pockets. Add mulch, being careful to keep mulch a couple of inches away from the trunk.

Growing Tips

Fertilize with an acid-forming or gardenia/ixora fertilizer. (Mussaendas are related to gardenias and ixoras, in the Rubiaceae family.) Cut back in late winter to encourage development of more flowering branches and to keep within bounds, size-wise.

Regional Advice and Care

You will have to grow these plants in containers in Central and North Florida. Fungal leaf spot can affect some plants; the pink is hardier than the salmon. Pruning after bracts fade will encourage more flowering in the same season. If the shrubs grow too large, cut back quite hard. Use the cuttings to propagate more. Legginess is a problem. In *Gardening in the Tropics*, R. E. Holttum and Ivan Enoch suggest planting mussaendas in a mixed border so shorter shrubs can conceal the trunks. Hard pruning is necessary because of the tendency to stretch and straggle. Holttum and Enoch also suggest that you place these shrubs carefully, because such continuous showiness can become tiresome.

Companion Planting and Design

A wonderful combination is pink mussaenda with Persian shield (*Strobilanthes dyerianus*), a silver-purple foliage plant, and cat palms or areca palms. Snowbush echoes the soft pink of *M. erythropylla* 'Dona Luz'.

Try These

Mussaenda erythrophylla, the red mussaenda, is a pretty plant. *Mussaenda glabra* is a dwarf form. *Mussaenda* 'Queen Sirikit' is a hybrid developed many decades ago that has lovely, soft-pink bracts.

Peace Lily

Spathiphyllum spp.

Botanical Pronunciation
spath-uh-FILE-um

Other Name White flag

Bloom Period and Seasonal Color
Summer blooms in white

Mature Height x Spread
12 inches to 4 or more feet x 12 inches to 4 or more feet

Zones 10B–11

One of the chief attributes of white flowers is their visibility in low light. And like a lighthouse beam in fog, the spathe of the peace lily is a small beacon in shadowy places. Dr. Bill Wolverton, formerly with NASA, did a famous study in the early 1990s showing that certain plants used indoors could remove pollutants such as formaldehyde, benzene, and carbon monoxide from the air. *Spathiphyllum* was among the top 10 of these in effectiveness for removing formaldehyde. In the garden, spathiphyllums like shade, moist soil, and plenty of air circulation. In nature, they love the margins of rivers and streams and even grow in swamps in the New World tropics. Most of the plants now sold are laboratory-created hybrids. (GBT)

When, Where, and How to Plant
Plant peace lilies any time from the beginning of the rainy season through midsummer. Choose a shady location with some protection against cold and well-draining soil. Use a high-nitrogen fertilizer for foliage plants, with a 3-1-2 ratio. In too much shade, the plants won't flower, although they will survive nicely. Today's cultivars have been developed to endure the ordeals of indoor abuse: they hold up well in low humidity, they hang on if not religiously watered, and they flower despite it all. Take the same plants outside, and they can flourish in medium to deep shade in well-drained soil. Peat moss, perlite, and bark make a great growing medium for these plants, whether in a bed or a container.

Growing Tips
Spaths like moisture and fertilizer in regular amounts. Water every other day or so, depending on conditions, keeping the soil evenly moist but not wet. A 3-1-2 fertilizer for foliage plants, or a fertilizer that's used generally for landscapes in South Florida, which is the palm special 8-4-12 can be used three or four times a year. Plants are susceptible to scale if air circulation is not optimal.

Regional Advice and Care
Potted plants can be moved outside in the summer to shaded patios or pool areas. You also may use spathiphyllum as a temporary groundcover during the summer in Central and North Florida.

Companion Planting and Design
These plants make wonderful potted specimens for use both indoors and out. As entryway plants they are showoffs, especially the large cultivars. Consider them for shady patios, porches, and interiors. Peace lilies and begonias in the same garden bed are wonderful compatriots. Both go up and down the size scale from huge to petite. Combine them with a tree fern and see if the textures aren't pleasing.

Try These
Spathiphyllum 'Clevelandii' is a big plant, with impressive leaves that are dark green. It's a showoff. Hundreds of cultivars exist, and you may select plants practically tailor-made for any situation.

Peperomia

Peperomia spp.

Botanical Pronunciation
pep-er-OH-me-ah

Bloom Period and Seasonal Color
Greenish flowers; usually at the end of summer

Mature Height x Spread
12 to 18 inches x 4 inches

Zones 10–11

Were you to venture into the Big Cypress Swamp, wade through the sloughs of the Fakahatchee Strand, or watch nature from the distinctly dry vantage of the boardwalk at Corkscrew Swamp Sanctuary near Naples, you would find *Peperomia obtusifolia*. It has round, succulent leaves and fleshy stems and is liable to drape itself atop fallen logs, sharing the ride with ferns and orchids. And were you to wander into a garden center, you would no doubt find them among the houseplants and dish gardens. In your garden, peperomias can easily serve as groundcovers, potted plants for the patio or waterfalls, fillers in the crags of shaded rocks around your pond, or roamers among the mulch in your hammock. (GBT)

When, Where, and How to Plant
Plant in spring or any time during summer. Select a shady, well-draining area that nonetheless can retain moisture. If you think about an old log, you can visualize the way water runs off, but moisture is kept in the decomposing bark and detritus. As a groundcover, plants may be spaced quite close or farther apart, depending on the leaf size. Plants will spread, though loosely. Some plants will clump up or mound slightly. You can multiply your groundcover easily from cuttings taken in the spring. Root them in a moist, 50-50 mix of peat moss and perlite, and keep them shady until roots have begun. Or plant cuttings directly into the bed, and keep well irrigated until the plants are growing well.

Growing Tips
A key ingredient to the successful culture of peperomias in the garden is mulch to keep the soil evenly moist. Fertilize with a 7-3-7 granular fertilizer containing micronutrients two or three times a year, or apply a slow-release fertilizer; apply less often if you use mulch and less often if you fertilize plants around which the peperomias grow.

Regional Advice and Care
Peperomias will creep along the ground, turning up their heads to the light. When they become too tall and flop into a heap, cut off the top few inches. These can be rooted in pots or directly in the ground. Keep the soil moist. These plants are too tender for widespread use in North and Central Florida, unless they are grown in containers. Watch for snails.

Companion Planting and Design
Peperomias make pretty hanging basket and container plants, particularly those with variegated leaves. As a groundcover with palms, this is a hardy plant for bright shade in areas with a lot of moisture. Ideal places for getting them started are tree stumps left in the garden or old logs brought in for character.

Try These
Peperomia caperata 'Emerald Ripple' is a beautiful bluish black color with ripples. *Peperomia clusifolia* var. *tricolor* has red, white, and green markings. *Peperomia sandersii* is nicknamed watermelon peperomia. There are many more.

Ti Plant

Cordyline spp.

Botanical Pronunciation
KOR-da-line

Other Name Cordyline

Bloom Period and Seasonal Color Irregular; winter peak November to December; spring March to April; leaves red and green, maroon, yellow/ivory, burgundy; flowers white; fruit red

Mature Height x Spread
6 feet x 20 inches

Zones 10B–11

If you were to dip feather dusters in a can of paint and insert them in the ground, feathers up, you would have a good idea of what a ti plant looks like. A sunburst of red wine coloration in the garden has long been the ti plant's contribution, but with extensive hybridization, color can now be copper, green, fuchsia, yellow, cream, and any and all combinations of these. New and beautiful cultivars include 'Iris Bannochie', tricolored with cream, red, and green; 'Peter Buck', orange suffused through the red; 'Little Rose', with older green leaves edged in red and new pink and red leaves; 'Hawaiian Flag', a cream and red combination; 'Yellow Bird', with butter yellow leaves that take on some green coloration with age. (GBT)

When, Where, and How to Plant

Plant any time from the beginning of the rainy season through midsummer. Plant in what is best described as high shade—akin to that beneath an oak, where light is bright without being direct. Ti plants can sunburn in summer in direct sun, but they can slowly decline in too much shade. Dig a hole larger than the rootball, add some peat moss or compost to enrich it (no more than one-third the total backfill should be organic), and water in the soil as you backfill the planting hole. In his monograph "The Cordyline," Frank Brown of Valkaria recommends planting mixed types of cordylines, being careful with the color red.

Growing Tips

Ti plants grow well in the rainy heat of summer, but their best color comes in fall and winter, when you ease off supplying so much water. They like to dry slightly in the dry season. Too much light and too much fertilizer can bleach the foliage. Organic fertilizer, such as compost or fish emulsion, is the gentlest, but slow-release is fine. Use a high-nitrogen fertilizer (10-5-5 or 30-15-15) for summer months, switching to a high-potassium (4-6-8 or 6-12-20) in fall to ready plants for winter. You can top cordylines when they are too tall and insert the cuttings into soil to root.

Regional Advice and Care

Watch for spider mites in winter, mealybugs in leaf axils, scales, and thrips. Ti cuttings easily develop roots. These are tender plants that are suitable for container culture in Central and North Florida. There are miniature ti plants that can work well in small containers, such as 'Minima', 'King Kamehameha', and 'Amazing Grace'.

Companion Planting and Design

Use colorful ti plants between billowy shrubs for flair; contrast a group of dark burgundy ti plants with variegated ginger; use the tricolor for bringing color interest to palm groupings.

Try These

Cordyline terminalis 'Tricolor' is a handsome plant, with enough oomph in its green, cream, and red combination to be noticed in the garden without being gaudy.

Traveler's Tree

Ravenala madagascariensis

Botanical Pronunciation
rav-en-ALLAH madgascar-EN-sis

Other Name Traveler's palm

Bloom Period and Seasonal Color
Summer; white

Mature Height x Spread
40 feet x 25 feet

As a landscape plant, the traveler's tree is most glorious when it is young, as that is when its remarkable head of leaves is closer to eye level. When young, this bird-of-paradise relative is trunkless and can remain so for several seasons. Eventually, the trunk emerges and comes to resemble a palm trunk. The mature display is a stunning bit of geometry, with leaves held on a single plane, like the cards held in a bridge hand. With a tall trunk and enormous leaves fanned across an axis, the traveler's tree makes quite a statement. The large flower bracts fill with water when it rains, as do the bases of the stems, offering to slacken the thirst of travelers. (GBT)

When, Where, and How to Plant
Plant at the beginning of the rainy season to midsummer. Plant in full sun or high, light shade, in a space large enough to accommodate the large head of leaves. Prepare a planting hole as deep and twice as wide as the rootball, and enrich with one-third compost before backfilling. Water in backfill to collapse air pockets. Mulch.

Growing Tips
Use a slow-release fertilizer, either balanced, such as 18-18-18, or high-nitrogen, high-potassium in the summer growing season, such as a 7-3-7. Use a balanced fertilizer on sand, or 8-4-12, on rocky soils, applying a small amount every couple of months. Traveler's tree likes plenty of water in the summer growing season, less in the winter. Apply a slow-release fertilizer three times a year after the plant has reached a fair size.

Regional Advice and Care
This tree is not suitable for Central and North Florida. Because they grow at about 3,000 feet in Madagascar, these plants can take a little more cold than other tropical plants. Suckers sometimes form at the base, and in smaller areas, it may be wise to remove them. The large leaves may become tattered in wind. When they look frayed, remove the outermost leaves.

Companion Planting and Design
As garden specimens, these are truly impressive and can overpower the rest of the garden as well as the house. A single plant grown next to a chimney dwelling in a larger setting may be just the right (landscape) architectural statement. When correctly used, a mature and solitary traveler's tree will be a stunning sculptural element in your garden—at the corner of a path or shrub bed, where rounded and low plants suddenly give way to exuberance.

Try These
This is the single species of *Ravenala*.

TURFGRASSES
FOR FLORIDA

reen vistas where children play, dogs run, and families entertain are still popular in home landscapes, but water concerns have caused many residents to consider downsizing their lawns. With an eye toward water conservation, residents are often limiting turf to only what's needed for family enjoyment.

Lawn grasses provide lots of benefits that make turf a valuable component of any landscape design. Adding a lawn offers a relatively inexpensive, quick groundcover that can be installed over minimally prepared bare ground. Turf removes pollutants from the air and runoff water. A healthy green lawn absorbs carbon dioxide from the air, returns oxygen for us to breathe, and helps cool the landscape. In addition, many gardeners just like the bragging rights of having an attractive, manicured lawn and love to share their secrets of success with fellow residents.

Many gardeners love the look of an attractive, manicured lawn.

Today the term *drought-tolerant* is prevalent when discussing lawns. All lawns have some drought-tolerance, but all need water to survive. St. Augustine and centipede are usually considered the least drought-tolerant, but they can go several weeks or more without water before suffering major decline. Due to their rooting structure, bahia, bermuda, and zoysia are the most drought-tolerant and can last for a month or more without major decline. One thing you need to know is all grass types are going to shrivel their leaves, assume a grayish green tinge, and eventually turn brown without water. There is no consistently green lawn without rains or irrigation during the dry times.

Planning the Lawn

Most grasses need full sun to grow their best, and only a few types have much shade tolerance. A general rule is if you have significantly more than 25 percent shade, better look for another groundcover. Also, lawns under trees not only have the shade to contend with but also have to deal with tree roots.

Landscapes are often planned with a green lawn near the entrance to the home. These areas can form focal points outlined with ornamental plantings. In some areas, lawns are giving way to other groundcovers as a way to conserve moisture, but most residents still like a little green grass out front.

Backyards traditionally have the most turf growing in the sunny to lightly shaded locations. This is the family area where the kids play and group gatherings take place. Lawns may occupy the entire backyard but are now often restricted to a few hundred to several thousand square feet. Lawns do require some care, and the more grass you add, the more you have to mow, feed, and provide with pest control.

Lawn Grasses at a Glance

Bahia: The Carefree Grass with a Durable Image

Gardeners who want a good-looking lawn with minimal care should consider bahiagrass. It's one of Florida's most drought-tolerant turf types, and it is tough enough to support most family backyard sports. Bahia has become the multipurpose turf used for home lawns, athletic fields, parks, and roadsides. It has the advantage of growing well from seed and is also easy to establish from sod. Some gardeners do not like its coarser look and the fact it goes dormant late fall through early spring. It has one common pest, the mole cricket, which seems to be pretty much under control through the release of natural predators by Florida researchers. There are two major selections usually used for home lawns. The variety 'Argentine' has a wide blade with the smallest number of seedheads and resists yellowing during the spring season. The 'Pensacola'

Bermuda

variety produces a narrower leaf blade and is the least expensive to start from seed, but it does have a tendency to yellow during spring and produces an abundance of tall seedheads.

Bahia lawns are normally mowed to a height of 3 to 4 inches and fed two to four times a year.

Bermuda: A Higher-Maintenance Turf with a Great Look

Florida's most impressive lawns are often bermudagrass. Gardeners like the fine texture and dense growth this turf offers, which creates a green carpet of durable grass for popular golf courses and athletic fields. Bermudagrass is also selected for its salt- and drought-tolerance plus good weed resistance. So-called "common" bermuda, a seeded type, has an open growth habit and coarse texture and is used mostly along the roadside. Improved seeded varieties of medium texture and dense growth, including the varieties 'Cheyenne', 'Sahara', 'Sundevil', and 'Jackpot', are useful in athletic fields, lawns, and parks. Some varieties are reproduced as sprigs, sod, or plugs. Popular types include varieties 'Celebration', 'FloraTex', 'Tifgreen', 'Tifway', and 'Tifway II', which have good density, a fine texture, and tolerance to varying cultural conditions. Bermudagrass does require your constant attention, because it is susceptible to most common turf pests, needs frequent mowing to between ½ and 1½ inches, and requires feedings three to six times a year.

Centipedegrass: Often Called the Poor Man's Turf

Gardeners familiar with centipedegrass know its ability to grow in infertile soils with minimal feedings. Centipede looks like a miniature St. Augustine with relatively narrow leaf blades forming in clusters along green runners. Gardeners like the turf's ability to grow in light shade and good drought tolerance. With the right care it can be quite vigorous, filling in bare spots and knitting a dense lawn in a few months. Some varieties of centipede include 'Common', 'Covington', 'Hammock', 'Santee', and 'TifBlair'. Gardeners in North Florida can grow the best-looking centipedegrass and with few pest problems. It also grows throughout the state, but nematodes and ground pearls affect lawns in the warmer sandy soils. This grass needs the fewest number of feedings, up to twice a year. Delay feeding until April in North Florida to prevent centipede decline, which is a melting out of the turf. Normally the grass is mowed when it's 2 inches tall. Water when sites begin to wilt for the best growth.

St. Augustinegrass: The Mainstay of Home Turf

St. Augustinegrass is still the most common turf for home lawns. Maybe gardeners just like the blue-green color and great vigor. Maybe it is the grass they are most familiar with and know how to care for. Many northern residents who head south find this turf a bit of a shock, as it's coarser and wirier than familiar back-home selections. But St. Augustinegrass is what they commonly find in their local neighborhoods, with most selections having good shade- and cold-tolerance, plus reasonable pest-resistance. Almost every gardener has heard of 'Bitter Blue' and 'Floratam' varieties. 'Bitter Blue' is now hard to find, but 'Floratam' is plentiful, although it only grows well in full sun locations. Other selections include standard sized 'Classic', 'DeltaShade', and 'Palmetto', which are all mowed to a height of about 3 to 4 inches. Dwarf varieties include 'Captiva', 'Sapphire', and 'Seville', which are mowed about 2 to 2½ inches high. Most of these standard and dwarf varieties have good shade-tolerance. St. Augustinegrass's one big problem is chinch bugs. It is probably best to consider all varieties as susceptible to this pest, because when a new selection with resistance is introduced, the pest seems to quickly overcome its tolerance. Caterpillars and brown patch, a turf disease, can also be common problems. St. Augustinegrass grows best with once- or twice-a-week watering during the dry times and feeding two to four times a year.

Zoysiagrass

Zoysiagrass: Growing in Popularity with Florida Residents

Maybe residents just like the fine-bladed look of zoysiagrass, whereas others have probably read the yearly promotions for a carefree lawn. Zoysia can grow a bright green carpet and, once established, usually beats out many weeds. It withstands normal wear, tolerates drought, is cold hardy, *and* salt-tolerant. But no matter what else you read or hear, zoysia does need some care. It only remains green if it has adequate moisture. Zoysia needs two to three feedings a year and may be affected by pests like other turf types. Some common varieties to grow in Florida include 'Diamond', 'El Toro', 'Emerald', 'Empire', 'JaMur', 'PristineFlora', and 'UltimateFlora'. During drought, zoysia is often the first lawn to turn brown, but it regreens and grows with the next rain or irrigation. Zoysia also turns brown for winter, which invites some residents to spray it green. It can also be slow to regreen in the spring. Its primary insect pests are bill bugs, and it may be affected by a disease called brown patch or large patch during the cooler months. It is hoped newer varieties have some resistance to nematodes, which have also plagued zoysia in the past. The best mowing height is 1 to 2 inches cut with a reel or rotary mower.

Soil Considerations

Most Florida soils are suitable for growing turf. Soils rich in organic matter or clay hold more moisture than sandy soils, but both are capable of growing a great lawn. All turf sites should have the proper pH. Most grasses like a slightly acidic to nearly neutral soil. A soil in the 5.5 to 7.5 pH range is generally ideal. Bahiagrass does seem to benefit from keeping the soil in the acid range of pH 5.5 to 6.5. In this acidic soil, extra iron is often available for the growing turf—bahia appears to need this iron more than other grasses.

Soil acidity can be adjusted by following soil test recommendations. In Florida dolomitic lime is usually used to raise the soil pH, soil sulfur to lower it. Have your soil tested at your local University of Florida Extension Office and follow the advice from their test to change the acidity of your soil. In some areas, such as the very alkaline soils of South Florida and in pockets of organic matter throughout the state, it may be impossible to adjust the acidity. If the soil pH cannot be changed, gardeners should grow the turf type best suited to their areas. Then be prepared to add minor nutrients that might be depleted at the extreme acidity levels.

The First Step

Starting a new lawn and filling in bare spots in older ones are similar processes. First remove debris and weedy growth. Unwanted vegetation can be dug out or killed with a nonselective herbicide. Choose a product that permits planting the turf immediately after the weeds decline. Once the weeds are removed, the soil is tilled. In shady areas lightly raking the soil's surface may be all that is possible because disturbing the tree roots could cause a tree's decline. This is the time to incorporate lime or soil sulfur if needed. Some gardeners also like to incorporate organic matter, including compost, garden soils, peat, and aged manures, into sandy soils. Adding organic matter is beneficial but usually only practical when dealing with small areas. After tilling or raking, smooth out the ground to establish a uniform planting surface as final preparation for planting. This can be performed with a rake or a drag.

Starting from Seed

Seeding a lawn should be performed during the warmer months of March through September, when the grass grows the best. In Florida, bahia is usually the most commonly seeded grass, but some bermuda, centipede, and zoysia varieties can also be seeded. For each area of the lawn, divide the amount of seed needed to cover it in half. Move back and forth across the lawn, spreading the first portion. Then move across the lawn in perpendicular directions and spread the remaining seed. Rake the lawn to cover the seed. Bahia seed germinates best if covered by the soil ¼ to ½ inch deep. Seeded lawns need frequent watering. Water daily to keep the surface of the soil moist until the grass begins to sprout. As the roots spread out into the surrounding soil, watering can be reduced to an as-needed basis.

Starting from Plugs

Grass plugs are well-established sections of grass 2 to 4 inches square that can be used to establish all but the bahia turf in home lawns. Some gardeners simply kill the existing weeds and old grass and then insert the plugs into the ground. Good lawns *can* be established this way, but they appear to fill in more slowly than when the ground is cleared before planting. After clearing, add the plugs to moist soil. Most are spaced 6 to 12 inches apart. The closer the spacing, the quicker the grass fills in to establish the lawn.

Some gardeners like to add a slow-release fertilizer to the planting hole. It may be beneficial, but it is also time-consuming. A good feeding shortly after plugging seems to give a similar response.

Keep the planted areas moist and the plugs will begin to grow. After two to three weeks of growth, a lawn fertilizer may be applied to encourage the grass to form a lawn. A lawn starter fertilizer that contains all the plant nutrients might be selected for this first feeding.

Starting from Sod

All types of turf can be established from sod, which gives an instant lawn and helps shut out weeds that may grow among seeded and plugged turf. Most sod is sold in rectangular portions about 24 inches long and 16 inches wide. A pallet of sod may contain 400 to 500 square feet, so ask about the quantity before you buy.

Have the soil prepared and moist when the sod arrives. If for some reason the sod cannot immediately be installed, keep it in a shady location. Sod that sits on the pallet for longer than 48 hours quickly declines. Install the sod by laying the pieces next to each other, abutting the edges. Cut sections into pieces to fill in the smaller spaces. It is best to water the sod as it is being laid and again thoroughly after installation. A good rule to follow to keep the sod moist is to water every day for the first week. The second week, water every other day, and the third week, water every third day. During extra hot or dry weather, extra watering may need to include misting during the heat of the day for the first week or two. After three weeks, water only as needed to keep the turf from wilting.

Gardeners should note that sod laid in the shade needs less water than do sunny locations. Too much water, especially during hot and humid weather, can cause the turf to rot, and the sod is often lost. Many growers recommend postponing sodding shady areas during the summer months.

After the sod has been growing for three to four weeks, the first application of lawn fertilizer can be provided. Consider using a starter fertilizer found at garden centers that contains all the needed nutrients. After this initial feeding assume a normal care program as recommended by your local University of Florida Extension Office.

Caring for the Home Lawn

All lawn types need seasonal care—there are *no* totally carefree lawns. Traditional care means feeding, mowing, and often some pest control. Try to learn as much about your lawn type as possible, and then begin a good care program. The lack of care often results in the loss of your good grass.

Feeding: Throughout most of Florida, two yearly feedings are usually adequate for bahia and St. Augustine lawns, once in March and again in early October. Centipede can grow with a single feeding, and both bermuda and zoysia benefit from extra feedings. Take note that in some areas of Florida ordinances are in force that prohibit feeding lawns June through September. Contact your local Extension Service Office for this information.

Use a fertilizer with a low phosphorus content, the middle number in the analysis, such as a 15-0-15 or a 32-0-10. Also select a product with slow-release properties that feeds the lawn over a longer period of time with little or no nutrient run off. Where permitted by local ordinances, a feeding may also be made during the summer season. This can be a slow-release nitrogen product, often with extra iron. Some gardeners find application of an iron-only product during the summer renews the green without producing a lot of growth.

Watering: Lawns need water to remain green and attractive. But don't provide the turf with more than it really needs. Allowing the grass to dry out just a little between watering forces it to grow a deeper root system. Avoid the daily watering schedule that encourages a shallow root system more susceptible to pests. It also encourages lush growth and pops up weeds. Surprisingly most lawns can go four days to more than a week without watering depending on the time of the year. All of Florida appears to be under some watering restrictions. In many areas it is twice a week on assigned days; in some areas or times of the year it is once a week. Check with your Extension Service Office for the watering rules in your area.

Feeding a lawn

It is best to let the grass tell you when it needs water. Wait until spots in the lawn start to wilt. You can tell when the turf is reaching this stage, as the leaf blades start to curl and turn grayish green. When several spots show these signs and during your next scheduled watering day, give the lawn a good soaking with ½ to ¾ inch of water.

Mowing: Home lawns need frequent mowing during the warmer months. March through October most lawns need cutting at least once a week. During the cooler months, cutting may not be necessary at all in North Florida and just every other week or so in Central and South Florida. Every grass type has its own cutting height that ranges from a ½ inch for bermudagrass to 4 inches for St. Augustine and bahia. The general rule is to remove no more than one-third of the grass blade at any one time. This practice keeps the grass from being burned after too close a mowing. Other good mowing tips include keeping a sharp blade, mowing in different directions across the lawn at each cutting, and allowing clippings to remain on the lawn.

Pest Control: Many pests affect lawns. Your University of Florida Extension Office has excellent bulletins to help with these problems and agents are always willing to look at turf samples brought by their office.

Chinch bugs love St. Augustine, whereas lawn caterpillars and mole crickets feed in most lawn types. Mole crickets can be a problem in Bermuda and bahia lawns, and bill bugs feed in zoysia. Learn the prevalent pests of your lawn type, and then inspect the turf regularly.

Diseases are a less frequent problem with most turf types. A fungus known as brown patch, also called large patch, can be a cool-season pest of St. Augustine and zoysia. With a good cultural program even these can be kept to a minimum. Grass that is under stress, in too much shade, or planted in areas with poor air movement is likely to have excessive disease problems.

Finally, all lawns get a few weeds. Again, good cultural conditions help prevent weeds. Digging or spot-killing the weeds when first noted offers a good quick control. Where there are too many weeds, a herbicide may help. First get the weed identified, and then locate a herbicide that can be applied to your turf types and provides the control needed. Always follow instructions carefully when using any pesticides in the lawn and landscape.

Bragging Rights

If you are thinking of adding a lawn, repairing an older one, or just giving your present turf good care, put this information to good use in selecting your lawn type, installing the lawn, and providing needed maintenance. You can also obtain a free guide to the grass you select from your local University of Florida Extension Office and read their bulletin on the common pests of home lawns and their control. All of this combined will help you win bragging rights in your neighborhood.

VINES FOR FLORIDA

My, my, how they get around, these vines. Shameless climbers, stealthy twiners, exuberant clingers, superlative sprawlers, midnight ramblers... cling to me like a vine, we say, and mean every word at the time.

The vining lifestyle must be the envy of the plant world. After all, everyone else stays put. Only the vines scramble hither and yon, scampering up trees and across fences, under guardrails and around poles. Look at kudzu. Look at morning glories. Look at passion vines. But look fast, or you'll miss them going by. Yes, we exaggerate—but only slightly.

Opportunity Climbs (and Twines, and Creeps, and...)

Vines are opportunists, seizing the moment, racing for the light. There is one in South Florida called cow itch vine because it can irritate even cattle. There is pull-and-haul-back, so named for its recurved thorns that won't let you move forward once it has

Confederate Jasmine

you in its grip. Then there is the parasitic dodder or love vine. It not only twines; it filches, too, stealing carbohydrates from its victims. Pothos, when it escapes (perhaps its revenge for imprisonment), runs up trees and does a quick change into the so-called hunter's robe, a vine with such big leaves that they are used as protection in rain. *Dioscorea bulbifera* is a wild yam that is an invasive exotic in the natural areas of South Florida. It gives kudzu a run for its money.

So really, the subtext of vine lore is that vines are poised to take over the world if presented with the possibility. You will have to exercise some control over the vines you introduce into your garden. Periodically take the machete to some of them.

On the other hand, there are spectacular effects to be had by running a bougainvillea or flame vine up a tree. Just make sure you want it there before you give it its head. Be especially careful with vining jasmines. They quickly become pests. The passion vine and the nasturtium bahuinia (*Bauhinia galpinii*) may also fling themselves about with abandon. Lightly prune vines periodically throughout the growing season, and cut them back hard after flowering or in early spring before they shoot out. Most vines like enriched soil and regular irrigation to keep going. Fertilize once or twice a year, in spring and fall. Keep the root zones mulched to reduce weeds and keep soils evenly moist.

Passion vine is susceptible to nematodes; keep it well fertilized and mulched, growing vigorously, to prevent damage. Like other pests and diseases, nematodes are more apt to attack a weakened root system than a strong one.

Passion vine has the added advantage of producing edible fruit. *Passiflora edulis* is one that can be grown for its tangy, hard-shelled fruit. As tropical fruits become more well known

Mandevilla

outside of California, Texas, and Florida, the passion fruit has captured a following. It has a puckery tang that enlivens sauces, salad dressings, ice cream, sorbet, desserts of all types, including soufflé and Key lime pie.

Vines Need Support (and Vice Versa)

Pergolas and rock walls are excellent support for vines. Pergolas and trellises can be used to create outdoor rooms or walkways, with vines adding colorful, natural decoration. A vine that has clusters of hanging flowers, such as the queen's wreath, makes a beautiful trellis plant.

In my (Georgia's) garden, I have a blue trellis on which I grow bridal bouquet, or *Stephanotis floribunda*. Its white flowers hang in clusters, become wonderfully fragrant at night to attract moth pollinators. Occasionally, a huge seedpod develops, matures over many weeks, and when it splits open, I harvest the seeds that otherwise would float away on silken threads. The thing about the vine is this: it now is holding together the trellis rather than vice versa. Sometimes a good vine serves many purposes.

Allamanda

Allamanda cathartica

Botanical Pronunciation
alla-MAN-da cath-AR-ti-kuh

Bloom Period and Seasonal Color
Spring, summer, fall blooms in yellow

Mature Length
5 feet vining

Zones 10–11

Allamanda is one of the plants that cheerily announce the warm season in South Florida. Although it does not have tendrils with which to cling, it sprawls and reaches with gusto. The large, trumpet-shaped flowers on this vine are especially showy, and yellow is a color that draws the eye. It is a member of the Apocynaceae family, and it has this family's white milky sap. This sap is toxic, so don't toss any leaves into your salad, and use gloves when working with the vine to avoid any allergic reaction. Cold weather will knock off some leaves, but the allamanda is a durable plant in almost all conditions and can grow for decades. The hottest weather may make it wilt. (GBT)

When, Where, and How to Plant

Plant any time except during the winter. Plant in full sun next to a structure that needs screening but can offer support. A trellis or arbor should be strong; a chain-link fence is ideal. Enrich the soil for this vine, mixing compost, peat moss, or good potting soil into the planting hole. Water in the backfill to eliminate air pockets, and mulch the root zone after planting. Keep the root zone moist while the plant becomes established.

Growing Tips

Allamanda grows vigorously in a fairly rich soil, and it loves fertilizer. Its leaves will become chlorotic, or yellow between the veins, when it is hungry. A complete slow-release fertilizer of 8-4-12 with micronutrients, applied in the spring and fall, can keep it vigorous. Allamandas are fairly drought-tolerant, but they need weekly watering in the dry season. When plant leaves begin to take on an overall yellow, a drench of iron can help return the color.

Regional Advice and Care

Few insects bother allamanda, with the exception of aphids in the spring. Let lady bird beetles control them, or use 1 to 2 teaspoons of liquid Ivory or baby shampoo plus 2 tablespoons of horticultural oil in a gallon of water. Cut back hard in early spring to remove crossed and woody stems. If using this plant as a shrub, you will have to prune it frequently. If you live in Central Florida, wait to prune until warm weather returns, or unexpected cold may damage or kill the plant. In colder parts of the state, grow this plant in a large pot with a trellis so it can be brought inside during cold weather.

Companion Planting and Design

Plants with yellow flowers often look great with blue-purple blossoms near them. If using this vine along a fence, think about a low planting of wild petunias, Mexican heather, or plumbago.

Try These

Allamanda schottii is a compact grower; *A. cathartica violacea* 'Cherries Jubilee' is a pink form; *A. × alba* is white; and a cultivar called 'Indonesia Sunset' is rich in sunset hues. There also are double forms.

Bougainvillea

Bougainvillea spp.

Botanical Pronunciation
boo-gan-VIL-ya

Bloom Period and Seasonal Color
Fall through spring in all colors

Mature Length
6 to 20 feet

Zones 9–11

A woody flowering perennial with grass-green leaves, thorns, and tiny flowers surrounded by spectacularly colored bracts, bougainvillea may be Brazil's most successful export. The shimmering and stunning color is in the papery bracts that surround small white flowers. Semithornless—often called thornless—varieties are good container plants for patios or balconies. (The plants are somewhat thorny when young, but lose that characteristic as they age.) There are a great number of cultivars these days, including a rose and white bicolor, bred from three basic species: *Bougainvillea glabra*, which is a compact grower and flowers throughout much of the year; *B. peruviana*, which flowers in the dry season; and *B. spectabilis*, which flowers after a dry spell. The purple-flowering *B. spectabilis* is more cold-tolerant than the others. (GBT)

When, Where, and How to Plant
Plant bougainvillea in the warm season in a site where the entire plant, including much of the root zone, can get sun and heat. The plant is not fussy about soil. It does not benefit from benign neglect, but flowers well with regular water and fertilizer. Dig a planting hole just as deep as the container and a little wider. Gently remove the pot from the plant, being careful of thorns, and position it in the hole. The trellis or fence should be in place behind it. Water in when backfilling to remove air pockets. Water regularly, keeping soil moist, but not wet, until the plant becomes established—sending out new growth.

Growing Tips
Mulch lightly. Bougainvilleas will wilt when they're too dry. They are tolerant of cold, but they will drop leaves if chilled. If frozen, they will come back from the ground. Bougies require a steady diet of fertilizer. Use a balanced fertilizer in the summer, followed by a bloom-booster such as 4-6-8 in the fall. Water and allow the soil to almost dry between watering.

Regional Advice and Care
Flowers develop on new growth, so in September you can prune back and shape the summer's growth. In more temperate areas, select a cultivar of *B. spectabilis*. Bougainvillea is readily grown in large terracotta pots, which won't keep the roots too wet, but may require frequent watering. They are fed upon by tiny green caterpillars, the larvae of small moths. Use a biological insecticide or wait for the cycle to run its course. The plants may lose leaves, but they sprout new ones.

Companion Planting and Design
This is another fence plant. It is supremely beautiful when colors are mixed and the long stems arch over and catch the light. Remember to use a white occasionally to make other colors stand out.

Try These
'Mary Palmer' has white and magenta colors in one flower, and it always makes you look twice.

Carolina Yellow Jasmine

Gelsemium sempervirens

Botanical Pronunciation
gel-SEM-ee-um semp-PER-vhir-ends

Bloom Period and Seasonal Color
Mid- to late winter blooms in yellow

Mature Length
20 feet

Zones 8–9

Carolina yellow jasmine offers a big splash of bright yellow blossoms that open in early February, when there is often a lack of color in the landscape. And you don't have to worry about a winter freeze damaging the flowers, as this plant is totally hardy. Set this jasmine to work hiding a fence or covering a wall. Create a planting at the end of a vista or on an arbor at the entrance to a garden. The leaves are bright green, lancelike in shape, and about 3 inches long. The shoots can grow to more than 20 feet in length, but this is not a vine that normally gets way out of control. *Note: All portions of the plant are poisonous if eaten.* (TM)

When, Where, and How to Plant

Carolina yellow jasmine can be planted throughout most of the year. The best planting time is during the cooler winter months. Carolina yellow jasmine vines need a trellis, fence, or similar support for good growth. The vines grow well in sandy Florida soils. Many gardeners like to improve the site with compost or peat moss and manure before planting, but it is not necessary. Dig a hole that's much wider than the rootball but not deeper. Position the vine at the same depth it was growing in the container or original planting site. The top of the rootball may be set a little higher above the soil level, especially in a poorly drained location. Gardeners should expect Carolina yellow jasmine vines to make lots of growth, and adequate room should be provided at the planting site. Prune when the plants fill the trellis and begin to grow out of bounds. Every few years the vine should be given an early spring pruning after flowering to renew growth before new spring shoots sprout.

Growing Tips

Carolina yellow jasmine vines should be watered daily for the first few weeks after planting; gradually taper off to watering as needed. The vines are drought-tolerant and need watering only during periods of drought—but for best growth, water weekly. Feed four to six weeks after transplanting by applying a light scattering of a general landscape fertilizer under the spread of the vine. Repeat feedings for established vines during March, May, and September.

Regional Advice and Care

The Carolina yellow jasmine is best suited to the colder portions of the state. Plant in North and Central Florida landscapes, Zones 8–9. No major pests affect the vines.

Companion Planting and Design

Plant as a space divider or backdrop for a patio or garden-opening late-winter blooms. Stage other flowers in front, including pentas, salvia, bush daisies, gaillardia, and caladiums.

Try These

Selections of the Carolina yellow jasmine have been made for a deep yellow bloom or unique flowering habit. One, the 'Pride of Augusta', opens clusters of fully double blossoms.

Confederate Jasmine

Trachelospermum jasminoides

Botanical Pronunciation
TRAY-key-loh-SPER-mum jass-men-OID-eez

Other Name Star jasmine

Bloom Period and Seasonal Color
Mid- to late spring blooms in yellow

Mature Length
15 to 20 feet

When springtime finally arrives, one plant can be counted on for attractive snow white flowers plus a great fragrance—it's the confederate jasmine. The plant needs just a little support for a dense view barrier or attractive vertical accent. It's an ideal wall covering for gardeners with just a little space. Once the blooms begin you can count on over a month-long display. Then the plant provides some great greenery from the masses of shiny oval leaves. When trained to a trellis, the confederate jasmine is kept at about 12 to 15 feet in height, but the vining shoots are capable of growing 30 to 40 feet long. One extra special feature with this vine is the leaves are held along the stems to the ground. (TM)

When, Where, and How to Plant
Add vines to the garden throughout most of the year. Unless you are using them as a groundcover, vines need a trellis, fence, or similar support. The vines grow well in sandy Florida soils. Many gardeners like to improve the site with compost or peat moss and manure before planting, but it is not necessary. Dig a hole that's much wider than the rootball but not deeper. Position the vine at the same depth it was growing in the container or original planting site. The top of the rootball may be set a little higher above the soil level, especially in a poorly drained location. Create a berm, and add a light layer of mulch. Vines used as a groundcover are planted in a similar manner and given a spacing of 3 to 4 feet.

Growing Tips
Water daily for the first few weeks after planting. Gradually taper off to watering on an as-needed schedule. The vines are drought-tolerant and only need watering during periods of drought—but for best growth, water weekly. Feed four to six weeks after transplanting by applying a light scattering of a general landscape fertilizer under the spread of the vines. Repeat for established vines during March, May, and September.

Regional Advice and Care
Prune when the plant fills the trellis and begins to grow out of bounds. Every few years renew the growth with a major spring pruning after flowering. Confederate jasmine grows well throughout all but the most southern portions of Florida, Zones 8–10. It's seldom affected by cold. Scale insects may need a control. Gardeners can apply a horticultural oil insecticide or another University of Florida-recommended pesticide.

Companion Planting and Design
Use with sun- or shade-loving plants. It makes a great plant for trellises set under oak, pine, sweet gum, and similar trees. Plant as a turf substitute in hard-to-mow areas.

Try These
Most plants are marketed as the species, but one selection, 'Variegatum', has green-and-cream-colored foliage that makes a good accent for a garden wall. Others include 'Tricolor' and 'Star'.

Coral Honeysuckle

Lonicera sempervirens

Botanical Pronunciation
lon-NEH-sir-ah sem-per-VHI-rens

Other Name Trumpet honeysuckle

Bloom Period and Seasonal Color
Spring through summer blooms in reddish orange and yellow

Mature Length
20 feet or more

Zones 8–10

Add this Florida native to a fence, masonry wall, or side of a building to enjoy a spring-through-summer display of reddish orange and yellow blossoms. The coral honeysuckle leads off with a massive flush of flowers during March and April and then gradually tapers to sporadic blooms by fall. Set a planting in easy view to watch the hummingbirds darting in and out to visit. When its blossoms fade, they are followed by shiny red berries that are food for birds. The foliage is bright green on top and blue-green on the bottom. Use the coral honeysuckle where you need reliable color for the early warm months. It serves as a good space divider and view barrier, keeping its foliage near the ground. (TM)

When, Where, and How to Plant
Vines can be added to the garden throughout most of the year. The best planting time is during the cooler winter months. Coral honeysuckle needs a trellis, fence, or similar support for good growth. Keep all vines off trees to prevent damage to the trunks and to keep from encouraging pests. Plant in full sun or a lightly shaded location. In shadier sites, flowering is greatly reduced. Coral honeysuckle tolerates sand, but provide an enriched soil for the best growth. Add peat moss or compost and manure to the planting site, and till it in several inches deep. Dig a planting hole that's several times wider but not deeper than the rootball. Plant at the same depth it was growing in the container or set the top of the rootball a little higher above the soil level, especially in a poorly drained location. Create a berm and add a light

layer of mulch. Prune when the plant fills the trellis and begins to grow out of bounds. Give the vine a renewal pruning in late spring every three or four years to ensure good coverage on the trellis.

Growing Tips
Water daily for the first few weeks after planting. Gradually taper the watering off to an as-needed schedule. Vines are drought-tolerant and need watering only during periods of drought—but when growth is desired, water weekly. Feed four to six weeks after transplanting by applying a light scattering of a general landscape fertilizer under the spread of the vine. Repeat for established vines March, May, and August.

Regional Advice and Care
Honeysuckles grow best in North and Central parts of Florida. They lack vigor if they don't experience some chilling winter weather. Coral honeysuckle plants usually remain pest-free.

Companion Planting and Design
This is a great Florida native for a fence or trellis in a sunny spot. It looks especially good with other natives firebush, yaupon holly, ornamental grasses, palms, and most perennials.

Try These
Several selections for the landscape are 'Sulphurea' and 'John Clayton', with yellow flowers; 'Magnifica', with intense red blooms; and 'Alabama Crimson', with improved color.

Flame Vine

Pyrostegia venusta

Botanical Pronunciation
pie-row-STEAG-ee-ah veh-NEW-stah

Bloom Period and Seasonal Color
Late winter to early spring, orange blooms

Mature Height
30 to 40 feet

Zones 9B–11

Set the flame vine where it has plenty of room to enjoy a month or more of late-winter to early-spring orange blooms. It can be used to cover an arbor, a fence, or a large trellis. This is a large growing vine that needs a good-sized yard to develop its full potential. The leaves are evergreen and only damaged in the most severe winters. Gardeners love to establish plants to produce the tubular orange blossoms when there is little other color in the landscape. Use it at the end of a vista to be enjoyed from a patio or family room. The vine is ideal for a minimal-maintenance landscape, being very drought-tolerant and needing little fertilizer. But don't let these vines get out of control. (TM)

When, Where, and How to Plant
Vines can be added to the garden throughout most of the year. The best planting time is during the cooler winter months. Flame vines need a trellis, fence, or similar support for good growth. Keep this often rampant vine from reaching trees, shrubs, and similar plantings to prevent them from being covered by its growth. Plant in full sun or a lightly shaded location. In the shadier sites, flowering is greatly reduced. Flame vines tolerate sand, and no additions to the soil are needed. Do dig a planting hole that's several times wider but not deeper than the rootball. Plant at the same depth it was growing in the container or set the top of the rootball a little higher above the soil level, especially in a poorly drained location. Create a berm and add a light layer of mulch. Prune when the plants fill the trellis and begin to grow out of

bounds. Give the vines a renewal pruning each year when flowering is over in early spring.

Growing Tips
Water daily for the first few weeks after planting. Gradually taper the watering off to an as-needed schedule. Flame vines are drought-tolerant and need watering only during periods of hot dry weather—but when growth is desired, water weekly. Feed four to six weeks after transplanting by applying a light scattering of a general landscape fertilizer under the spread of the vine. Repeat for established vines during March, May, and August if needed for growth.

Regional Advice and Care
Flame vines are cold-sensitive, and both foliage and flowers can be damaged by frosts and freezes. Most years the plants receive minimal damage and produce the colorful flower displays. Plant in the warmer spots of colder locations. Use the spring pruning to remove any cold damage. Because this is a very vigorous vine, continual care is needed to keep it in bounds in all locations.

Companion Planting and Design
Grow with other drought-tolerant plantings of ornamental grasses, yaupon holly, firebush, shrimp plant, African iris, viburnums, and ligustrums.

Try These
This plant is usually marketed only as the species.

Mandevilla

Mandevilla splendens

Botanical Pronunciation
MAN-deh-vill-ah splend-ENZ

Other Name Pink allamanda

Bloom Period and Seasonal Color
Warmer months but best during the summer
with pink blooms

Mature Height
15 to 20 feet

Zones 9B–11

Mandevilla flowers are intense pink and trumpetlike, making them an attractive accent against its dark green leaves. This very durable plant is drought- and salt-tolerant. Most gardeners like to train them over a fence, up at trellis, or over and around a mailbox. Some of the prettiest displays have been on white picket fences enclosing a yard. When used in this manner they form a backdrop for other annuals and perennials. In colder locations with frosts and light freezes, mandevilla vines decline during the winter but usually grow back come spring. In the really cold sites they have to be replanted each year or can be grown in containers. All portions of this plant are poisonous, and some gardeners are sensitive to the sap. (TM)

When, Where, and How to Plant

Mandevilla are best planted in the late winter or spring in the cooler portions of the state; any time in warmer sites. Plant in full sun or a lightly shaded location. In the shadier sites flowering is usually reduced and plants are more open in growth habit. Mandevilla tolerate sands, but care may be a bit easier if the sites are improved with organic matter additions. Dig a hole that's several times wider but not deeper than the rootball. Plant at the same depth it was growing in the container, or set the top of the rootball a little higher above the soil level. Create a berm, and add a light layer of mulch. Prune when the plants fill the trellis and begin to grow out of bounds.

Growing Tips

Water daily for the first few weeks after planting. Gradually taper the watering off to an as-needed schedule. Mandevilla are drought-tolerant and need watering only during periods of hot dry weather—but when growth is desired, water weekly. Feed four to six weeks after transplanting by applying a light scattering of a general landscape fertilizer under the spread of the vines. Repeat feedings for established vines during March, May, and August if needed for growth.

Regional Advice and Care

Trimming is usually needed in all areas of the state at the end of winter. In some areas it is to remove cold damage that can kill the plants to the ground. Or the plantings may just need a reshaping to prepare them for spring growth. Pests are few, but oleander caterpillars and aphids may feed in the foliage. Use a natural insecticide for these pests.

Companion Planting and Design

Stage as a background vine with seasonal flowers, including begonias, marigolds, salvia, and zinnias. Or consider planting with some longer-lasting perennials, such as bush daisy, perennial salvias, and roses.

Try These

Two plants make up locally marketed mandevilla. One is sold as mandevilla and the other dipladenia. There is considerable confusion over their relationship, but most likely they are separate species with a number of hybrids.

Passion Vine

Passiflora spp.

Botanical Pronunciation
pass-a-FLOOR-ah

Other Name Passion flower

Bloom Period and Seasonal Color
Summer blooms in pink, red, blue, purple, white, and greenish yellow

Mature Length
Indeterminate

Zones 9–11, depending on the species

The *Passiflora* genus produces a marvelously complex flower. With as many as 10 sepals and petals, the sexual parts are elaborately displayed. The flowers are tiny to several inches across in colors from pink to red, blue or purple, white, and greenish yellow. All the reds are perfumed, and bees are crazy in love with them. Some produce delicious fruit. *Passiflora coccinea* is the red species; *P. alatocerulea* is the common blue passion flower that seems to perform well in South Florida. The corky-stemmed *P. suberosa* is South Florida's native, and it can be found at native plant sales. It is a larval food plant for Zebra Heliconian butterflies. *P. incarnate*, a purple species, is a larval food plant for Gulf Fritillary and Julia butterflies and is another native. (GBT)

When, Where, and How to Plant
Plant in the spring. Plant in full sun, against a support such as a fence or trellis, but away from trees—unless you're prepared to find the vine looking down at you one morning. Plant in fast-draining soil. Potting soil or organic amendments may be added to a planting area. Dig a planting hole that's several times wider but not deeper than the rootball. Plant at the same depth it was growing in the container. Create a saucer around the root zone and add a 2- to 3-inch layer of mulch. Keep the roots well irrigated until the vine is growing vigorously.

Growing Tips
Passion vines are quick growers. Use a slow-release 8-4-12 with micronutrients. Too much nitrogen may result in foliage production only. The vines can grow in slightly alkaline soil, but they will become chlorotic in very alkaline soils. If chlorosis occurs, use an iron drench or a foliar spray of micronutrients with a spreader sticker, or both. When root suckers appear, they may be transplanted.

Regional Advice and Care
The blue passion flower is more cold-tolerant than is the red or purple. The edible passion fruit are *Passiflora edulis* (purple) and *P. edulis* f. *flavicarpa* (yellow), with fruit maturing in midsummer. A local passion fruit that grows well in South Florida is *P. edulis* 'Possum Purple', named by tropical fruit grower Robert Barnum, who first grew it at his Possum Trot Nursery. It may produce a bushel of fruit on one vine.

Companion Planting and Design
Build an arbor at the entrance to your garden, and run an edible *Passiflora* over it. These plants make perfectly splendid garden specimens because they flower freely in the summer and attract loads of butterflies.

Try These
South Florida's native *Passiflora suberosa*, the corky-stemmed passion vine, has small leaves and tiny flowers and fruit. When in sun, it hosts larvae of Gulf Fritillary and Julia butterflies; in the shade, it is the larval host for Zebras.

Queen's Wreath

Petrea volubilis

Botanical Pronunciation
pee-TREE-ah voh-LUBE-ah-liss

Other Name Sandpaper vine

Bloom Period and Seasonal Color
Spring blooms in blue-purple

Mature Length
To 35 feet

Zones 10B–11

One reason to spend early spring in South Florida is to see the flowering of the queen's wreath. The darker violet petals fall after a few days, leaving the lighter blue for several more weeks of color. With age, the vine develops a trunk that is quite thick. Twining vines will circle whatever support they are climbing, growing in a direction that has been encoded genetically, rather like being either right- or left-handed. At Fairchild Tropical Botanic Garden, *Petrea volubilis* clambers up the beautiful stone columns of the vine pergola originally constructed by the Civilian Conservation Corps (CCC) in the 1930s. It is a plant loved around the world. (GBT)

When, Where, and How to Plant
Plant queen's wreath in fall for flowers the following spring or at the start of the rainy season to provide a long growing period until the next flowering season. This kind of vine can slink around a wooden arbor or even wires, but not up the sides of walls, as do clinging vines like *Ficus pumila*, the creeping fig. Because it is a vigorous vine, no matter where it is grown, *Petrea* species must be supported by a pergola or arbor. Without tendrils, the vine twines, and it twines best on a craggy surface. Dig a hole slightly larger than the rootball and add some peat moss, compost, or well-aged manure. Slide the rootball out of the container, making sure the top of it is at the same level in the ground as it was in the container when placing it in the planting hole. Water in the backfill, and mulch to keep soil moisture and temperature well modulated.

Growing Tips
Fertilize three times a year, in spring, summer, and fall. Water two or three times a week in summer and twice a week in winter.

Regional Advice and Care
The queen's wreath has few pests, other than those normally found in the landscape: scale and mealybugs. Spider mites can be a problem in dry weather. Give the affected areas a hard spray of water. The queen's wreath is a vigorous vine that can be cut back hard after it has flowered. It can be pruned in late winter. A tender plant that will be hurt by cold, this vine needs a protected, sunny spot in Central Florida. It is not a plant for North Florida.

Companion Planting and Design
Because it is so strongly seasonal, the vine wants to show off when it finally does flower. Using it at an arching gate, or on a pergola or trellis of some sort, is ideal. Give it a place to show off.

Try These
Petrea volubilis var. *albiflora* is the albino form.

Wisteria

Wisteria sinensis

Botanical Pronunciation
WISS-tear-ee-ah sigh-NEN-sis

Bloom Period and Seasonal Color
Spring blooms in lavender

Mature Height
Shoots to 24 feet

Zones 8–9

What is the one vine most gardeners would like to grow? It's probably the wisteria. It is restricted to the cooler portions of the state, but lucky gardeners in these areas can enjoy a spring display of exquisite purplish blossoms. The flowers open in long hanging clusters just before the foliage, so the color is especially easy to see. Flower clusters of some vines are fragrant. Plantings need room to grow, and too much trimming delays flowering. After flowering, the vines quickly fill with large pinnate leaves that add extra enjoyment during the summer and fall months. Even during the winter months when the vines are bare, the twisting limbs add interest to the landscape. *Note: seed producing portions are poisonous if eaten.* (TM)

When, Where, and How to Plant

Vines can be added throughout the year, but the best planting time is during the winter. Wisteria needs a trellis, fence, arbor, or similar support. Keep all vines off trees to prevent damage to the trunks and to avoid encouraging pests. Wisteria vines are tolerant of sandy sites. Dig a planting hole that's several times wider but not deeper than the rootball. Plant at the same depth it was growing in the container or set the top of the rootball an inch or so higher. Create a berm and add a light layer of mulch. Planting can easily invade other plantings, so regular control of the vining growths is needed. Prune when the vines begin to grow out of bounds. Good times to do the trimming are after flowering and during late summer.

Growing Tips

Water daily for the first few weeks after planting. Gradually taper the watering off to an as-needed schedule. Wisteria vines are drought-tolerant and need watering only during drought; for extra growth, water weekly. Feed four to six weeks after transplanting, by applying a light scattering of general landscape fertilizer under the spread of the vines. Repeat for established vines during March, May, and September for the first year or two, and then reduce the feedings to once or twice a year.

Regional Advice and Care

Wisteria grows best in Northern and Central Florida where the vines receive some cold. It's hardy in these areas and needs no special care. Wisteria plants may have mite or thrip pests. Apply a soap, oil, or another University of Florida–recommended pesticide.

Companion Planting and Design

Train to a trellis against a wall as an accent or space divider. Add contrasting perennials and bulbs of crinums, bird-of-paradise, caladium, salvia, wild petunia, gaura, and pentas.

Try These

A number of selections have been made for the flowering features, including 'Alba', a white; 'Caroline', a good blue; 'Plena', with double lavender blooms; and 'Purpurea', with good purple flowers. A native American wisteria is also available and includes varieties 'Magnifica' (lavender) and 'Nivea' (white).

GLOSSARY

Alkaline soil: soil with a pH greater than 7.0. It lacks acidity, often because it has limestone in it.

All-purpose fertilizer: powdered, liquid, or granular fertilizer with a balanced proportion of the three key nutrients—nitrogen (N), phosphorus (P), and potassium (K). It is suitable for maintenance nutrition for most plants.

Annual: a plant that lives its entire life in one season. It is genetically determined to germinate, grow, flower, set seed, and die the same year.

Balled and burlapped: describes a tree or shrub grown in the field whose soilball was wrapped with protective burlap and twine when the plant was dug up to be sold or transplanted.

Bare root: describes plants that have been packaged without any soil around their roots. (Often young shrubs and trees purchased through the mail arrive with their exposed roots covered with moist peat or sphagnum moss, sawdust, or similar material, and wrapped in plastic.)

Barrier plant: a plant that has intimidating thorns or spines and is sited purposely to block foot traffic or other access to the home or yard.

Beneficial insects: insects or their larvae that prey on pest organisms and their eggs. They may be flying insects, such as ladybugs, parasitic wasps, praying mantids, and soldier bugs, or soil dwellers such as predatory nematodes, spiders, and ants.

Berm: a narrow, raised ring of soil around a tree, used to hold water so it will be directed to the root zone.

Bract: a modified leaf structure on a plant stem near its flower, resembling a petal. Often it is more colorful and visible than the actual flower, as in dogwood or poinsettia.

Bud union: the place where the top of a plant was grafted to the rootstock; usually refers to roses.

Canopy: the overhead branching area of a tree, usually referring to its extent including foliage.

Cold hardiness: the ability of a perennial plant to survive the winter in a particular area.

Composite: a flower that is actually composed of many tiny flowers. Typically, they are flat clusters of tiny, tight florets, sometimes surrounded by wider-petaled florets. Composite flowers are highly attractive to bees and beneficial insects.

Compost: organic matter that has undergone progressive decomposition by microbial and macrobial activity until it is reduced to a spongy, fluffy texture. Added to soil of any type, it improves the soil's ability to hold air and water and to drain well.

Corm: the swollen energy-storing structure, analogous to a bulb, under the soil at the base of the stem of plants such as crocus and gladiolus.

Crown: the base of a plant at, or just beneath, the surface of the soil where the roots meet the stems; the head of a palm.

Cultivar: a CULTIvated VARiety. It is a naturally occurring form of a plant that has been identified as special or superior and is selected for propagation and production.

Deadhead: a pruning technique that removes faded flower heads from plants to improve their appearances, abort seed production, and stimulate further flowering.

Deciduous plants: unlike evergreens, these trees and shrubs lose their leaves in the fall.

Desiccation: drying out of foliage tissues, usually due to drought or wind.

Division: splitting apart perennial plants to create several smaller-rooted segments. The practice is useful for controlling the plant's size and for acquiring more plants; it is also essential to the health and continued flowering of certain ones.

Dormancy: the period, usually the winter, when perennial plants temporarily cease active growth and rest. Dormant is the verb form, as used in this sentence: Some plants, like spring-blooming bulbs, go dormant in the summer.

Established: the point at which a newly planted tree, shrub, or flower begins to produce new growth, either foliage or stems. This is an indication that the roots have recovered from transplant shock and have begun to grow and spread.

Evergreen: perennial plants that do not lose their foliage annually with the onset of winter. Needled or broadleaf foliage will persist and continues to function on a plant through one or more winters, aging and dropping unobtrusively in cycles of three or four years or more.

Foliar: of or about foliage—usually refers to the practice of spraying foliage, as in fertilizing or treating with insecticide; leaf tissues absorb liquid directly for fast results, and the soil is not affected.

Floret: tiny flower, usually one of many forming a cluster, that makes a single blossom.

Germinate: to sprout. Germination is a fertile seed's first stage of development.

Graft (union): the point on the stem of a woody plant with sturdier roots where a stem from an ornamental plant is inserted to join with it. Roses are commonly grafted.

Hands: groups of female flowers on a banana; hands develop into bananas. A well-grown banana produces about 15 hands of bananas. The entire bunch is called a head.

Hardscape: the permanent, structural, nonplant part of a landscape, such as walls, sheds, pools, patios, arbors, and walkways.

Herbaceous: plants having fleshy or soft stems; the opposite of woody.

Hybrid: a plant that is the result of intentional or natural cross-pollination between two or more plants of the same species or genus.

Low water demand: plants that tolerate dry soil for varying periods of time. Typically, they have succulent, hairy, or silvery-gray foliage and tuberous roots or taproots.

Mulch: a layer of material over bare soil to protect it from erosion and compaction by rain and to discourage weeds. It may be inorganic (gravel, fabric) or organic (wood chips, bark, pine needles, chopped leaves).

Naturalize: *(a)* to plant seeds, bulbs, or plants in a random, informal pattern as they would appear in their natural habitats; *(b)* to adapt to and spread throughout adopted habitats (a tendency of some non-native plants).

Nectar: the sweet fluid produced by glands on flowers that attract pollinators such as hummingbirds and honeybees, for whom it is a source of energy.

Organic material, organic matter: any material or debris that is derived from plants. It is carbon-based material capable of undergoing decomposition and decay.

Peat moss: organic matter from peat sedges (United States) or sphagnum mosses (Canada), often used to improve soil texture. The acidity of sphagnum peat moss makes it ideal for boosting or maintaining soil acidity while also improving its drainage.

Perennial: a flowering plant that lives over two or more seasons. Many die back with frost, but their roots survive the winter and generate new shoots in the spring.

pH: a measurement of the relative acidity (low pH) or alkalinity (high pH) of soil or water based on a scale of 1 to 14, 7 being neutral. Individual plants require soil to be within a certain range so nutrients can dissolve in moisture and be available to them.

Pinch: to remove tender stems and/or leaves by pressing them between thumb and forefinger. This pruning technique encourages branching, compactness, and flowering in plants, or it removes aphids clustered at growing tips.

Pollen: the yellow, powdery grains in the center of a flower. A plant's male sex cells, they are transferred to the female plant parts by means of wind or animal pollinators to fertilize them and create seeds.

Raceme: an arrangement of single-stalked flowers along an elongated, unbranched axis.

Rhizome: a swollen, energy-storing stem structure, similar to a bulb, that lies horizontally in the soil, with roots emerging from its lower surface and growth shoots from a growing point at or near its tip, as in bearded iris.

Rootbound (or potbound): the condition of a plant that has been confined in a container too long, its roots having been forced to wrap around themselves and even swell out of the container. Successful transplanting or repotting requires untangling and trimming away of some of the matted roots.

Root flare: the transition at the base of a tree trunk where the bark tissue begins to differentiate and roots begin to form just before entering the soil. This area should not be covered with soil when planting a tree.

Self-seeding: the tendency of some plants to sow their seeds freely around the yard. It creates many seedlings the following season that may or may not be welcome.

Semievergreen: tending to be evergreen in a mild climate but deciduous in a rigorous one.

Shearing: the pruning technique whereby plant stems and branches are cut uniformly with long-bladed pruning shears (hedge shears) or powered hedge trimmers. It is used when creating and maintaining hedges and topiary.

Slow-acting fertilizer: fertilizer that is water insoluble and therefore releases its nutrients gradually as a function of soil temperature, moisture, and related microbial activity. Typically granular, it may be organic or synthetic.

Succulent growth: the sometimes undesirable production of fleshy, water-storing leaves or stems that results from overfertilization.

Sucker: a new-growing shoot. Underground plant roots produce suckers to form new stems and spread by means of these suckering roots to form large plantings, or colonies. Some plants produce root suckers or branch suckers as a result of pruning or wounding.

Tuber: a type of underground storage structure in a plant stem, analogous to a bulb. It generates roots below and stems above ground as with dahlias.

Variegated: having various colors or color patterns. The term usually refers to plant foliage that is streaked, edged, blotched, or mottled with a contrasting color—often green with yellow, cream, or white.

White grubs: fat, off-white, wormlike larvae of Japanese beetles. They reside in the soil and feed on plant roots (especially grass) until summer when they emerge as beetles to feed on plant foliage.

Wings: *(a)* the corky tissue that forms edges along the twigs of some woody plants such as winged euonymus; *(b)* the flat, dried extension of tissue on some seeds, such as maple, that catch the wind and help them disseminate.

BIBLIOGRAPHY

Barwick, Margaret. *Tropical & Subtropical Trees, An Encyclopedia*. Portland, Oregon: Timber Press, 2004.

Bar-Zvi, David, Chief Horticulturist, and Elvin McDonald, series editor. *Tropical Gardening*. New York: Pantheon Books, Knopf Publishing Group, 1996.

Batchelor, Stephen R. *Your First Orchid*. West Palm Beach: American Orchid Society, 1996.

Bechtel, Helmut, Phillip Cribb, and Edmund Launert. *The Manual of Cultivated Orchid Species, Third Edition*. Cambridge, MA: The MIT Press, 1992.

Bell, C. Ritchie and Byron J. Taylor. *Florida Wild Flowers and Roadside Plants*. Chapel Hill, NC: Laurel Hill Press, 1982.

Berry, Fred and W. John Kress. *Heliconia, An Identification Guide*. Washington and London: Smithsonian Institution Press, 1991.

Black, Robert J. and Kathleen C. Ruppert. *Your Florida Landscape, A Complete Guide to Planting & Maintenance*. Gainesville, FL: Cooperative Extension Service, Institute of Food and Agricultural Sciences, University of Florida, 1995.

Blackmore, Stephen and Elizabeth Tootill, eds. *The Penguin Dictionary of Botany*. Middlesex, England: Penguin Books, Ltd., 1984.

Blombery, Alec and Tony Todd. *Palms*. London, Sydney, Melbourne: Angus & Robertson, 1982.

Bond, Rick and editorial staff of Ortho Books. *All About Growing Orchids*. San Ramon, CA: The Solaris Group, 1988.

Brookes, John. *The Book of Garden Design*. New York: Macmillan Publishing Co. and London: Dorling Kindersley Ltd., 1991.

Broschat, Timothy K. and Alan W. Meerow. *Betrock's Reference Guide to Florida Landscape Plants*. Cooper City, FL: Betrock Information Systems, Inc., 1991.

Brown, Deni. *Aroids, Plants of the Arum Family*. Portland, OR: Timber Press, 1988.

Bush, Charles S. and Julia F. Morton. *Native Trees and Plants for Florida Landscaping*. Gainesville, FL: Florida Department of Agriculture and Consumer Services.

Calkins, Carroll C., ed. *Reader's Digest Illustrated Guide to Gardening*. Pleasantville, NY and Montreal: The Reader's Digest Association, Inc., 1978.

Campbell, Richard J., ed. *Mangos: A Guide to Mangos in Florida*. Miami: Fairchild Tropical Garden, 1992.

Courtright, Gordon. *Tropicals*. Portland, OR: Timber Press, 1988.

Dade County Department of Planning, Development and Regulation. *The Landscape Manual*. 1996.

Dehgan, Bijan. *Landscape Plants for Subtropical Climates*. University Press of Florida, 1998.

Editors of Sunset Books and Sunset Magazine. *Sunset National Garden Book*. Menlo Park, CA: Sunset Books Inc., 1997.

Gerberg, Eugene J. and Ross H. Arnett, Jr. *Florida Butterflies*. Baltimore: Natural Science Publication, Inc., 1989.

Gilman, Edward F. *Betrock's Florida Plant Guide*. Hollywood, FL: Betrock Information Systems, 1996.

Graf, Alfred Byrd. *Tropica*. East Rutherford, NJ: Roehrs Co., 1978.

Hillier, Malcolm. *Malcolm Hillier's Color Garden*. London, New York, Stuttgart, Moscow: Dorling Kindersley, 1995.

Holttum, R.E. and Ivan Enock. *Gardening in the Tropics*. Singapore: Times Editions, 1991.

Hoshizaki, Barbara Joe. *Fern Growers Manual*. New York: Alfred A. Knopf, 1979.

Kilmer, Anne. *Gardening for Butterflies and Children in South Florida*. West Palm Beach, The Palm Beach Post, 1992.

Kramer, Jack. *300 Extraordinary Plants for Home and Garden*. New York, London, Paris: Abbeville Press, 1994.

Llamas, Kirsten Albrect. *Tropical Flowering Plants, A Guide to Identification and Cultivation*. Portland, Oregon: Timber Press, 2003.

Lessard, W.O. *The Complete Book of Bananas*. Miami, 1992.

MacCubbin, Tom. *Month-By-Month Gardening in Florida*. Nashville, Tennessee: Cool Springs Press Inc., 1999.

MacCubbin, Tom. *Florida Home Grown: Landscaping*. Orlando, Florida: Sentinel Communications, 1989.

Mathias, Mildred E., ed. *Flowering Plants in the Landscape*. Berkeley, Los Angeles, London: University of California Press, 1982.

Meerow, Alan W. *Betrock's Guide to Landscape Palms*. Cooper City, FL: Betrock Information Systems, Inc., 1992.

Morton, Julia F. *500 Plants of South Florida*. Miami: E.A. Seemann Publishing, Inc., 1974.

Myers, Ronald L. and John J. Ewel, eds. *Ecosystems of Florida*. Orlando: University of Central Florida Press, 1991.

The National Gardening Association. *Dictionary of Horticulture*. New York: Penguin Books, 1994.

Neal, Marie. *In Gardens of Hawaii*. Honolulu: Bishop Museum Press, 1965.

Nelson, Gil. *The Trees of Florida, A Reference and Field Guide*. Sarasota: Pineapple Press, Inc., 1994.

Perry, Frances. *Flowers of the World*. London, New York, Sydney, Toronto: The Hamlyn Publishing Group, Ltd., 1972.

Rawlings, Marjorie Kinnan. *Cross Creek*. St. Simons Island, GA: Mockingbird Books, 1942. Seventh Printing, 1983.

Reinikka, Merle A. *A History of the Orchid*. Portland, OR: Timber Press, 1995.

Rittershausen, Wilma and Gill and David Oakey. *Growing & Displaying Orchids, A Step-by-Step Guide*. New York: Smithmark Publishers, Inc., 1993.

Scurlock, J. Paul. *Native Trees and Shrubs of the Florida Keys*. Pittsburgh: Laurel Press, 1987.

Stearn, William T. *Stearn's Dictionary of Plant Names for Gardeners*. New York: Sterling Publishing Co., Inc. 1996.

Stevenson, George B. *Palms of South Florida*. Miami: Fairchild Tropical Garden, 1974.

Tasker, Georgia. *Enchanted Ground, Gardening With Nature in the Subtropics*. Kansas City: Andrews and McMeel, 1994.

Tasker, Georgia. *Wild Things, The Return of Native Plants*. Winter Park, FL: The Florida Native Plant Society, 1984.

Tomlinson, P.B. *The Biology of Trees Native to Tropical Florida*. Allston, MA: Harvard University, 1980.

Vanderplank, John. *Passion Flowers, Second Edition*. Cambridge, MA: The MIT Press, 1996.

Walker, Jacqueline. *The Subtropical Garden*. Portland, OR: Timber Press, 1992.

Warren, William. *The Tropical Garden*. London: Thames and Hudson, Ltd., 1991.

Watkins, John V. and Thomas J. Sheehan. *Florida Landscape Plants, Native and Exotic, Revised Edition*. Gainesville, FL: The University Presses of Florida, 1975.

Workman, Richard W. *Growing Native*. Sanibel, FL: The Sanibel-Captive Conservation Foundation, Inc., 1980.

INDEX

PHOTO CREDITS

William Adams: pages 42, 51, 53, 62, 65, 75, 83, 120, 134, 147, 148, 192, 196

Alamy: pages 63 (Zuma Wire Service), 106 (Florapix), 112 (blickwinkel), 122 (National Geographic Image Collection)

Steve Asbell: page 194

Liz Ball & Rick Ray: pages 18, 29, 32, 41, 74, 89, 91, 140, 169, 225

Creative Commons: pages 21 (Rufino Osario/CC-BY-SA-2.5), 56 (Tato Grasso/CC-BY-SA-2.5), 57 (Tillman/CC-BY-2.0), 107 (Arturo Reina/CC-BY-SA-3.0), 153 (Guettarda/CC-BY-SA-3.0), 174 (Aroche/CC-BY-2.0)

Michael Dirr: page 159

Dreamstime: page 66 (Nicolas Iskoan/Dreamstime.com)

Thomas Eltzroth: pages 8, 11, 12, 16, 17, 19, 20, 22, 23, 25, 26, 28, 31, 34, 37, 40, 46, 50, 52, 60, 68, 69, 70, 72, 76, 80, 81, 84, 86, 88, 94, 98, 99, 102, 103, 104, 111, 116, 118, 121, 123, 130, 138, 139, 142, 146, 151, 152, 154, 156, 158, 161, 163, 164, 166, 167, 168, 172, 182, 190, 195, 197, 198, 200, 202, 203, 205, 206, 207, 209, 214, 215, 216, 217, 218, 222, 223

Katie Elzer-Peters: page 212

Lorenzo Gunn: pages 61, 67, 149, 150, 188, 219

Roger Hammer: pages 64, 78, 92, 136, 157, 160, 170, 176

Pam Harper: pages 55, 77, 115, 173, 204, 220, 224

Bruce Holst: pages 96, 145, 183, 187

iStock: pages 82, 127, 137

Dency Kane: pages 128, 178, 180

Kirsten Llamas: pages 39, 43, 100, 101, 108, 109, 113, 155, 162, 171, 177, 179, 181, 186, 189, 191

Joani MacCubbin: pages 38, 45, 71, 126, 129, 131, 133, 135, 221

Charles Mann: pages 47, 93

Jerry Pavia: pages 24, 27, 30, 33, 35, 36, 48, 73, 119, 124, 125, 141, 143, 184

Stephen G. Pategas/Hortus Oasis: pages 95, 105, 114, 165, 201

David Price: page 97

Shutterstock: pages 85, 87, 199

Ralph Snodsmith: page 175

Forrest & Kim Starr: pages 59, 193

Georgia B. Tasker: pages 49, 54, 79, 110, 117, 132, 144

©2002 Mark Turner: pages 6, 44, 90, 185

MEET THE AUTHORS

Tom MacCubbin has been helping gardeners throughout Florida for over 40 years. Some readers may be familiar with his "Plant Doctor" column and features articles for the *Orlando Sentinel*. Others may recognize him as the co-host of *Central Florida Gardening* and his work with Central Florida News 13 or his 25 years as co-host with his wife, Joani of *Better Lawns & Gardens Radio*.

MacCubbin graduated from the University of Maryland with degrees in Horticulture, plus he received advanced training at the University of Florida. He was an Extension urban horticulturist before retiring. In addition to this book for Cool Springs Press, he co-authored the first edition of the *Florida Gardener's Guide* with Georgia Tasker. He is the author of *Month-by-Month Gardening in Florida*, and co-author with Georgia Tasker of *Florida Gardener's Handbook*, all for Cool Springs Press.

MacCubbin has been honored for his media contributions with numerous awards, including the Best Horticultural Writer Award by the Florida Nurseryman and Growers Association as well as the Garden Communicators Award by the American Nurseryman's Association. Tom was recognized nationally as the teacher of the year by the American Horticultural Society. In 2007, Tom was promoted to the distinguished position of Extension Agent Emeritus with the University of Florida upon his retirement after 37 years of service.

Active in their community, Tom and his wife, Joani, live near Apopka.

Georgia Tasker is a staff writer at Fairchild Tropical Botanic Gardens. She also writes for *The Tropical Garden* magazine, has a blog on gardening on Fairchild's website, and has written three handbooks in her on-going series, *Gardening with Fairchild*. Prior to joining the Gardens staff in 2009, she was a garden writer with *The Miami Herald* and author of three garden books (including the original edition of this book).

She is a graduate of Hanover College in Indiana and received the first certificate in tropical botany from FIU in 1984. She was a Pulitzer Prize finalist and a Knight Journalism Fellow at Stanford University. She has been awarded the Barbour Medal from Fairchild and the first lifetime achievement award from the Tropical Audubon Society.

Tasker is a photographer, amateur birder, butterfly gardener, and passionate traveler, having visited the Arctic and the Antarctic, Madagascar, Africa, Borneo, Papua New Guinea, Australia, China, Japan, all of Europe, Central America, and much of South America.